POWER, TREASON AND PLOT IN

TUDOR ENGLAND

Margaret Clitherow, an Elizabethan Saint

This book is dedicated to the memory of Jeffrey and Olwen Morgan.

POWER, TREASON AND PLOT IN

TUDOR ENGLAND

Margaret Clitherow, an Elizabethan Saint

TONY MORGAN

PEN & SWORD HISTORY

AN IMPRINT OF PEN & SWORD BOOKS LTD.
YORKSHIRE - PHILADELPHIA

First published in Great Britain in 2022 by
PEN AND SWORD HISTORY
An imprint of
Pen & Sword Books Ltd
Yorkshire – Philadelphia

ISBN 978 1 39909 797 0

Typeset in Times New Roman 11.5/14 by
SJmagic DESIGN SERVICES, India.
Printed and bound in the UK by CPI Group (UK) Ltd.

Pen & Sword Books Limited incorporates the imprints of Atlas, Archaeology,
Aviation, Discovery, Family History, Fiction, History, Maritime, Military, Military
Classics, Politics, Select, Transport, True Crime, Air World, Frontline Publishing,
Leo Cooper, Remember When, Seaforth Publishing, The Praetorian Press,
Wharncliffe Local History, Wharncliffe Transport, Wharncliffe True Crime and
White Owl.

For a complete list of Pen & Sword titles please contact
PEN & SWORD BOOKS LIMITED
47 Church Street, Barnsley, South Yorkshire, S70 2AS, England
E-mail: enquiries@pen-and-sword.co.uk
Website: www.pen-and-sword.co.uk

Or

PEN AND SWORD BOOKS
1950 Lawrence Rd, Havertown, PA 19083, USA
E-mail: Uspen-and-sword@casematepublishers.com
Website: www.penandswordbooks.com

Contents

Freepost Plus RTKE-RGRJ-KTTX
Pen & Sword Books Ltd
47 Church Street
BARNSLEY
S70 2AS

✂ DISCOVER MORE ABOUT PEN & SWORD BOOKS

Pen & Sword Books have over 4000 books currently available, our imprints include; Aviation, Naval, Military, Archaeology, Transport, Frontline, Seaforth and the Battleground series, and we cover all periods of history on land, sea and air.

Can we stay in touch? From time to time we'd like to send you our latest catalogues, promotions and special offers by post. If you would prefer not to receive these, please tick this box. ☐

We also think you'd enjoy some of the latest products and offers by post from our trusted partners: companies operating in the clothing, collectables, food & wine, gardening, gadgets & entertainment, health & beauty, household goods, and home interiors categories. If you would like to receive these by post, please tick this box. ☐

We respect your privacy. We use personal information you provide us with to send you information about our products, maintain records and for marketing purposes. For more information explaining how we use your information please see our privacy policy at www.pen-and-sword.co.uk/privacy. You can opt out of our mailing list at any time via our website or by calling 01226 734222.

Mr/Mrs/Ms ....

Address..

....

Postcode.................................... Email address...

Website: www.pen-and-sword.co.uk Email: enquiries@pen-and-sword.co.uk

Telephone: 01226 734555 Fax: 01226 734438

Stay in touch: facebook.com/penandswordbooks or follow us on Twitter @penswordbooks

Chapter One

Introduction

The majority of people in societies down the ages have obeyed their governments. Some have done so willingly, believing in what they were told; others have acquiesced reluctantly, for the sake of a quiet life, or to protect themselves and their families; many have considered they had little option but to conform. There has, however, usually been a minority who refused to obey. These rebels, the enemies of the state, have acted due to their conscience, or through sheer bloody-mindedness.

Under Elizabeth I the Protestant-leaning Church of England began to gain a level of stability. The laws of the land changed, and the population was ordered to attend a new church. Most did so, but some, from paupers to lords, retained their original faith. Many crossed their fingers. On Sundays and holy days, these 'Church Catholics' or 'Church Papists' frequented Protestant services, before sneaking off to attend an illegal Catholic Mass. A smaller number of Catholics, known as recusants, were more openly defiant. They refused to attend Church of England services and often paid the price.

From the 1580s onwards their resistance movement was supported by seminary and Jesuit priests, smuggled into England and Wales by the Catholic Church. Their mission included keeping the old faith alive until a new Catholic monarch could be placed upon the throne. When this happened, the Church would be restored to its former glory and the country reconciled with Rome. We now know this wasn't to be.

Between 1535 and 1681 it's estimated that over 600 people, including clergy, laymen and women, died in England and Wales for their adherence to the Catholic faith.[1] Selected details of the life and death of many of them were recorded and are still available. In other cases, very few records remain. Little is known about the martyrs, other than their names.

Margaret Clitherow, now Saint Margaret Clitherow, is one of those 600. For a butcher's wife who lived in the sixteenth century, we know a great deal about her life and subsequent death. For this, we owe a debt of thanks to her first biographer, Father John Mush, one of the Catholic priests she harboured in her home in the Shambles in York.

In the weeks following Margaret's death, Father Mush wrote *A True Report of the Life and Martyrdom of Mrs Margaret Clitherow*. He gathered information wherever he could, using a range of sources to supplement his own knowledge. Of course, like everyone else, the priest had his own thoughts and his own agenda.

A number of different versions of Father Mush's manuscript remain intact.[2] The transcription most often quoted in this book was created by a Jesuit priest, John Morris, in his compilation *The Troubles of the Catholic Forefathers Related by Themselves*. Father Morris adapted the contents to align with contemporary late nineteenth century English.[3] There are one or two other differences between Father Morris's version and earlier interpretations, which we'll highlight later.

This book seeks to examine the life and death of Margaret Clitherow in the context of the wider events that influenced her life, and the lives of many others. In 1970 Margaret was canonised. She was made a saint by Pope Paul VI, as one of the Forty Martyrs of England and Wales. All suffered a somewhat similar grisly fate.

Margaret lived in York in the sixteenth century. For a time, she attended the slowly reforming Protestant Church of England, before converting to Catholicism in early adulthood. After serving several prison sentences for refusing to attend official church services, she was arrested and charged with a more serious crime. In 1586 she was brought before the York Lent assizes court, accused of the newly established capital offence of aiding or harbouring Catholic priests.

Margaret's story is remarkable for a number of reasons. In a society where virtually all the power and wealth were held by men (with the obvious exception of Queen Elizabeth), she made a committed stand against the authorities and their legal system. Under tremendous pressure, and facing barbaric execution, she refused to recognise the jurisdiction of the court that was attempting to try her. Although her actions were considered subversive by the Protestant authorities, she wasn't calling for a revolution. Margaret Clitherow simply wanted the freedom to worship the way her parents had thirty years earlier.

Of course, things were more complex than this. National politics, local rivalries and family intrigue all played their part in the events which led to her arrest. Fearing rebellion and invasion, the Queen and her government were cracking down on the Catholic population of England and Wales. The local authorities, the Council of the North and Corporation of York, were often at loggerheads. Both wished to be seen in a positive light by the Queen and Privy Council. Prosecuting Catholics was a good way to achieve this.

Margaret was a family woman with children. She was married to a Protestant butcher. At the time of her arrest, there were claims she was pregnant. During the court proceedings which followed, she was accused of betraying her husband by sleeping with the Catholic priests she hid in their home. Remarkably, her stepfather, Henry Maye, had only just been elected lord mayor of York. With Margaret's Catholicism a political embarrassment to him, could he have been complicit in his stepdaughter's arrest, even her execution?

In telling Margaret's story, this book examines the bigger picture of Elizabethan times. Margaret's example may have been an extreme case, but the circumstances surrounding it were a microcosm of the wider events which affected so many people's lives in a society scarred by, and scared of, religious divisions and power games.

Some readers may hold religious convictions. Others will not. Either way, please consider the role religion played in the life and culture of people at the time. For the vast majority, religion was far more important than it is to many of us – though not all – today.

Before you read on, I'd like to make a personal admission. When I began working on this book, I believed I knew many of the 'facts' surrounding Margaret Clitherow's life and death. I'd previously carried out a great deal of research for my novel *The Pearl of York, Treason and Plot*, which tells Margaret's story through the eyes of her youthful neighbour, Guy Fawkes. By the time I completed the first edit of this book, I started questioning parts of my analysis. In certain cases, I changed my mind. I hope you'll be open to changing yours.

My parents lived through the Second World War. My father joined the Royal Navy in his late teens. He served as a ship's gunner, protecting the vital Atlantic convoys which kept Britain fed and armed. My mother worked for a while as a cook in a famous school near London, temporarily removing herself from her more usual life in rural Wales. This book is dedicated to their memory.

It's too late now, but how I wish I'd spent more time talking to them, getting to understand more about their young lives. In particular, I wish

I'd asked how they felt when the war was going badly, and Nazi invasion appeared to be imminent. It must have been a desperate time.

This thought takes me back to the second half of the sixteenth century. Queen Elizabeth I's reign is sometimes viewed as a golden age filled with adventure, the seafaring tales of Raleigh and Drake and defeat of the Spanish Armada. But for many it was a time of turmoil. What emotions filled the hearts and minds of 'ordinary' Elizabethans?

In England and Wales thousands of Catholics were being persecuted; some suffered dreadfully. What was their reaction? Did a minority, perhaps even a majority, believe the tide would change and Catholicism would soon be restored as the state religion? It had happened once before during Queen Mary's reign. As the laws against them became harsher, how many Catholics lived in dread, racked with fear, waiting to be arrested, as Margaret Clitherow had been? Did they feel like members of the resistance in early 1940s Europe?

Queen Elizabeth I and her supporters had a different problem. Their side was in the ascendancy, but how long could it last? Since the middle of the reign of her father, Henry VIII, the direction of the Church in England and Wales had changed four times. Some saw treason, plot and Spanish invasion everywhere and in everything. Was this simple paranoia or understandable concern? How many hours were plagued with nightmarish thoughts of the Queen's assassination, the overthrow of her government and Protestants burning at the stake, as they had so recently under 'Bloody' Queen Mary?

Even within these two segments of the Elizabethan population, we shouldn't forget there were many other wide-ranging views and differing concerns. How useful it would be to understand how the country's people felt. If only we had a time machine. What insights could we gain?

The events depicted in this book are largely described and examined in chronological order. After all, like my parents and members of the resistance movement, the people of the sixteenth century didn't know what would happen next, or which side would prevail. They lived their lives fearing the worst and hoping for the best. By examining and attempting to better comprehend their worries, aspirations and motivations, we seek to gain an improved understanding of why things happened the way they did.

Occasionally, it's useful to push our assumptions aside for a moment and generate empathy for the people who lived and died on both sides of this religious divide. What was important to them? What might we have done if we'd been wearing their shoes?

Following initial scene-setting, the majority of this book is structured in three concentric layers. At the core, we explore the power games and religious tensions of the Tudor period. In the middle we examine a time slice of the history of York, the city where Margaret Clitherow was born, lived and died in. Finally, on the surface, is the story of this remarkable woman, Margaret Clitherow.

Sometimes these layers interacted. The tectonic plates shifted. Lava erupted and flowed onto the surface. When this happened, communities were torn apart. Margaret Clitherow's circle was amongst them. There were many others.

There are a whole host of notable players in Margaret's story. They range from kings and queens, popes, archbishops, earls, judges, mayors and sheriffs to the more 'ordinary' people, the tradesmen, servants, husbands, wives, parents, children, friends and priests. Each had an influence on Margaret's life. They all played a part in what happened in York before, during and after March 1586. Of course, similar events and tragedies were taking place across the rest of England and Wales and all over Europe.

For ease of reading, the years examined in this book are described in a modern Gregorian-based calendar format. Each year is considered as beginning on 1 January, rather than on 25 March. In addition, a single standard spelling of many people's names has been adopted. Readers carrying out further reading and research may find slight variations in stated years and the spelling of certain names when referring to different sources.

Chapter Two

Power and Religion (Prior to 1547)

Henry VIII – Beginning of the Reformation

While this book isn't focused on pre-Elizabethan England, the events described in this chapter had a material effect on what happened next in England and Wales, in the city of York, to Margaret Clitherow and to many others. As such, it would be remiss not to include them.

We begin our examination immediately prior to the Reformation. In the early 1500s Roman Catholicism was the long-standing and virtually all-pervasive faith of the country. By 'the country' I refer here to a combination of England and Wales. As a proud Welshman, I cough a little nervously at this point, but let me explain.

The Laws in Wales Acts, enacted by Parliament in 1535 and 1542, were introduced by Henry VIII. Although Henry Tudor (Tudur) was of Welsh origin, the new laws effectively annexed the country and made it formally part of the kingdom of England. The jurisdiction of English law was extended to include the people of Wales.[1]

In some ways, this was a positive measure. For the first time, the Welsh were given the same legal rights as their English neighbours. On the other hand, the Welsh language was badly impacted, as English became the primary language of officialdom in Wales. A detailed study of the Laws in Wales Acts would be an interesting project, but it's not this one. Along with Yorkshire, Wales holds a special place in my heart, but for historical accuracy and ease of writing, when I refer to 'the country' I mean both England and Wales.

In the early years of the sixteenth century only a tiny minority of the people in the country questioned the validity of the Catholic Church. There was no drive for change from the top, neither was there a widely supported grass roots movement within wider society.

In the early years of his reign, Henry VIII had been something of a religious traditionalist. Published in 1521, his theological treatise *Assertio*

Septem Sacramentorum ('Defence of the Seven Sacraments') was a robust rebuttal of the work of the German monk Martin Luther.[2] This vigorous defence of traditional Catholicism resulted in Pope Leo X bestowing Henry with the title of *'Fidei Defensor'* ('Defender of the Faith').

Over time, what Henry craved most was a legitimate male heir. When, in the 1520s, the King concluded that his first wife, Catherine of Aragon (the mother of their daughter Mary), was no longer capable of providing this, he faced a dilemma. The only man who could grant his divorce from Catherine was the Pope, and he'd be unlikely to do so, at least without strong justification.

Eventually, Henry and his advisers believed they had a compelling case, but it would take some arguing. Pope Clement VII would need to be persuaded to backtrack on one of his predecessors' judgements. The submission was simple enough – Henry didn't need a divorce, as his existing marriage to Catherine wasn't valid. It never had been.

To understand this, we need to go further back. When Catherine was just three years old, England and Spain agreed she should wed Henry's older brother, Arthur, Prince of Wales and heir to the throne, as soon they were old enough. The couple married in 1501, when Catherine was fifteen. A few months later, a tragedy occurred. Arthur died.

This left the prince's father, King Henry VII, with an unwanted hole in his financial accounts. If Catherine returned to Spain, he'd be unable to claim the second half of her dowry. Worse still, he'd have to repay the first half to her father, so a new deal was made. Catherine would now marry Arthur's younger brother, Henry, the new heir to the throne. However, this time, the prospective groom wasn't old enough. Henry was eleven when Arthur died.

Papal dispensation would be needed anyway. Church scholars believed the words of Leviticus in the Bible indicated a man wasn't permitted to marry his own brother's widow. Therefore, before any proposed wedding between Henry and Catherine could go ahead, the Pope would have to agree.

Catherine eventually testified that her marriage to Arthur hadn't been consummated. In church law, this meant the marriage wasn't valid. Accordingly, Pope Julius II provided his approval for the proposed union. In 1509, shortly before his eighteenth birthday, Henry wed Catherine. For most of her twenty-three years, Catherine had been treated as a chattel, a marital and financial asset, with little sway over the events of her life.

Almost two decades later, in 1527, Henry argued Pope Julius's dispensation had been invalid. His marriage to Catherine should never have been allowed: it was void. Therefore, there should be no just impediment to prevent him marrying someone else, Anne Boleyn, for example.

If Henry had been hoping for a quick decision from Rome, he was disappointed. Pope Clement VII and the Catholic Church repeatedly delayed and deferred their judgement. While the Pope had no wish to upset the king of a Catholic country, neither was he keen to overturn an important adjudication made by his predecessor.

And then there was Catherine. Finally, she might have some say in matters. If she was cast aside by the King, what would become of her? The Queen and her advisers argued vigorously against the annulment. As the Pope dithered, the process dragged on, and on, for years.

By 1532 Henry gave up all hope of achieving positive approval for the divorce through Rome. With encouragement from his increasingly influential adviser, Thomas Cromwell, Henry concluded that a decision would only fall in his favour if it was made closer to home. Consequently, a momentous decision was made. The Church in England should break away from Rome.

In May 1532, under pressure from Henry and his aides, the Church of England renounced its authority to make church laws without royal approval. By early 1533 Henry realised he had to move quickly. Anne Boleyn was pregnant. The couple were married in a secret ceremony performed by the new Archbishop of Canterbury, Thomas Cranmer. For the wedding to be legal, Henry's marriage to Catherine would have to be invalidated.

Thomas Cromwell proposed a new act of Parliament. The Statute in Restraint of Appeals declared, 'This realm of England is an Empire ... governed by one Supreme Head and King ... he being also institute and furnished, by the goodness and sufferance of Almighty God, with plenary, whole, and entire power, pre-eminence, authority.'

Effectively, the act stated that final authority for legal and religious matters within the English 'Empire' was the King's. By adding, 'And if any person or persons ... provoke or sue any manner of appeals ... to the said Bishop of Rome ... shall incur and run into the dangers, pains, and penalties,' the act made it illegal for the King's subjects to appeal to Rome.

Once the new act was passed, a hearing was held in May 1533 to consider Henry's divorce. Archbishop Cranmer decreed the Papal dispensation that allowed Henry's marriage to Catherine was invalid. A few days later the Archbishop confirmed that, as Henry hadn't been legally married to Catherine, his marriage to Anne Boleyn was indeed lawful and therefore Anne was his rightful Queen.

Although Catherine continued to refer to herself as Henry's lawfully wedded wife and England's one and only Queen, once more she lost control of her life. The previous Queen was shifted between several English residences, until her death in 1536.

In the meantime, in September 1533 Anne Boleyn gave birth to a daughter. The baby princess would grow up to become Elizabeth I. If Elizabeth had been a healthy boy, perhaps her mother's life would have been different – and lasted longer.

Once the divorce was achieved, Henry is thought to have favoured mending the relationship with Rome. However, in 1534 Pope Clement finally declared Henry's marriage to Catherine was valid. Therefore, to Rome, she remained Queen of England, and Henry's marriage to Anne was illegal. Henry was furious.

In the same year, the English Parliament passed a new Act of Supremacy stating, 'The king, our sovereign lord, his heirs and successors, kings of this realm, shall be taken, accepted, and reputed the only supreme head in earth of the Church of England.'

The act formally confirmed Henry (rather than the Pope) as the head of the Church of England. It continued, by stating that the King, 'shall have and enjoy … all honours, dignities, preeminences, jurisdictions, privileges, authorities, immunities, profits and commodities to the said dignity of the supreme head of the same Church.'

Although Henry had had no strong desire to see the practices of the Church change, he did have lavish tastes, a country to run and expensive wars to fight. With the Church of England being the country's wealthiest institution, his new-found ability to 'have and enjoy' its 'profits and commodities' was too good an opportunity for him to turn down.

In 1535 Henry appointed Thomas Cromwell as his 'Vice-Gerent in spirituals'. This placed Cromwell in a unique position in English history.[3] He was now the King's deputy in all matters relating to the Church. Unfettered by Rome, Cromwell had greater power than the country's archbishops. The only question was how he would use those powers.

Cromwell's motivations have long been argued over by historians. Some believe they were twofold. He maintained until his death that his actions were driven only by his unswerving loyalty to the King. While he may have done many things on Henry's behalf, it does appear he also had a religious motivation.

In order to progress his religious agenda, Cromwell knew he would have to keep Henry happy. As 'Vice-Gerent in spirituals', Cromwell set about liquidating Church assets to give the King direct access to some of the 'profits and commodities'.

The first step was to understand what assets were available. In 1535 Cromwell ordered 'The Visitation'. This was a variant on a traditional process whereby a bishop or head of a religious order would visit and inspect a religious house. This time the visitors were Cromwell's representatives, and the financial details were to be recorded in the *Valor Ecclesiasticus*, a new national ledger listing the Church's assets.

Cromwell set out to create a record of all the property and valuables owned by the Church (and as such by King Henry) in religious houses right across the country. This included a multitude of monasteries, friaries, priories and convents. In addition to the financial details, Cromwell's commissioners were tasked with collecting evidence of dubious moral, financial or other behaviour which might prove useful if there was future resistance to Cromwell's plans.

Abbots, nuns, monks, friars and others were ordered to work with Cromwell's men as they built up an accurate view of each house's land, assets and incomes. As they did so, many must have suspected and feared what would happen next.

In early 1536 the Suppression of Religious Houses Act, or Act for the Dissolution of the Lesser Monasteries, was passed in Parliament. All religious houses with an annual income (as assessed by the *Valor Ecclesiasticus*) of less than £200 were to be dissolved and their assets transferred to the Crown, unless special exemption was granted by the King. Around 300 of these houses were adjudged as such. Cromwell ordered his men to act quickly; if they didn't, the disposable wealth of many of the houses would be transferred elsewhere, for example, to the larger religious houses, or perhaps vanish altogether.

Each house was visited by Cromwell's commissioners. Any ecclesiastical staff were told to move on. The most valuable assets, including gold and silver items, were collected and the lead removed from roofs. Bronze bells and other precious metals were stripped from their locations. Saleable items of a lower value were sold locally. Suitable properties were rented out. When the commissioners weren't looking, the local residents descended, taking away as much as they could carry of anything that remained for use as building materials and so on.

Although he's remembered for dissolving the religious houses, Cromwell's vision included subtly changing the direction of the Church. He wanted to morph the Church of England into something a little more Protestant in nature. To achieve this, he knew he would need to manipulate the bishops. There was certainly not going to be a religious revolution. Thomas Cromwell knew that neither the conservative bishops nor the King would support such an action. If he pushed things too far, or too quickly, it wouldn't work.

There appears little doubt Cromwell was a shrewd man. He'd helped the King achieve his divorce and marry his new wife. Even though Anne Boleyn was executed in 1536, Henry soon remarried. Not long afterwards, in 1537, he was blessed with the son he'd waited so long for. Sadly, Henry's third wife, Jane Seymour, died just two weeks later, following complications after the birth of Prince Edward.

Henry remained angry with Rome and wanted even more money. If Cromwell could keep bringing in the cash and keep the King away from the details, he believed he could gradually reform the Church. He attempted to prod and direct the bishops, ensuring it was they, not he, who put forward and published the amendments he wished to make. Should Henry be unhappy with a specific development, the fault could be laid at their door, and the policy reversed until the time was right to try again.

It's fascinating to wonder what Cromwell's thoughts were at this time. Did he sit happily in his office, confident he could continue to get away with things? Or did he lie in bed at night, worrying he'd soon be exposed by his enemies as they plotted his downfall? Cromwell's actions were certainly carefully planned, even if everything didn't come off. The direction of the Church began to change.

In 1536 the Church of England published a short statement called the 'Ten Articles'. Whereas the Catholic Church practised seven sacraments (activities regarded as imparting divine grace onto the persons involved), the Lutheran Protestant reformers argued there should only be two (baptism and the Lord's Supper or Eucharist). The Ten Articles included a compromise, by identifying three (baptism, the Eucharist and penance). This wasn't well received by the conservative bishops. In the subsequent publication, the *Bishops' Book*, the four missing sacraments were added back in, although they were moved to a separate section to emphasise their lesser importance.[4]

One of Cromwell's most significant changes was announced in 1537. A decree was issued that every parish church in the country should possess an English language (rather than Latin) Bible within the next two years. Cromwell worked to ensure sufficient bibles were printed and made available. For the first time, ordinary parishioners, assuming they could read English, would be able to examine the contents of the Bible for themselves rather than through their priest.

Cromwell also took action against a number of items many Protestants considered to be Catholic superstitions rather than religious practices. For example, minor feast days were changed from holidays into working days, and pilgrimages discouraged. Use of religious relics was banned and relics were ordered to be removed from churches.

One of Cromwell's less religiously driven injunctions has since proved itself a fantastic resource for historians and anyone wishing to trace their family tree. All parishes were instructed to create and maintain an accurate register of births, marriages and deaths.

Of course, not everyone was happy. There were many examples of regional discord. The most significant of these was the Pilgrimage of Grace, which we'll explore shortly. However, such protests were largely unsuccessful.

In 1539 the Second Suppression of Religious Houses Act, or the Act for the Dissolution of the Greater Monasteries, was passed through Parliament. This opened the door for the dissolution of the larger monasteries and many other religious houses. More than 500 institutions in total were included, as wholesale liquidation of the Church's assets continued.

Despite the wealth he'd generated for Henry, things began to go awry for Cromwell. Rightfully or wrongfully, the King blamed him for his mismatched marriage to Anne of Cleves, which had taken place in January 1540. With Cromwell's influence in the royal court weakening, his enemies seized their opportunity. In June 1540 Cromwell was arrested at a Privy Council meeting and imprisoned in the Tower of London.

A Bill of Attainder was passed in the House of Lords, condemning Cromwell to death without trial. The charges against him included treason, heresy and Protestant sympathy. Although he made a plea for mercy to King Henry, the man he'd faithfully served ignored his request. Cromwell was beheaded on the same day Henry married his fifth wife, Catherine Howard.

The Reformation stalled. Even before Cromwell's death, the more conservative clerics had begun to regain their influence. Although the rift with Rome appeared permanent, the Church of England began to adopt a more Catholic stance in religious matters.

Henry married his sixth and final wife, Catherine Parr, in 1543. Catherine was thought to be a Protestant sympathiser, but there was little change in Church policy during the course of their marriage. If one thing did continue, it was Henry's need for money. Ongoing wars with France and Scotland continued to drain the economy. Once more, the King turned towards the Church for a source of funding. With the dissolution of the lesser and larger religious houses almost complete, Henry was forced to consider even the smallest institutions.

The first Chantries Act was passed in 1545. This authorized a review of the chantries (for example, dedicated chapels on private land), colleges, hospitals, free chapels, guilds and stipendiary services. The assets of any body found to be poorly governed could be stripped and passed to the Crown. Although investigations began, the work lacked Cromwell's vigour. Progress was slow and little revenue was raised before Henry's death in January 1547.

York – Decline, Dissolution, Pilgrimage and Progress

The city of York is located 200 miles north of London. Down the centuries it has been a regional capital for invading Romans and Vikings, and during his wars with the Scots, King Edward I briefly made the city his capital. These days, the marauding invaders are mainly tourists. They visit the Minster, walk along the historic walls and wind their way through York's well-preserved medieval streets, such as the Shambles, where Margaret Clitherow once lived.

In 1396 King Richard II granted York a royal charter. This transformed the city into a corporate borough, independent of the wider shire.

York was a county in its own right. The city council, known as the Corporation of York, established a structure for local government which remained largely in place until well into the nineteenth century.

Administrative affairs, taxation and justice were managed locally. Answerable only to the Crown, the Corporation was headed by a mayor and twelve additional aldermen. As the city's justices of the peace, the aldermen presided over many of the court hearings within their jurisdiction. Working with their colleagues in the next tier of administration, the Twenty-Four, the aldermen maintained local laws, non-religious policies and much else in the city.

While the number of aldermen was fixed at thirteen (the mayor and his twelve colleagues), the Twenty-Four often varied in size, above and below two dozen. The Twenty-Four were supported by a wider Common Council, sometimes known as the Forty-Eight. While the Common Council played a minor role, it did provide a voice for junior freemen in the city and, for some, a route into the higher echelons of York's government.

The first step onto the corporate ladder for a freeman in York was to be appointed in a minor administrative role, such as bridgemaster or chamberlain. Subsequently, in time, a freeman might be invited to join the Forty-Eight.

The next step was more significant. Each year, two men were elected to serve as one of the city's sheriffs. When their annual term was complete, both retiring sheriffs would traditionally be invited to join the Twenty-Four.

A man could only become an alderman when an existing incumbent died or, more rarely, retired from the role due to ill-heath or disgrace. Either way, the remaining eleven aldermen and the mayor would get their heads together and elect one of the Twenty-Four to join their number. On an annual basis, the aldermen also elected one of their own to become the new mayor. An alderman could be the mayor on multiple occasions, although not in successive years.

The mayor held a number of important powers. He set the Corporation's agenda, had the casting vote in meetings, could sometimes fix prices in the city's markets and even had the ability to order arrests on certain occasions. Ultimately, the mayor was responsible for law, order and behaviour in the city. Effectively, he reported directly to the King or Queen of the day. During the Tudor period, as in London, the people of York bestowed their leader with the grand title of lord mayor of the city.

The higher echelons of the Corporation were dominated by merchants. More than seventy per cent of aldermen in York during the sixteenth century could be classed as merchants or wholesale traders. Another twenty-five per cent were craftsmen or retailers and five per cent lawyers or gentlemen. The Twenty-Four tended to have a lesser concentration of merchants. Men in certain trades and crafts would know the Twenty-Four was as far as they could go. Of the twelve butchers in the Twenty-Four during the sixteenth century, not one was invited to become an alderman.[5]

The Corporation operated for many years alongside an even more powerful body, the Catholic Church. At the beginning of the Tudor period, York was home to a cathedral (York Minster), four monasteries, one nunnery, four friaries, forty parish churches and a myriad of chapels, hospitals, chantries and almshouses, run by a variety of religious houses and orders.

Together, these Catholic institutions provided a place of worship for York's citizens and a roof and vocation for hundreds of clergy, monks, friars, nuns and clerics. The Church had its own courts and prisons focused on religious matters. In combination, the religious houses created an economic powerhouse for the city, providing employment and business for many tradesmen, labourers and others in York and beyond.

The Archbishop of York held a powerful position. In terms of the Church of England's hierarchy, he was second only to the Archbishop of Canterbury. Above these two men were the Pope and the cardinals in Rome, although Christopher Bainbridge and Thomas Wolsey, both Archbishops of York in early Tudor times, eventually became cardinals themselves. The archbishop's official residence was, and still is, located at Bishopthorpe Palace on the banks of the River Ouse, to the south of the city.

Another important local body with relevance to the contents of this book was the Council of the North. Established in 1472 by King Edward IV, its headquarters were initially located ten miles north of York at Sheriff Hutton Castle. Edward's vision was for a royal body to oversee important matters in the northern counties of Cumberland, Derbyshire, Durham, Lancashire, Northumberland, Nottinghamshire, Staffordshire, Westmorland and, of course, Yorkshire.

Edward appointed his brother Richard, later Richard III, as the first Lord President of the Council. Following Richard's subsequent defeat by Henry VII, which ended the Wars of the Roses, the Council waned in importance for a time, although it returned to play a major role during the reigns of Henry VIII and Elizabeth I.

At its peak during the Middle Ages, York had been the most populous city in the whole of England, bar London. The population may have been as high as 15–16,000. By the time of the Tudor era, the numbers were in decline. The reasons were varied. Epidemics and disease, such as bubonic plague, swept across most of the country during the Middle Ages. Larger locations, such as York, were often disproportionately affected due to urban populations living closely together in poor sanitary conditions. Numbers in the city directly declined due to the death rate caused by multiple outbreaks. There was an indirect impact too, as people became more wary of living in a city.

A change in the industrial landscape was also a factor. Cloth-making had long been one of England's major industries. However, the Yorkshire heartland of the trade had begun to migrate westward from towns and cities such as Beverley and York to Leeds, Halifax and elsewhere in the West Riding. Elements of the population followed. Consequently, York's direct trade with Europe through the port of Hull was also in decline, further reducing prosperity.

Insurrection and war played their part too. For example, the Wars of the Roses had an adverse impact on York's population, with people killed, wounded, or displaced by the fighting and ongoing unrest. For example, men from the city fought and died on both sides at the Battle of Towton in 1461.[6] Some York men fought with the losing Lancastrians while others supported the victorious Yorkist forces.

The Wars of the Roses finally ended in 1485, when the first Tudor king, Henry VII, defeated Richard III. Due to York's links with the previous regime, the aftermath was a concerning time for the city. Henry VII visited York in 1486 and 1487. The mayor, aldermen and sheriffs were all keen to make a good impression and avoid any further hardship for the city. The Corporation claimed to Henry that York's population had declined by half since its peak, although the number may have been overstated in an attempt to avoid taxation and gain financial aid.

During the first half of the sixteenth century York was impacted by further outbreaks of bubonic plague and the mysterious sweating sickness. There was also another significant factor at play – the dissolution of the religious houses during the 1530s. Although no definitive records are available, it's likely the city's population sank to a low point of around 8,000.

In 1536, for the first time, York was directly impacted by the dissolution. Clementhorpe Nunnery and Holy Trinity Priory in Micklegate were closed during the summer months. These shutdowns were part of the suppression of the lesser monasteries, initiated at a national level by Thomas Cromwell. Such changes weren't well received in the religiously conservative north, and across Yorkshire in particular.

The Pilgrimage of Grace was the largest of a number of public uprisings against Cromwell's policies. The Pilgrimage began in Beverley in the East Riding of Yorkshire in early October 1536. Within weeks the uprising's leader, the lawyer Robert Aske, led a group of around 9,000 men towards York. The city's gates were opened and the rebels largely welcomed inside. Once within York's walls, Aske set about arranging for expelled monks and nuns to be returned to their religious houses and for the restoration of full observance of Catholic rituals in the city's churches.

By the time the 'Pilgrims' neared Doncaster a few weeks later, it's estimated Aske was accompanied by a sizeable army, possibly of 30,000 men. They soon encountered a smaller force of less than 10,000 led by the king's representatives, the Duke of Norfolk and the Earl of Shrewsbury. Heavily outnumbered, Norfolk had little choice but to negotiate with Aske from a position of weakness.

Aske and his followers were eventually promised they'd receive pardons, and many of their demands would be met. These included a reprieve for the religious houses until Parliament could meet without any royal interference. Upon hearing this, Aske stood his men down.

Following a lesser rebellion, unrelated to Aske's own activities, a series of arrests were made. Aske and many of the other ringleaders and churchmen associated with the Pilgrimage of Grace were tried, found guilty of treason and executed. Robert Aske was hanged in chains outside Clifford's Tower at York Castle in July 1537.

The dissolution and the suppression of the religious houses continued apace. Between 1538 and 1539 York's remaining priories and friaries were dissolved. This included the largest two houses, St Mary's (or York) Abbey and St Leonard's Hospital. Forty other monasteries across the country which owned property in the city were also closed down. The immediate impact on the local economy was severe.

Many of the monastic buildings and friaries were dismantled for building materials. The closed hospitals could no longer support the poor, sick or destitute. Friars, nuns, monks and canons were turfed onto the streets. The ownership of between twenty and thirty per cent of the city's housing stock, previously owned by York's or other religious houses, was transferred to the King. Henry and his advisers sold many of them off. For example, over 400 houses were bought by one London alderman, Sir Richard Gresham.

As money and wealth flooded from the city, there was an outbreak of plague. The demand for goods and services driven by the needs of the religious houses collapsed. Merchants, tradesmen, labourers and others were all badly affected. For example, the butchers and wax chandlers saw sales of meat and beeswax products reduced as they were no longer needed to feed and light the religious houses.

Despite the savage reprisals after the Pilgrimage of Grace, Henry was determined to keep a closer eye on Yorkshire and the other potentially rebellious northern counties. He reinstated the Council of the North and installed Robert Holgate as the new lord president. The Council was to meet up for four annual sessions – one each in York, Durham, Newcastle and Hull. Following the dissolution of St Mary's Abbey in York, the abbot's house was retained for the King's use. Known as the King's Manor, it was allocated to the Council in 1539.

In addition to reinstating the Council of the North, Henry VIII decided he needed to demonstrate his personal power. The King's Northern Progress in 1541 was a show of force that ended in York. While staying there, Henry was due to meet King James V of Scotland. Accompanied by his fifth wife, Catherine Howard, and around 5,000 soldiers, Henry reached Fulford Cross on the outskirts of the city on 16 September. He was met there by the lord mayor, the aldermen and other local dignitaries. As the King approached, York's leaders sank to their knees, and the city's recorder read out a lengthy, prewritten apology and submission on behalf of the people of York for their role in the Pilgrimage of Grace.[7]

York's citizens claimed to be repentant from 'the bottoms of their stomachs'. In future, they would 'spend their all in royal service'. The local dignitaries showered the royal couple with gifts, including a large silver cup for both the King and Queen. These were filled with as much gold as the cups could hold.

Henry and his force remained in York until 27 September, by which time it was clear the Scottish King wasn't going to show up. The Progress withdrew and travelled south. It must have been an uncomfortable eleven days for York's population, living under what must have felt like an occupation. Fortunately, there were no major disturbances during the King's time there.

The remaining years of Henry's reign were a difficult time for many in York. Wealth and employment fell, and with many of the religious houses, hospitals and grammar schools closed, healthcare, education and other services were hard to come by. For some though, life went on as usual.

Margaret's Story – Turners and Middletons

Margaret Clitherow, née Middleton, was born six years after Henry VIII's reign in 1553. One of her biographers, Katharine Longley, has researched Margaret's immediate ancestry.[8] Her maternal grandparents were Richard and Margaret Turner. They ran The Angel, a large hostelry located outside the city walls on the street of Bootham.

Like virtually everyone else in the country at the time, the Turners were Catholics. When Richard Turner wrote his will in 1531, the document stated the majority of his estate should be shared out between his wife and elder son, Thomas. In addition, twelve shillings were to be donated to each of the religious orders who ran York's four friaries. When Richard died in 1534, these friaries were still very much ongoing concerns. We assume they accepted his money gratefully and spent it wisely. If not, it would soon be passed on to the coffers of the Crown.

Richard Turner's will included a request for his body be buried at St Olave's Church, which was located in the same parish as The Angel, just a few yards away in Marygate. The church was built next to St Mary's (or York) Abbey. At the time, the area around the abbey would have been a bustling hive of activity.

Richard and Margaret had two sons. The elder lad, Thomas, followed in his father's footsteps, running The Angel after Richard's death. The other, Robert Turner, became a Catholic priest. The boys had three sisters, but they didn't share in the inheritance left by their father. Born in 1515, Jane Turner was the youngest of them. In the years to come, she would give birth to a daughter called Margaret.

Not a great deal is known about the background of Margaret's father. From the properties detailed in Thomas Middleton's will, it appears his family may have been from Ripon, twenty-five miles north-west of York. We do know Thomas completed his apprenticeship in York as a wax chandler. In 1530 he became a freeman of the city.

Two years later, in 1532, Thomas Middleton married Jane Turner. After their wedding ceremony, Jane departed the family home in Bootham. The newlyweds moved into a relatively large property in Davygate in central York in the parish of St Martin's Church, Coney Street.

The couple set about building a business and creating a family. At a time when every workplace, every home and place of worship needed candles for lighting and much more besides, a wax chandlery was a prosperous trade. Thomas Middleton would have been a busy man.

Wax chandlers like Thomas used beeswax to manufacture and sell a variety of products. In addition to different shapes and sizes of candles, wax was used to make torches and seals, and for medical purposes. Seals made of beeswax were an invaluable security aid for correspondence and contracts. Officials, tradesmen and religious officers used wax-coated tablets as portable and reusable devices for detailing notes and transactions on their journeys and in their homes and places of work.[9]

Prior to the Reformation, the biggest demand for beeswax products came from the churches and religious houses. Vast quantities were needed to make candles, tapers and images for lighting, decoration and other purposes. For example, candles were used in Catholic churches to help speed the souls of the recently deceased through Purgatory into Heaven.

Beeswax candles were made by melting and staining beeswax. This was a skilled and lengthy process. Cauldrons of water were heated over fires, and when the water boiled, measured amounts of beeswax were placed into the simmering liquid. For coloured candles, dyes were also added. Positioned high above the cauldron was an intricate system of wooden planks. Each held one or more rows of dangling wicks, typically made from rush stalks.

Melted beeswax is lighter than water. When it reaches a certain temperature, the wax floats to the surface. Once the wax was sufficiently melted, the wicks were dipped into the mixture to take up the wax and form candles. However, only a limited amount of wax could be added at one time.

Following each dip, the planks had to be lifted and dipped into cold water. After this, they were lifted again, and the wax allowed to cool in the air.

Once the partially formed candles were sufficiently cool, additional wax was added to the reheated water and the wicks dipped once more. The procedure was repeated until the candles reached the desired size. Afterwards, they were trimmed to create uniform shapes, and stored until sold.

In addition to living accommodation, the premises in Davygate contained areas for the manufacture, storage and sale of candles and other beeswax products. Although the cauldrons and fires were hot and the dipping process tiring and uncomfortable, beeswax candle production had one positive side effect: it created a pleasant smell, in stark contrast to the pungent aromas made by tallow chandlers, whose lower-cost candles were created by melting animal fats.

Sighting, managing and collecting wax from beehives were all part of the wax chandler's trade. The beehives themselves were frequently kept in orchards and other locations outside the city. Many large estates had their own hives. The production of honey and mead were welcome by-products of beeswax production, although some may consider it to be the other way around.

In 1540 Jane's mother, Margaret Turner, died. In her will Margaret requested her body be buried at St Olave's Church, alongside her husband's. The main inheritors from Margaret's estate were to be her two sons, although six silver spoons and a rosary, made from a pair of ivory beads, were bequeathed to Margaret's daughter Jane.

This time, the family couldn't make any donations to York's friaries and priories. St Mary's Abbey and the city's other major religious houses were all closed. Their land and chattels had been passed to the King's Commissioners as part of the dissolution. The friars, monks and nuns who'd inhabited them were gone. In addition, the dissolution was beginning to have a negative impact on the trade of the wax chandlers, who saw significant falls in demand for their beeswax candles and related products.

Inside the city walls in Davygate, the Middleton family was expanding. Jane gave birth to a daughter, Alice. A year later the couple's first son, named Thomas after his father, was born. What the growing family thought of the Pilgrimage of Grace, the execution of Robert Aske, the Northern Progress and destruction and pillage of the religious houses in the streets around them, we can only imagine.

Chapter Three

Turmoil and Decline (1547–1558)

Edward VI and Mary I – Changing Times

In 1547 Henry VIII was succeeded by the son he'd longed for, but there was a problem. When Edward VI was crowned he was just nine years old. To maintain stability, Henry arranged for a Regency Council to be put in place after his death. This would rule the land until the boy came of age. It would be led by Edward's maternal uncle, Edward Seymour, who adopted the title Lord Protector Somerset.

One of Somerset's first challenges was to consider the country's ailing finances. In 1547 Parliament passed a second Chantries Act. This amended and accelerated the earlier plans to get the Crown's hands on the assets of the smallest religious houses. Commissioners were sent to visit the chantries and the other minor religious buildings. Their land and valuables were often confiscated, liquidated and the proceeds injected into the royal coffers. Although the dissolution of the chantries is often overlooked due to the emphasis placed on the larger houses, the impact on the local population was often far greater.

Like Thomas Cromwell before him, Somerset found himself in a power struggle with the more conservative members of the Church and Privy Council. Equally, his views on religion didn't fully align with the young King's. Despite his age, Edward was a significantly more radical Protestant than his Lord Protector.

To the consternation of the conservatives, Parliament passed a new Treason Act, which repealed many of the previous rulings regarding heresy and censorship. The people of the country would now be allowed to discuss, debate and write about religion without any fear of arrest. A raft of religious pamphlets and books were soon written. Others were imported from Europe. Often, these publications contained radical Lutheran ideas.

When the Act of Uniformity was passed in 1549, it declared the contents of the 1549 Book of Common Prayer – written in English rather than Latin – to be the only legal form of worship in England. Communion, matins and evensong services were all to be conducted in English. Even if most services followed the same order as the previous Latin services, and the Eucharist was defined in Catholic terms, this was a huge change. Permission was also given for clergymen to marry.

The act was hugely controversial. The governing classes and parts of the country were split down the middle. Ten bishops voted for it, eight against. The book was criticised by Catholics for containing too much Protestant content, and by Protestants for not being radical enough and for retaining too many elements of Catholic beliefs.

The man behind the prayer book was the Archbishop of Canterbury, Thomas Cranmer. During Henry VIII's time, Cranmer had declared the King's marriage to Catherine of Aragon to be void. In Henry's later years, particularly following Cromwell's execution, Cranmer had been sidelined by the more conservative bishops. Now, during Edward's reign, he regained his influence.

Somerset's leadership didn't last very long. In addition to increasing religious divisions, the country's economic problems persisted. Despite the income from the chantries, the continuing attrition with France and Scotland was expensive and showed little sign of abating, and there was unrest in rural areas following illegal enclosures of common land.

Popular uprisings took place in Norfolk, the West Country and elsewhere. All had to be put down. The Privy Council lost patience and seized power from the Lord Protector in the latter half of 1549. Somerset was arrested, released, and later rearrested, before finally being executed in 1552. The young King summarised his uncle's death in a rather blasé manner in a letter, 'The Duke of Somerset had his head cut off upon Tower Hill between eight and nine o'clock in the morning.'

The man who replaced Somerset as the country's new ruler, until the King came of age, was John Dudley, the Earl of Warwick. Also known as the Duke of Northumberland and Lord President of the Council, Dudley adopted the title Lord President Northumberland. In an attempt to court favour with the King, Northumberland opened the door to more radical religious reforms. To limit opposition, a number of the country's leading Catholic bishops, including the Bishop of Winchester, Stephen Gardiner, were arrested and imprisoned in the Tower of London. Once inside, they were replaced by more ardent reformers.

In the meantime, Thomas Cranmer was busy. In 1552 a second Act of Uniformity was passed. This confirmed the updated Second Book of Common Prayer as the legally binding basis for all church services. The new edition addressed many (though not all) of the complaints previously made by Protestant reformers about the first edition. Many traces of Catholicism and Mass were removed. Attendance of Church of England services became mandatory. Clergy and lay people accused and found guilty of non-attendance could be fined and imprisoned.

Firmly in the ascendency, the reformers planned to go further. Cranmer created a document called the Forty-Two Articles, which he intended to use as the basis of a new and much more Protestant Church of England. However, by the time of Edward's death in 1553 the Forty-Two Articles hadn't yet become law and the opportunity was lost.

Before the young King's death, there was a flurry of activity. Suspecting his illness could be terminal, Edward, Lord President Northumberland and the Privy Council drew up a plan of succession designed to prevent restoration of the Catholic Church. The King's young cousin, Lady Jane Grey (who just happened to be Northumberland's daughter-in-law), was named as Edward's heir, rather than one of his half-sisters, Mary or Elizabeth.

This decision was hotly disputed. Following Edward's death, Jane was swiftly deposed and disposed of. Both she and her father-in-law Northumberland were executed. Edward's elder half-sister, Mary, the staunchly Catholic daughter of Henry VIII and his first wife, Catherine of Aragon, was crowned Queen Mary I of England.

One of the many men arrested in the aftermath was Henry Hastings, son of the second Earl of Huntingdon. Although Hastings had supported Northumberland's plans, upon his release from prison he swore loyalty to the Queen, despite her Catholicism and his own Puritanical leanings. Hastings will come back into the book later, as a future Lord President of the Council of the North.

The Catholic bishops were freed from the Tower and their cells refilled with Protestants. Stephen Gardiner was appointed the Queen's Lord Chancellor. Clergymen were once again banned from marrying. Anyone who'd taken up the option was ordered to give up their wife and family or be deprived of their parish.

In September 1553 the Catholic Mass was reintroduced. In July 1554, to ensure a Catholic succession, Mary married King Philip II of

Spain. Their royal union caused much resistance and hostility around the country, from Protestants and Catholics alike.

In November 1554 Parliament passed a second Act of Repeal, which put an end to the royal supremacy. The act repealed many of the laws relating to religion created under Henry VIII as part of the breakaway from Rome. Papal authority was now restored. England reconciled with Rome, and the Church of England again became part of the wider Roman Catholic Church.

The heresy laws repealed under Edward were re-enacted by Parliament, and there was a period of intense religious persecution against Protestants. Mary's new Lord Chancellor, Stephen Gardiner, who'd spent time in the Tower under Edward, argued strongly against this. Equally, he opposed Mary and Philip's marriage, fearing these actions might split the country and turn many of the Queen's subjects against her. His advice was ignored.

Stephen Gardiner died of natural causes at the end of 1555. With Thomas Cranmer in prison, Reginald Pole was appointed as the new Archbishop of Canterbury. Pole had been a vociferous opponent of Henry VIII's divorce and the breakaway from the Catholic Church. Afterwards, he'd been summoned to Rome by the Pope, who made him a cardinal. In response, Henry branded Pole a traitor and ordered the arrests of his mother and brother. Both were eventually executed. Pole hadn't forgotten. He was determined to work with Mary to stamp out what he saw as the heresy that had polluted his country.

Around 300 Protestants were put to death during Mary's short reign.[1] This included three bishops, Cranmer, Latimer and Ridley, who became known as the 'Oxford martyrs'. Former Archbishop Cranmer was forced to watch while his colleagues, Latimer and Ridley, were burnt in the same fire at Balliol College in Oxford in October 1555. Cramer was eventually burned at the stake in March 1556. These actions and many others earned the Queen her infamous nickname of 'Bloody Mary'.

A number of prominent Protestant churchmen, including a future Archbishop of York, Edwin Sandys, escaped execution by fleeing abroad. Some of the exiles worked with others on the Continent to write anti-Catholic publications and import them back into the country to fuel unrest.

Gardiner's predictions proved to be well founded. Mary's popularity waned, although her desperate desire to have Philip's child didn't. Despite widespread protests against Spanish control of England, Mary initially indicated in her will that if she died after childbirth, Philip should be regent until the child came of age. However, no infant was born. When Mary fell ill in 1558 she confirmed her half-sister, Elizabeth, daughter of Henry VIII and Anne Boleyn, as her successor. Knowing Elizabeth had been raised a Protestant, it must have been a bitter pill for the dying Catholic Queen to swallow.

When Mary died – probably of cancer – in November 1558, she was forty-two. Coincidentally, her Archbishop of Canterbury, Reginald Pole, died the same day after suffering, like many others at the time, from a severe bout of influenza.

Mary's husband, Philip II, the King of Spain, didn't appear too heartbroken when he heard the news of his wife's death. In a letter to his sister, he wrote, 'I felt a reasonable regret.' There was to be no Catholic king of England, and no longer a Catholic queen. The Counter-Reformation was over.

York – Reformation, Counter-Reformation and Pestilence

The eleven-year period which spans the reigns of King Edward and Queen Mary was a difficult time for York. In common with many other towns and cities in the north, York was religiously more conservative and Catholic leaning than London. The reforms driven under Edward were difficult for York's clergymen and merchant classes to accept.

The city continued to suffer from ongoing economic depression. Food prices were rising, and there was significant national and local inflation. In addition, the population was impacted during both reigns by continued epidemics, which struck down the city with alarming severity.

The dissolution of the chantries and smaller religious houses during Edward's reign had a significant impact on York. Many of these institutions provided charity, healthcare and welfare services to the city's least fortunate residents. Over a hundred chantries, colleges and religious guilds were closed and their valuables auctioned off. To add to this, around 500 more domestic houses were transferred to the Crown to be sold to the highest bidder.

To reduce costs and raise funds, the Church took advantage of government legislation. A decision was made to shut down or merge twelve or thirteen parish churches in the city between 1548 and 1550. Although the plan wasn't fully completed, several churches were sold off to members of the Corporation of York at very low prices.[2]

Many of the remaining churches were impacted by the Protestant-leaning changes in the Church and in law. A number of Catholic practices were forbidden. In some churches, the altars were forcibly removed. York's clergymen were given the option to marry, although it's not clear how many men in the city took advantage of this.

During Edward's reign York was struck down by both bubonic plague and sweating sickness. Records show particularly heavy rates of mortality in 1550 and 1551. The parish of St Martin's, Micklegate, for example, may have lost half its population. The situation wasn't helped by the weather. In 1551 the city was hit by a great storm, with winds so severe they brought down the steeples of Trinity Church on Micklegate and St John's. There was also a series of poor harvests, causing malnutrition in certain quarters of the city. The death rate remained high in both winter and summer months. It was around this time that York's dwindling population reached a low point of less than 8,000.

Mary's coronation in 1553 was largely welcomed in the city. The Corporation sent a letter of allegiance to their new monarch whom they considered to be, 'So noble, Godly and most rightful a Queen'. The majority of the people in the city also responded positively to the Counter-Reformation. Many of the parish churches were gradually repaired and restored, and the altars removed during Edward's reign were replaced. The work sometimes took place slowly, when individual parishes and parishioners were able to afford the changes needed.

Recognising the need for improved healthcare, the Corporation wrote to Cardinal Pole requesting the restoration of St Leonard's hospital. This had been closed during the dissolution, leaving a significant gap for the care of the city's sickest and poorest. Although no positive reply was received, there was better news for the Corporation in 1556 when the Crown handed back revenue to the city from many of the former chantries and colleges removed from local control during Edward's reign. Records indicate the city got its hands on an additional £157 a year from this.[3] Each and every pound, shilling and penny would have been gratefully received.

In 1555 Nicholas Heath was appointed the new Archbishop of York. Although he didn't know it at the time, Heath would be the last Catholic to serve in the post. In contrast to many other places across England, and in London in particular, there were no prosecutions or executions for heresy or treason in York during Queen Mary's reign. Partially at least, this was down to Archbishop Heath's efforts. They may not have realised it, but York's citizens had much to thank him for.

Bad news was to follow, however. York was struck down by pestilence once again. It's believed the 'new ague' was a particularly virulent strain of influenza which swept across the country. York itself was severely impacted in 1558 and 1559, and death rates in the city were once again very high. As news reached the north that their Catholic Queen was ill and likely to be replaced by her Protestant half-sister, the outlook for the city looked bleak indeed.

Margaret's Story – Early Childhood

The reign of Edward VI brought with it challenges to the Middleton family in Davygate. Although no records indicate significant deaths in the immediate household due to the epidemics in the city, it's unlikely the family remained unaffected. Equally, the closing of the chantries and the Protestant reforms of the Church of England led to reduced demand for beeswax candles and products.

The Middletons, however, were not paupers. They employed servants, who were supervised by Jane as mistress of the house. When Thomas was away, checking his beehives, visiting suppliers or on other business, responsibility for running the chandlery would fall on her shoulders. Jane Middleton would have been adept at managing orders, planning deliveries and making sales. She also had a growing family to support. A second son, George, was born, who would grow up to be a draper in the city.

The religious beliefs and levels of piety within the Middleton household at this time are not recorded, but it's known that conversion to Protestantism in the North of England during Edward's reign was patchy at best. When the young King's short reign ended, Mary I re-established the Catholic Church. Her bishops set about restoring the old faith and ways of worship. One of the impacts of this change was a sudden upsurge in the demand for beeswax. Even if the Middletons had temporarily converted to Protestantism for pragmatic reasons, it's likely they would have warmly welcomed the latest change in direction of the state religion.

In 1553, the year of Queen Mary's coronation, Jane Middleton is believed to have given birth to her younger daughter, the subject of this book. The exact date of Margaret Middleton's birth is unknown. Some sources state 1556, although 1553 appears more likely.[4] Either way, at her baptism she was named after her maternal grandmother.

The early years of Margaret's life coincided with the Counter-Reformation of Queen Mary's reign. It was a busy time in Davygate, and hopefully a happy one. The family would certainly have been financially better off than many in the city. Business would have been booming and everything must have looked rosy and bright for the future. With the Catholic Church restored and more elaborate use of beeswax products back in vogue, the sweet smell of candle production would have wafted around the family's house and premises once more.

In 1555 Margaret's father, Thomas Middleton, began a three-year term as one of four churchwardens at the family's parish church of St Martin's, Coney Street. Katharine Longley's research indicates Thomas and his three companions set about completing the refurbishment of the church, returning it to Catholic standards in time for the year's Easter services.

Tasks included re-establishing the rood (the crucifix positioned between the chancel and nave of the church) and the rood screen beneath it, procuring new candlesticks to illuminate it (populated no doubt with fine Middleton candles) and repairing the Easter Sepulchre. This was the arched recess where the crucifix and other sacred elements relating to the resurrection were located between Good Friday and Easter Sunday. The wardens also arranged for the purchase and fitting of new materials for the altar cloth. They bought charcoal for the Easter vigil service and funded repairs for the damaged stalls for the choir and congregation.

As a young child, Margaret would have accompanied her parents and siblings to Catholic Mass, as well as other services at St Martin's. It's easy to imagine her father proudly pointing out the improvements he'd made around the church, and her parents talking to the priest, their neighbours, friends and churchwardens. Margaret, meanwhile, may have stood next to them, gazing in wonder at the redecoration around her. Some of her earliest memories may have been in this church: the theatre of Mass, the sound of spoken Latin, the smells of incense and the sights of her father's candles.

It's equally likely she would have spent some time with her local relatives, for example the families of her mother's brothers and sisters. Her uncle Richard Turner was now a Catholic priest, but his brother Thomas was running The Angel on Bootham. It appears Thomas's business was prospering sufficiently for him to acquire at least one other adjacent property on the street.

It's likely there was a close relationship between Thomas Turner's family and the Middletons. As a young child, Margaret may have frequently visited the Turners in Bootham and played with her cousins. On other occasions, Thomas and his wife may have dined with her parents in Davygate. Margaret may have placed her head around the door, before being sent to bed.

Thomas Turner was now in an up-and-coming profession. Innkeeping had previously been much less prestigious. At one time, innkeepers had been barred from becoming aldermen in York. However, in 1540 John Beane became the first man in the trade to be elected to the lofty position of alderman. Later, he served as one of York's Members of Parliament and twice as lord mayor, although over time his business interests expanded, and by then he was classified as a merchant.[5]

Like many others in York, Thomas Turner died during the influenza epidemic of 1558. His brother-in-law Thomas Middleton (Margaret's father) witnessed and supervised the will. The Turners were keen to ensure The Angel remained in the family. Richard Turner, Margaret's first cousin, became the new innkeeper, while his brother Edward inherited the family's adjacent property on Bootham.

Thomas Turner's will was typically Catholic in nature. It committed his soul to Almighty God and beseeched the Virgin Mary and the holy company in heaven to pray for him. At his burial at St Olave's church in Marygate, he made a request for a dirge to be sung. This was a solemn mourning hymn that would include a cry of lament for the deceased's soul.

The timing of Thomas Turner's death coincided with a moment of significant and lasting change in the country. In Westminster, 200 miles south of York, the body of another Catholic lay in state, awaiting burial. Queen Mary I was dead. She was to be succeeded by her Protestant half-sister, Elizabeth. The temporary resurgence of the Catholic Church in England had come to an abrupt end. Given the level of religious turmoil of the previous three decades, nobody could have possibly known how permanent, or otherwise, this change might be.

Chapter Four

Change and Slow Recovery
(1558–1570)

Elizabeth I – Supremacy and Uniformity

Following the death of Mary I in November 1558, her half-sister, Elizabeth, daughter of Henry VIII and Anne Boleyn, was crowned Queen. The coronation procession to Westminster Abbey in January 1559 was led by Sir Thomas Leigh of Warwickshire. His granddaughter Catherine would one day marry Robert Catesby, the man who'd lead the Gunpowder Plot against Elizabeth's Protestant successor, James I.

Queen Elizabeth was now twenty-five years old. In addition to the crown on her head, she carried heavy burdens on her shoulders. The country remained at war with both France and Scotland and continued to struggle economically. The final years of Mary's reign had been blighted by serious epidemics, including the widescale outbreak of influenza which had killed the Archbishop of Canterbury. Mary's marriage to Philip of Spain had been hugely unpopular. Given her age, it was expected Elizabeth would marry soon. The country hoped she'd select a better match, but on the thorny issue of religion the nation remained divided.

One of Elizabeth's first actions was to appoint William Cecil as Secretary of State and leader of the Privy Council. Cecil was an experienced and skilful politician, who'd served Somerset and Northumberland during King Edward's time. Despite his Protestant faith, he'd survived Mary's reign and remained true to the Crown. He was one of the men Elizabeth would come to rely on.

With the new Queen's parents' marriage still judged to be invalid by the Pope, in Rome's eyes Elizabeth was illegitimate. As she and her advisors set out to create a revised religious settlement, the Catholic Church watched nervously. Which way would it go?

Her coronation service was led by a surprise choice, the relatively lowly but very Catholic Bishop of Carlisle. Sections of the service were said in Latin and other parts in English. It was almost as if there was an attempt to reach out to both sides of the religious divide. However, during the coronation oath, Elizabeth committed to rule her country by the 'True profession of the Gospel established in this Kingdom'.

William Cecil's brother-in-law, Nicholas Bacon, was appointed Lord Keeper of the Great Seal, an important role in Parliament. At the opening of Elizabeth's first Parliament, Bacon made the following declaration on the Queen's behalf:[1]

> Now the Matters and causes whereupon you are to Consult, are chiefly and principally three points. Of those the first is of well making of Laws, for the according, and uniting of these people of the Realm into a uniform order of Religion, to the Honour and Glory of God, the establishing of the Church, and Tranquillity of the Realm. The second, for the Reforming and removing of all Enormities, and Mischiefs, that might hurt or hinder the Civil Orders and Policies of this Realm. The third and last is, advisedly and deeply to weigh and consider the Estate and Condition of this Realm, and the Losses and Decays that have happened of late to the Imperial Crown thereof; and therefore to advise the best remedies to supply and relieve the same.

Parliament's first priority would be to unite the country's people under a 'uniform order of Religion'. The second was to address any sources of potential rebellion, while the third was to take action to remedy the country's economic decline.

Parliament debated and eventually passed the Acts of Supremacy and Uniformity. As a potential olive branch to the Catholic Church, the Act of Supremacy saw Elizabeth confirmed as the Supreme Governor of the Church of England, rather than its Supreme Head. However, the intention behind the subsequent wording, to 'restore to the Crown the Jurisdiction over the State Ecclesiastical and Spiritual, and abolishing all Foreign Power repugnant to the same,' was clear enough.

An important element of the Act of Supremacy was to ensure the loyalty of those who wanted to hold high office, take a university degree, or do many other things. Anyone who refused to take the new oath of supremacy could be barred from certain positions and privileges.

The objective of the Act of Uniformity was to establish one 'uniform order of Religion'. This would be based on the 1552 Book of Common Prayer created by Thomas Cranmer during Edward VI's Protestant reign. However, the bill faced stiff opposition, particularly in the House of Lords, where concessions had to be made to gain sufficient votes to squeeze the act through.

Church services were amended to include additional Catholic elements; communion was to follow a more Catholic approach than had been originally intended, such as the belief in the presence of Christ in the Eucharist; vestments and ornaments were set to mimic Catholic Mass; and church ministers were positioned in the same manner as Catholic priests.

However, many of the Catholic bishops still weren't convinced. They continued to argue against the bill and attempted to vote it down. The Queen's supporters persuaded as many lay peers as possible to vote in favour. Finally, the Act of Uniformity was passed into law by the narrow margins of just three votes.

The act was to be supplemented by a number of royal injunctions. These removed altars from churches to placate Protestants and allowed some imagery to remain to appease Catholics. As is often the case with such compromises, neither side was particularly satisfied with the changes made.

The Church of England set about establishing the new uniform service, which included elements of Protestant and Catholic proceedings. However, it would be possible for some priests with Catholic leanings and largely Catholic congregations to conduct their services in a way that would be barely different from Mary's time ... unless there was a way to check on them.

Six new commissions were set up to verify that the Acts of Supremacy and Uniformity were properly implemented and adhered to. The commission leaders were selected largely from Protestant clergy, including some men recently returned from exile on the Continent, having escaped to evade persecution and death during Mary's time.

A number of Catholic bishops refused to swear the oath of royal supremacy. These men were removed from office and replaced by Protestants. In addition, Elizabeth appointed her mother's former chaplain, Matthew Parker, as the new Archbishop of Canterbury. The role had been vacant since Reginald Pole had passed away on the day of Mary's death.

Given their outlook, many of the new commissioners had little inclination to follow the compromises agreed in Parliament and described in some of the royal injunctions. In a number of places they ordered items they considered as idolatrous – such as the rood crucifix and screen of the type lovingly restored at St Martin's by Thomas Middleton – to be removed from the churches and burned. In certain parishes, altars and images were taken down and hidden so they could be reinstalled on the fateful day when Catholicism returned, as had happened following the transition from Edward to Mary.

The commissioners called together the senior clergy in each area to ensure their adherence to the royal supremacy, the prayer book and royal injunctions. Despite the compromises made, many refused to attend. Some were incensed by what they saw as vandalism being carried out in their churches. As a punishment, those who continued to dissent were removed from their parishes. Following widespread outbreaks of influenza and other epidemics, these dismissals resulted in an acute shortage of clergymen in some areas

In response, Elizabeth attempted to make a further compromise. She determined that rood crucifixes should be allowed to return to the parish churches. This time the Protestant bishops protested, including two future archbishops of York, Edmund Grindal and Edwin Sandys. Knowing she couldn't afford to lose her Protestant bishops, as well as the Catholic ones, Elizabeth backed down.

The pace of change and level of adherence to the new acts and injunctions varied widely between dioceses and locations, depending on the bishop and views of the local clergy. In the areas with the largest numbers of dismissals, often clerics were forced to administer multiple parishes. Some churches were left empty.[2]

The most significant change to the Church of England during Elizabeth's time was yet to come. Before his execution under Queen Mary, Thomas Cranmer, as Archbishop of Canterbury, had led development of the Forty-Two Articles. He'd intended the document to become the basis of a more Protestant Church of England. Now, during the early years of Elizabeth's reign, the new Archbishop of Canterbury, Matthew Parker, set out to complete Cranmer's work.

Parker began by organising the Convocation of 1563. This brought together leading reformist clerics from across England and Wales. The objective was to initiate a review of the content of Cranmer's Forty-Two

Articles. The Convocation was held in St Paul's Cathedral in London and ran for three months, in parallel with a sitting of Parliament.

The result of the Convocation was an updated list of articles. Once fully defined and agreed, these could be used to confirm the position and practices of the Church of England, particularly in relation to Catholic and Protestant doctrines. The intention was to create an updated 'uniform order of Religion', but there was much work still to be done. The result was the Thirty-Nine Articles, although this didn't become law until 1571, some eight years later.

Of course, religious challenges weren't the only ones facing Elizabeth. There were wars, economic issues and unfulfilled plans for her marriage. Although military conflicts with France and Scotland were much reduced due to focus being placed upon internal issues, tensions remained. In 1568 Elizabeth's cousin, Mary Stuart, the deposed Queen of Scots, escaped after being imprisoned by rebel Scots lords. She raised a small army and faced down the rebels in battle. Mary was subsequently defeated and travelled to England to request aid from Elizabeth, with the aim of gaining support to regain her throne in Scotland.

The aid she wanted wasn't forthcoming. Instead, new commissions were established, first in York and then in Westminster, to review the events that had occurred in Scotland and recommend what should be done about Mary. When the results of these political inquiries were inconclusive, Mary was retained in custody in England and held in a series of comfortable castles and houses.

York – Slow Recovery

York's population greeted Elizabeth's coronation with much less enthusiasm than her half-sister's. However, in some ways the city fared better under Elizabeth than during the reign of any other Tudor monarch. After the influenza outbreak of 1559, there wasn't another major epidemic in the city until the plague returned a year after Elizabeth's death in 1604.

Following the population decrease of previous decades, York's parish registers finally began to record higher numbers of births than deaths. Immigration, primarily from elsewhere in England, began to increase. For decades many of York's professional guilds had allowed tradesmen to take on apprentices from outside the city. During the population rises of the 1560s this became much less common. In 1568 the Common Council introduced controls to prevent 'strangers' from being enfranchised for less than £10.[3]

As the Corporation's finances improved, the city began to make a number of civic improvements. These were certainly needed in 1564. The bridge over the river Ouse was seriously damaged when a deluge of water swept down the river following a heavy snowfall and sudden thaw. Two bows of one arch and twelve houses were completely washed away, and a dozen people drowned. The Corporation, aided by donations from wealthy merchants, completed the repairs in 1566. A year later, the river was dredged. Following this, the riverbank was built up to protect the city from future deluges. This wasn't fully successful, and the city continues to be regularly affected by flooding today.

The driving force behind York's improving economy was the establishment of two major institutions inside the city. They would come to play a prominent role in Margaret Clitherow's story. Both also brought a major influx of wealth, power and people into the city.

Although the Council of the North's main offices were already in York (at the King's Manor in the former grounds of St Mary's Abbey), it sat annually in four different locations. In 1560 the Council made a request to William Cecil for York to become its sole meeting place, on the basis this would benefit the city's flagging economy, as well as make life much easier for Council officials. A year later, Cecil agreed the change.

During the 1560s several men fulfilled the role of Lord President of the Council of the North. Most prominent amongst them was Thomas Young, who held the position between 1564 and 1568. Young had replaced his deposed Catholic predecessor, Nicholas Heath, as Archbishop of York. By holding both roles, Young demonstrated the close connections which existed between the Council and Church at the time.

The Ecclesiastical Commission for the Northern Province was a brand-new body created by royal letters patent in 1561. Once established, the new Commission was based in York and presided over by the Archbishop. The Ecclesiastical Commission would soon become the second most important court in the north of the country, subservient only to the Council of the North. Both would come to play a major role in the battle to enforce religious uniformity, in alignment with the wishes of the Queen and Parliament.

Archbishop Young knew there was much work to be done in York and the surrounding area. At the beginning of Elizabeth's reign the Queen's commissioners had sought to ensure adherence to the royal supremacy and the new prayer book. When the commissioners called together the district's senior clergy, they summoned ninety men. But only twenty-one of them appeared and subscribed to the new policy. Sixteen sent proxy representatives in their stead. Thirty-six appeared but declined to subscribe, and seventeen didn't respond at all.[4]

A number of dissenting clergy, including Henry Moore, the rector at St Martin's in Micklegate, were forcibly removed from their parishes. This punishment caused some, including Moore, to relent. After promising to conform, these men returned to their churches. With so many clergy having died during the disease-ridden 1550s, there were insufficient numbers left to allow wholescale change in the short term. Negotiations and time would be needed to persuade York's clergy and the city's wider population to adhere to the new course of the Church.

Archbishop Young and the new Ecclesiastical Commissioners took to their task. Protestants were actively recruited to join the city's clergymen, for example in York Minster, although the pace of change in a number of the parishes was slower. Some churches, including the Middletons' own place of worship at St Martin's, Coney Street, actively resisted the removal of their altars and images. A few only did so under duress, as late as the end of 1562. Many roods weren't dismantled until the end of the decade.

A level of friction began to grow between the Council of the North and the Corporation of York. In 1564 the Council raised a formal complaint against the Corporation for not actively preventing 'the use, service and administration of the sacraments' in some of York's churches. This was to be the first of many such diatribes.

In the same year Archbishop Young made a report to the Privy Council in which he questioned the religious beliefs and loyalty of many of the city's aldermen. In 1566, under his authority as lord president, the Archbishop ordered that the Corporation's lord mayor, James Simpson, be removed from office and imprisoned. Although the exact charges against Simpson aren't clear, he was one of the men the archbishop had accused of 'non-favouring' the state religion in his letter to the Privy Council.

Following the arrest, and no doubt wishing to be seen in a favourable light in the royal court and Westminster, Archbishop Young reported to the Privy Council that his jurisdiction was now in good order, apart for 'a few gentlemen' he'd sent to prison.

In 1568 the Archbishop's attention began to turn to the thorny issue of non-attendance of church services. Thirty-two York citizens were charged. All were ordered to more appropriately conform with the law in future, but none were severely punished. This was to be the first of a number of clampdowns on York's recusants. It also proved to be one of the archbishop's final acts. Thomas Young died later that year and was buried at York Minster.

Following Young's death, the Dean of York, Matthew Hutton, a forthright character, wrote to William Cecil requesting the swift appointment of a strong replacement. Hutton described York's population as 'ignorant ... rude and blind'. However, the announcement of a new archbishop wasn't forthcoming, although Thomas Radcliffe, the Earl of Sussex, replaced Young as the new Lord President of the Council of the North.

In 1569 York's loyalties were tested in a different manner. A major rebellion had flared up in England's northern extremities. The Rising of the North (or Northern Rebellion, or Earls' Rebellion) was instigated by the Earls of Northumberland and Westmoreland. Although the restoration of Catholicism was one of their stated aims, their action came as a response to wider concerns.

In a joint proclamation, the Earls stated: 'Diverse disordered and well-disposed persons about the Queen's Majesty, have, by their subtle and crafty dealings to advance themselves, overcome this Realm, the true and Catholic Religion towards God, and by the same abused the Queen, disordered the Realm, and now lastly seek and procure the destruction of the nobility.'

Both men had become increasingly concerned by their dwindling influence in the royal court, especially in comparison to 'crafty' men like William Cecil. Some of the changes in the law introduced by Cecil and his supporters had negatively impacted their finances. The earls considered Cecil's work an attack on themselves, and part of a wider assault on the English nobility, particularly in the north.

In response, the earls continued, 'We, therefore, have gathered ourselves together to resist by force.' The two men ended their statement with 'God save the Queen' to demonstrate their loyalty to the Crown, and immediately set about rallying men to take up arms in support of their cause. In addition, they wrote to the Pope requesting he garner support from the Catholic powers in mainland Europe.

One of the Rising's first acts was to march on Durham Cathedral. Protestant images were torn down and Catholic Mass was heard. The force then marched south through Darlington, Northallerton and Richmond. Wherever they stopped, they held Catholic Masses and gathered more men. By the time the rebels had reached Ripon, their army had grown to around 6,000 men.

The earls continued south, halting at Boroughbridge and Bramham, near Wetherby. By this time, the Rising had two immediate aims. The first was to force the release of Mary Stuart. However, they soon discovered the former Queen of Scots had been moved to Coventry, ensuring she was held beyond their immediate reach. Their second goal was to take York. The walled city would make a mighty prize and provide a fortified base for future operations. However, unlike in the Pilgrimage of Grace, the city's gates weren't thrown open to the rebels. Only four men from York are known to have joined the earls' army.

Instead, the Corporation threw its support behind the Council of the North. As the two organisations worked together to prepare for a siege, Sussex, the Lord President of the Council, assembled an army of several thousand men. All were loyal to the Queen and ready to defend the city.

Having discovered York was stoutly defended, the earls and their followers received more bad news. A royal army had been despatched to engage them. The rebels retreated north, taking Hartlepool, hoping it would soon become a welcoming port for Spanish reinforcements. When the Spanish didn't come, the rebels laid siege to Barnard Castle, which they captured. Soon after, with the royal army closing in on them, the earls, and a number of their wealthier followers, abandoned their men and fled to Scotland.

The Earl of Westmorland travelled as far north as Aberdeen. From there he escaped to Flanders, where he eventually died in exile in 1601. His lands and assets had been forfeited to the Crown. The Earl of Northumberland wasn't so fortunate. After being captured by a Scots lord, he was imprisoned and ransomed. After this, he was sold back to Elizabeth in 1572 and transported south to York. More on this later.

In summary, the 1560s was a turning point for York. Public health and the economy had begun to improve. In small steps, the city's leaders, and some of its people, had begun to accept, if not embrace, the government's diluted version of Protestantism. Equally, although the decade had ended turbulently, the city had demonstrated its loyalty to the Queen and her government.

Margaret's Story – Youth and Family Changes

Margaret Middleton was six years old when Elizabeth ascended to the throne of England. During the following years, Margaret and her family witnessed many changes in their parish church of St Martin's. Over time, the finery and decorations lovingly restored by her father and others were removed, as churches up and down the land began to conform to a simpler, less Catholic form of worship.

We can only guess what Margaret may have recalled from the time. It's possible she remembered her parents, Thomas in particular, bemoaning the changes and the renewed drop in demand for beeswax products. However, despite his reservations, Thomas Middleton had ambitions to rise up the ranks of the Corporation. For this to happen, he and his family would have to conform. When the direction of the Church changed, so did his family. Outwardly at least, the Middletons, like many others in York, became Protestants.

Each Sunday and holy day they attended the Church of England service, as the law ordered. The Church of St Martin's and their God may have been the same, but the language, sacraments and emphasis of the service were changing. From some point during the early years of Elizabeth's reign, Margaret was raised as a Protestant, although there must be doubt about just how Protestant the Middleton household really became.

In the next few years two relatively insignificant events occurred in York. Although these would go on to change Margaret's life, she was blissfully unaware of them at the time. At this stage, Margaret knew nothing of the two men who would bring security and conflict into her life.

In 1560, when Margaret was seven, her future husband, John Clitherow, became a freeman of York, having served his apprenticeship as a butcher. His premises, like those of the other butchers in the city, were located in the Shambles, a narrow lane of interconnected buildings, a few hundred yards away from Davygate.

A year later, in 1561, a young man named Henry Maye arrived in York. It's believed he came from Hampshire. Many migrants were being attracted to the city at this time, due to the establishment of the Ecclesiastical High Commission and the permanent placement of the Council of the North. Both bodies brought wealth and employment to the city, including many visitors who needed somewhere to eat and sleep.

Although Henry Maye brought with him a knowledge of inns, the wine trade, hard work and ambition, this wouldn't be enough for him to succeed in the city. Lacking wealth and social standing, Henry needed to somehow find his way onto York's social and corporate ladders. Luckily, he was prepared to wait for his chance. For the next five or six years he worked in the city's inns, made connections, and scoured the city for opportunities.

In 1564 John Clitherow's father, Richard, died. Richard had been a tailor but John's mother (whose name we don't know) was a butcher's daughter. The oldest son of three, John inherited the bulk of his father's estate, including property and grazing land at Cornborough near Sheriff Hutton.[5]

The eleven-year-old Margaret Middleton knew none of this. Her focus was on growing up in what was often a difficult time for her family. Her father's health was poor. At times, Thomas Middleton suffered from various bouts of illness, including gout, but somehow he managed to struggle on. It's likely that Jane Middleton worked hard to keep the chandlery business afloat.

Despite his ailments, Thomas retained his ambitions to progress in the Corporation of York. In September 1564 he was included on the short list for election as one of the two Sheriffs of York for the coming year. He was vying for these positions with Edward Richardson, a pewterer, William Thompson, a victualler, and Gregory Paycoke, a merchant.

The lord mayor at the time was James Simpson, one of the aldermen whom Archbishop Young had suspected of having Catholic tendencies, but this was before his future arrest. Lord Mayor Simpson chaired a session at the Corporation's headquarters in the Common Hall. The objective was to agree which of the four candidates should be elected as sheriff. The attendees included representatives from the aldermen, the Twenty-Four and wider Common Council, of which Thomas was already a member.

The city house-books recorded the result as follows: 'This worshipful presents, by their most voices, have elect and chosen the said Thomas Middleton and William Thompson to be Sheriffs for this year to come.'[6]

Unfortunately, there was a twist in Thomas's story. The house-book also states, 'William Thompson was sent for, and came before the said presents and took the oath of Sheriff-ship. And for that, the said Thomas Middleton lay on his bed, sick with the gout, and could not come.'

Luckily for Thomas, Mayor Simpson was determined the wax chandler's infirmity shouldn't prevent him from taking office. 'The worshipful presents agreed that Mr Appleyard, Mr Bean and Mr Watson, aldermen, Mr Maskew, Sheriff, George Goodyear, Richard Ainley, John Johnson and diverse others of the Common Council should go to Thomas Middleton's house to hear him take his oath accustomed … and that done, the said aldermen and others returned again to the Common Hall to the presents there assembled, and then and there declared all their doings in the premises accordingly.'

Thomas must have had a very large bed chamber. Membership of the Twenty-Four was now tantalisingly close, but being a sheriff was an expensive and exhausting business, due to a series of time-consuming responsibilities. The sheriffs made and ordered arrests, managed prisons and prisoners, supported important trials and even attended executions. They also selected which citizens should sit on York's juries.

Unfortunately, Thomas's health prevented him from fulfilling a number of his duties. The victualler William Thompson was forced to carry out many tasks in Thomas's stead. Things were hardly better a year later, when the two men stood down from being sheriffs and were invited to join the Twenty-Four. Once again, Thomas was too ill to travel. He couldn't attend his own swearing-in ceremony in the Common Hall. 1564 and 1565 must have been busy years for William Thompson.

It was a busy time too for Jane Middleton. Nursing her sick husband, she tirelessly raised their children and managed their waning wax chandlery business. As her husband's health deteriorated, it's possible she may have sometimes looked towards the future, though it's doubtful she had that much time.

In May 1567 Thomas Middleton finally succumbed to his ailments. Margaret's father's death marked the beginning of a sombre time for her. Thomas was buried at the church at St Martin's, which he'd attended for most of his adult life, and served and refurbished as a churchwarden a decade before.

Thomas had written his will six years earlier, making a note even then that he was 'sick in body'. The document makes fascinating reading. The contents include significant implications for Margaret and her family.

> The 14th day of December, in the year of our Lord God 1560, I, Thomas Middleton of the city of York, chandler, of whole mind and good memory, being sick in body, do ordain and make this my last will and testament, in manner and form following: First, I bequeath my soul to God Almighty and my body to be buried within the church of St. Martin, in Coney Street, in the middle aisle before the high choir [...]
>
> I give to Thomas Middleton, my son, one close, lying in the horse-fair at Ripon of 14s by year, in the holding and occupation of William Swayn, to him and his heirs lawfully begotten for ever, and he to enter to it at the day of my death.
>
> I give to Jane, my wife, the residue of all my lands and leases during her natural life.
>
> I give to George, my son, one house and two shops lying in the Market Place in Ripon, with five roods of meadow lying in the Upper Ings in Ripon fields, after decease of my wife, to him and his heirs for ever; and if the said George die before that he come to lawful age, that then I will and give the said lands to Thomas Middleton the one moiety (part), and to Margaret Middleton the other moiety (part), my daughter, and to their heirs for ever [...]
>
> I give to Margaret, my daughter, one house lying in Davygate within the city of York, after decease of my wife, to her and to her heirs of her body lawfully begotten, and for default of such issue, then I will that it shall go to the right heirs of me, the said Thomas, for ever.
>
> Also I give to the said Margaret one silver goblet and half a dozen of silver spoons, provided always I will that my daughter Alice and Thomas Hutchinson, my son-in-law, be content with those goods that I gave him with her the day of their marriage for her full child's portion [...]

I give to William Hutchinson one silver spoon. I give to Agnes Hutchinson one silver spoon.

I give to the four wards of poor folks within this city to every ward 3s and 4d to pray for me. Also I give to Myles and to Matthew and to Ellis, my servants, to enrich one of them one ewe to pray for me. Also I do give to the residue of all my servants, to every one of them, to pray for me 12d.

Also I will and do ordain and make supervisors of this my last will and testament Edward Turner and Thomas Jackson, and either of them to have for their pains 5s. The residue of all my goods and chattels, my debts paid and my funerals made, I do give to Jane Middleton, my wife, whom I do ordain and make my sole executrix by herself.

Apart from the rented property in Ripon, which would pass immediately to her brother Thomas, Margaret's father had left most of his estate to his widow, Jane, for her to enjoy 'during her natural life'. At the time of Jane's death, the remains of his legacy would transfer to some of their children.

This would make Margaret's younger brother, William, a wealthy man, as he'd inherit additional properties in Ripon. Margaret's sister, Alice, and her husband, Thomas Hutchinson, though, must have received a decent dowry at the time of their marriage. The couple would have to make do with what they already had.

When her mother died, Margaret was to inherit the family home in Davygate. We'll examine the implications of this later. Additionally, Margaret inherited a few pieces of silver, as did Alice's children. Thomas gave three of his servants a sheep each. The rest received 12d and a request for them to pray for him. He also made a donation to the city's poor, with a further request they pray for his soul.

Execution of the will was supervised by Thomas Jackson and Edward Turner. The latter was Margaret's older cousin, the son of Thomas Turner (the former innkeeper of The Angel) and the brother of Richard Turner (the current innkeeper). The profession of innkeeping was to become more familiar to Margaret in the years ahead.

At the time of her father's death, Margaret was fourteen. Her mother, Jane, was around fifty. She was wealthy and favourably thought of by many in the city. She was an attractive prospect, perhaps for an older man, or a wealthy widower with children of his own. In Tudor times, widows and widowers often remarried within a year. Jane was no exception, though two things stood out – quite how quickly she remarried and the man she decided to wed. Just four months after the death of Thomas, Jane's choice of second husband came as quite a surprise.

*****

Henry Maye was around half Jane's age. The man was a foreigner, from the south of England. What's more, he hailed from a lower social class. Henry wasn't a merchant, or a tradesman. Tongues must have been wagging in the houses and workshops around Davygate and Coney Street.

How long Henry Maye had had his eyes on Jane Middleton, we don't know. He may have been watching her from the shadows or approached Jane more openly as they waited for the inevitable to happen to her ailing husband. Unable to fulfil his official duties and too ill to leave the house, the signs for Thomas Middleton hadn't been good for some time.

Some things were more certain. Henry Maye was ambitious. He wanted to run his own tavern. Gaining a licence to do so wouldn't be easy for a man of his social class. He lacked standing and wealth and he wasn't from York, or even from one of the Yorkshire Ridings. What he needed more than anything was an upstanding, local and very wealthy wife.

It's easy to imagine the cogs in Henry's mind turning over. The Middletons' house and chandlery were located in a prime city centre location. Davygate would make an ideal spot for a tavern. A well-located hostelry, if carefully managed, could earn a lot of money. Jane was older than Henry, but she'd been raised in an inn and was experienced at running a business. The woman was bright and hard working. What she didn't know, she'd learn quickly from Henry, or pick up from her nephew, Richard, who ran The Angel across the city.

The couple were married in September 1567. Six months later, in February 1568, and boosted by his new wife's lofty standing, Henry was appointed as a chamberlain by the Corporation of York. With this appointment, he placed his foot firmly on the first rung of York's corporate ladder. Additional steps would soon follow.

Two months later, following a dispute between York's existing vintners, Henry was given permission to run his own tavern and licensed to sell wine in the city. The second appointment was a fairly exclusive arrangement, with Henry becoming one of only eight men allowed to sell wine in York. Beeswax and candle production ceased in Davygate, and the stock was sold off. In a matter of weeks, Henry Maye converted the Middletons' house and premises into a tavern.

Jane's older children had left the family home by this time. As detailed in their father's will, Alice was married to Thomas Hutchinson, a local locksmith. Thomas junior had served his apprenticeship and was earning his living making bricks and tiles. Only Margaret and the second brother, George, remained at home.

Margaret watched as events unfolded around her. It couldn't have been easy. Her father was dead, and her mother remarried. The way of life she'd known had been brought to an end, replaced by frantic change. When her stepfather moved into Davygate, he was closer to Margaret's age than her mother's. Their house had been transformed into a tavern. If she'd ever wondered what life was like for her cousins in The Angel, she found out. Things weren't the same.

In October 1568 the Davygate tavern was bursting at the seams. A commission was hosted in York to determine what should be done about Mary Stuart, the deposed Queen of the Scots, and the city's inns and taverns were crowded with officials, their lackeys and hangers on. Talk in the bars came cheap. Some cursed the Catholic Queen of Scots, while others bemoaned her situation. A few held their tongues, for fear of being overhead. Margaret's stepfather stood on the other side of the bar, listened to his customers, watched them with a smile, and counted his money.

Like Thomas Middleton before him, Henry Maye recognised the need to conform. It's likely this prompted his Protestantism rather than any religious conviction. Apart from gout and chandlery, Henry set out to grasp everything else Margaret's father Thomas had achieved or hoped for.

Nothing is written down about what fifteen-year-old Margaret thought of these events, or of her attitude to her stepfather during this time. It's quite possible the Middletons attended church services but secretly retained a level of Catholicism behind closed doors. We can only speculate what Margaret thought of Henry Maye as he replaced her father's legacy and used his new-found wealth and her mother's position to create a new life for himself, and his new family. It's possible

Margaret resented Henry's actions. Alternatively, she may have admired his dynamism, and been happy to see her mother holding court in the trade to which she'd been born.

Margaret's first biographer, Father John Mush, tells us she grew up to be an attractive young woman. 'God gave her a body with comely face and beauty correspondent.' A commercially minded man like Henry Maye would probably have put her to work in the tavern to earn her keep. As the young Margaret served drinks and carried food to the tables, it's hard to imagine, at times, she'd didn't have to fend off unwanted advances from drunken patrons and revellers.

Perhaps Henry propositioned his pretty young stepdaughter? Without making any direct claim about sexual advances, Father Mush implies as much with these words about Henry in *A True Report*: 'Let him remember whether he himself had not good proofs of this martyr's constant honesty at all times when she was in her mother's house.'

If Henry tried it on with Margaret, she rejected his advances. Maybe she threatened to tell her mother. The best way for a woman to protect herself during Elizabethan times was to find herself a good husband, one who'd look after her and protect her from this type of behaviour.

Chapter Five

Family and Marriage (1570–1574)

Elizabeth I – Papal Bull and Plot

When Parliament passed the Acts of Supremacy and Uniformity at the beginning of Elizabeth's reign, England broke away from Rome for a second time. Surprisingly, the new Queen wasn't immediately excommunicated. Perhaps the main thing preventing this was the hope she might one day marry a Catholic.

In 1570 Queen Elizabeth had been on the throne for more than a decade, but she remained unmarried. Pope Pius V was now in receipt of the correspondence issued to him by the Earls of Northumberland and Westmoreland at the beginning of the Rising of the North. The earls had requested his support in their struggle against the 'subtle and crafty dealings to [...].overcome this Realm, the true and Catholic Religion towards God.'

Although the two earls had been routed and the rising was over, Pope Pius wanted to demonstrate the Catholic Church's support for their cause. In 1570 he issued a Papal Bull, '*Regnans in Excelsis*' ('Reigning on High'), against Elizabeth. Documented as, 'Given at St. Peter's at Rome, on 27 April 1570 of the Incarnation; in the fifth year of our pontificate,' the Bull was a devastating attack on the queen of England.

'She has followed and embraced the errors of the heretics. She has removed the royal Council, composed of the nobility of England, and has filled it with obscure men, being heretics; oppressed the followers of the Catholic faith; instituted false preachers and ministers of impiety; abolished the sacrifice of the mass, prayers, fasts, choice of meats, celibacy, and Catholic ceremonies; and has ordered that books of manifestly heretical content be propounded to the whole realm.'

With these words, Pope Pius aligned himself closely with the earls' agenda. Rather than call Cecil and his associates 'crafty', he damned them for being 'obscure men' and 'heretics'. Most of all, his ire fell on

Elizabeth. The Pope was clear about what he believed she'd done wrong, and explicit about what should be done about it.

'We do out of the fullness of our apostolic power declare the foresaid Elizabeth to be a heretic and favourer of heretics, and her adherents in the matters aforesaid to have incurred the sentence of excommunication and to be cut off from the unity of the body of Christ.'

Elizabeth was excommunicated from the Catholic Church. More than that, the Bull demanded she should be deprived of her throne and the Catholics in her realm absolved of any oaths they had sworn to support her.

'Moreover (we declare) her to be deprived of her pretended title to the aforesaid crown and of all lordship, dignity and privilege whatsoever [...] The nobles, subjects and people of the said realm and all others who have in any way sworn oaths to her, to be forever absolved from such an oath and from any duty arising from lordship, fealty and obedience; and we do, by authority of these present, so absolve them and so deprive the same Elizabeth of her pretended title to the crown and all other the above-said matters.'

Anyone who considered themself a member of the Catholic Church was instructed to disobey the Queen's orders. Refusing to obey the mandate could result in an English or Welsh Catholic's excommunication.

'We charge and command all and singular the nobles, subjects, peoples and others afore said that they do not dare obey her orders, mandates and laws. Those who shall act to the contrary we include in the like sentence of excommunication.'

At the stroke of his quill, Pope Pius had made life and governance of the country much more dangerous for Elizabeth. Not only had the Pope excommunicated her, he'd ordered her subjects to break the law and given them freedom and absolution to deprive her of the throne. The only practical ways to achieve this would be through the Queen's assassination or arrest and execution.

Unwittingly perhaps, Pope Pius had also made life significantly more troublesome and hazardous for the country's Catholics. There'd inevitably be a backlash against them from the English authorities. A harder line would be taken.

Elizabeth had made an attempt to follow a middle way, retaining some elements of Catholic worship while nurturing a level of Protestant reform. Until now, most Catholics had grudgingly gone along with the situation, even if they'd acted differently behind closed doors. Few had continually refused to go to church. Most who retained the older faith had been satisfied to do so quietly, kneeling in their pews with their fingers crossed, before sneaking off to attend a secret Catholic Mass.

The majority of Catholics had sworn their oath to support the Queen. Better this than risk control by a foreign power, as had been widely feared during Mary I's reign, following her marriage to Philip of Spain. Many had seen religion and loyalty to the Crown as distinct and separate issues.

Now though, the Pope was telling them they dare not 'obey her orders, mandates and laws' for fear of their own excommunication. The choice was clear. Obey the Queen of England and the laws of her land or comply with the Pope and the Catholic Church. The Pope appeared to be sewing the seeds for a mass campaign of civil disobedience. The Queen and her subjects faced a dilemma. How should they react?

In 1571 the work of the Archbishop of Canterbury, Matthew Parker, was allowed to come to fruition. The Thirty-Nine Articles, the set of practices which described the revised position of the Church, were integrated into an updated version of the English Book of Common Prayer. A clear distinction was made between the Church of England and the Catholic Church. The sacraments were finally limited to two – baptism and communion.

One of the Thirty-Nine Articles, XXXVII, includes two key statements: 'The King's Majesty hath the chief power in this Realm of England, and other his Dominions, unto whom the chief Government of all Estates of this Realm, whether they be Ecclesiastical or Civil,' and 'The Bishop of Rome hath no jurisdiction in this Realm of England.'[1]

This confirmed there would be no reconciliation with Rome. Views on both sides of the religious divide became more entrenched. In 1571 Parliament passed a new Treason Act in response to the Papal Bull. Anyone considering, carrying out or inciting harm to the Queen, or collaborating with foreigners to invade the country, or claiming Elizabeth was a heretic, or not the rightful owner of the Crown would be committing high treason.

> An act whereby certain offences be made treason [...] if any person or persons whatsoever [...] within the realm or without, compass, imagine, invent, devise, or intend the death or destruction, or any bodily harm tending to death,

destruction, maim, or wounding of the royal person of the same our sovereign lady, Queen Elizabeth; or to deprive or depose her of or from the style, honour, or kingly name of the imperial crown of this realm or of any other realm or dominion to her majesty belonging, or to levy war against her majesty within this realm or without, or to move or to stir any foreigners or strangers with force to invade this realm […]

Or shall by writing, printing, preaching, speech, express words, or sayings maliciously, advisedly, and directly publish, set forth, and affirm that...our said sovereign lady, Queen Elizabeth, is a heretic, schismatic, tyrant, infidel, or an usurper of the crown of the said realms or any of them; that then all and every such said offence or offences shall be taken, deemed, and declared, by the authority of this act and parliament, to be high treason. [2]

Some in the country were still wishing to see a Catholic monarch wear the English crown, and in Mary Stuart they had a ready and waiting replacement. In 1571 William Cecil and his followers foiled one of a growing number of Catholic plots against Elizabeth. Devised by Roberto Ridolfi, a banker from Florence, the conspiracy became known as the Ridolfi Plot.

Ridolfi was a committed Catholic. The gist of his plan was as follows. The Duke of Norfolk would marry Mary Stuart, before overthrowing Elizabeth with military support from Spain. Finally, Mary would be placed onto the thrones of both England and Scotland as their Catholic monarch.

When the plot was uncovered, Ridolfi was already in France, out of reach of the English authorities. The Duke of Norfolk wasn't. In 1572 he was arrested and executed. Elizabeth's ears remained deaf to her advisors' pleas to pass the same sentence on her cousin Mary Stuart. Instead, Mary remained imprisoned in England, although Elizabeth's opinion of her was severely diminished.

Across the rest of Europe religious tensions were rising. In August 1572 thousands of French Huguenot Protestants – men, women and children – were murdered by Catholic mobs. Centred in Paris, the slaughter was witnessed by Francis Walsingham.

In 1573 Walsingham was appointed Elizabeth's Principal Secretary. Many believe his experience in France was the key motivation behind the policy changes he sought to make against the country's Catholic population. One day, he feared, a similar bloodbath might happen in England.

York – Friction between Council and Corporation

For the men who'd been involved in the Rising of the North, the future was bleak. The Earls of Northumberland and Westmoreland may have fled, but retribution was planned against their abandoned followers. Forces loyal to the Queen were ordered to make a series of raids across the border into Scotland. Once there, they harried, captured and killed the fleeing rebels and anyone foolish enough to support them.

For those who hadn't fled, the situation was little better. In a letter dated 10 January 1570, the Earl of Sussex, Lord President of the Council of the North, gave orders to the local authorities to execute 200 local men who'd followed the earls. Many of those rounded up were hanged in Ripon. The people of York must have issued a collective sigh of relief that they hadn't been involved. A few months later, in March 1570, a special commission was held in York and a further eleven men were sentenced to death. Four of them were executed in York.

Following the Rising of the North, and subsequent receipt of the Papal Bull, Elizabeth was more determined than ever to exert control over the northern counties and prevent any possibility of a future reoccurrence. She valued the loyalty of men like William Cecil and was keen to appoint similarly loyal men to key roles in the northern institutions, many of which were based in York.

If still alive, Thomas Young may have validly claimed that his leadership of the Church in York, the Council of the North and Ecclesiastical Commission had been instrumental in ensuring the city's loyalty to the Queen. However, his approach to religious uniformity had been more subtle. He'd often sought to use the powers of persuasion and time, rather than direct use of force and the law.

In May 1570 Elizabeth announced Edmund Grindal as the new Archbishop of York. Grindal had been a chaplain for her half-brother, Edward VI, but had fled the country and lived in exile during Mary's reign. Upon his return to England he'd been appointed as the Bishop of

London. A little Puritan-leaning in nature, he was certainly anti-Catholic. When he arrived in York, Grindal wrote to William Cecil, complaining the locals were not 'well-affected to Godly religion,' and 'superstitious practices remained'.

In his mission to correct York's religious shortcomings, the new archbishop placed a significant focus on re-education. If this didn't work, he acted to replace the local clergy. In 1571 he issued a set of injunctions that were to be enforced before and during his upcoming visitation to the city's parish churches. The injunctions identified a range of Catholic practices which Grindal perceived were still being carried out in some churches. All had to be eradicated.

Archbishop Grindal set about addressing the thorny issue of non-attendance of Church of England services. Although many in York retained a Catholic persuasion, most did so unobtrusively. These 'Church Papists' did their best to avoid the attention of the authorities. They sought to evade a summons before the minor courts or the Ecclesiastical High Commission, and the punishment this might bring.

Since the death of Queen Mary, a smaller number of more radical Catholics had been prepared to break the law in the name of their faith. Recusants considered attendance of the English-language Church of England service to be heresy, due to the disregard for Catholic doctrine and lack of recognition of all seven sacraments.

At the beginning of Archbishop Grindal's tenure in York, only a small number of recusancy cases were being brought before the High Commission. For example, in May 1571 George Turton, Jonathan Hall and Emot Halliday were fined. One woman, Dorothy Vavasour, the 'wife of Thomas Vavasour MD', was also fined.[3] The Vavasours will come to play a more significant role in the following chapters.

One month later the High Commission imprisoned Stephen Branton of York for 'refusing expressly to communicate or come to the church'. In the same month, the High Commission heard the case of Edward Besley, a man who'd been a Member of Parliament for Ripon, Thirsk and Scarborough during Queen Mary's reign. A fervent Catholic, Besley was found guilty and jailed. One of Besley's relatives (probably his son), George Besley, would go on to become a seminary priest and be executed for treason in 1591.[4]

In addition to former Members of Parliament, officials in the higher echelons of the Corporation of York discovered they weren't immune to being called before the Ecclesiastical High Commission. One alderman, and soon to be lord mayor, William Alleyn, was accused and chastised for the disparaging remarks he'd made about the celibacy of the clergy and for making the sign of the cross.

There are two possible causes why more recusancy cases weren't being heard at this time. Either the level of church attendance by York citizens was remarkably high, or the churchwardens and/or the Corporation weren't capturing and passing on the full list of names of the people who were skipping services.

Convinced that the number of recusants in York was much higher than the volume of cases being brought before the courts, Archbishop Grindal demanded the Corporation take immediate action. Reluctantly, the aldermen promised to make a more regular list of absentees. To show they were doing something, they fined the city's sheriffs for negligence in their duties. In addition, the Corporation abolished the annual Corpus Christi play and York's Yule festivities. Both were considered to be superstitious Catholic traditions by the Ecclesiastical High Commission.

In 1572 the Earl of Sussex, the man who'd so severely punished the rebels following the Rising of the North, left York for London to become Lord Chamberlain. The man appointed to replace him as Lord President of the Council of the North was Henry Hastings, the Earl of Huntingdon. Like Archbishop Grindal, Huntingdon was a fervent Protestant. The two men began to work closely together to crack down on what they saw as unacceptable Catholic practices and activities still taking place in York.

The year 1572 saw a significant event in the city. The Scots lord who'd been holding the Earl of Northumberland following his flight to Scotland finally agreed terms with Elizabeth's advisors. In return for a huge payment of £2,000 he handed Northumberland back to the English authorities, and the earl was taken to York.

A scaffold was erected on the Pavement in the centre of the city. This was a few yards from both Davygate and the Shambles. To warn what might happen to anyone who dared to rebel against the Queen and the state, the earl was publicly beheaded. Afterwards, his head was placed on a spike and positioned prominently on a high pole above York's traitors' gate, Micklegate Bar, to be seen by anyone entering or leaving the city.

The city's records indicate the head was mysteriously removed two years later, in 1574, by 'persons unknown'. Before then, a curious case had been brought before the Ecclesiastical High Commission.

In November 1572 William Tessimond was taken into custody by the sheriffs of York. Under questioning, he confessed to possessing whiskers from the executed earl's beard.

Tessimond admitted he'd trimmed the hair from the earl's beard himself. The posthumous shave had taken place when the earl's head was temporarily stored in the tollbooth on Ousebridge, before it was placed on display above Micklegate Bar. The prisoner was also found guilty by the High Commission for persistent non-attendance of church and sent to jail.

Although the case is a strange one, it indicates the fondness some Catholics retained for possessing relics made from body parts of the dead. This was one of the 'superstitious' practices the Protestant authorities were keen to stamp out.

Increasingly, Archbishop Grindal and Lord President Huntingdon began to exert pressure on the Corporation to take a harder line against the city's remaining Catholics. From 1573 every new lord mayor and sheriff had to take the Oath of Supremacy to the Queen, as well as swear their own oath of office. Although it appears unlikely the previous holders would have refused to do so, having the action forced upon them was clearly a signal they were being watched. If they stepped out of line, their loyalty would be questioned in ways they wouldn't much like.

Margaret's Story – Marriage to John Clitherow

The year 1570 marked the beginning of an important time for Margaret Middleton's stepfather. Once again, Henry Maye was treading in Margaret's father's footsteps, as he began the first of two three-year terms as a churchwarden at St Martin's, Coney Street. His parish duties included identifying anyone around him, even his family, friends and neighbours, who failed to attend Sunday and holy day services. What the Corporation would do with the information afterwards was open to question.

One of Henry's tasks was to ensure the church was a suitably Protestant place of worship in accordance with the law. This was particularly important in 1570, ahead of the scheduled autumn visitation from Archbishop Grindal. Before the archbishop's inspection could take place, all traces of the church and congregation's previous Catholic leanings had to be removed.

After a successful visit from the archbishop in September, Henry invited his fellow churchwardens and a few others back to his inn on Davygate where they shared a fine meal. This may have been an early celebration. A few days later, on 21 September 1570, the lord mayor, Richard Calom, his fellow aldermen and the Twenty-Four elected Henry as one of the two sheriffs of York. His meteoric rise was almost complete.

A week later, as was customary, on Michaelmas Day, 29 September 1570, Henry Maye was sworn in as sheriff. No doubt he left the ceremony with a broad smile on his face. After all, he'd made it. His demeanour must have been in stark contrast to Thomas Middleton's gout-induced grimace when he'd been made sheriff from his sickbed in Davygate,

The role of sheriff didn't come cheap, but after two-and-a-half years of running a successful tavern, Henry Maye could afford it. Being one of the city's sheriffs took time and effort, but Henry was his own boss, and in any case, he knew he could rely on his wife to run things smoothly when he was busy elsewhere.

Bizarrely, the other sheriff that year was called Thomas Middleton. Although Margaret's older brother, Thomas, was around the right age, he never became a sheriff. This Thomas Middleton was a tanner. His son Peter was also a tanner and became a sheriff himself almost four decades later, in 1618.

One example of Henry Maye's tasks in the role of sheriff was noted in the court records, which survive from the time. In December 1570 Peter Wilkinson was brought before the High Commission charged with standing in High Pavement on market day, 'speaking seditious and slanderous words against the Queen to the profanation of God's word'. Wilkinson was found guilty and fined £3. Henry was tasked with ensuring the fine was paid.

In his dual roles of churchwarden and sheriff, Henry Maye met many people. One of these was a butcher, John Clitherow. John was a widower with two young sons. He'd recently placed his own foot on York's corporate ladder by beginning a year-long term as one of the Corporation's bridgemasters.

The city's bridgemasters were responsible for looking after York's bridges. The main one, Ousebridge, crossed the river Ouse. This was the bridge that had been repaired following the major damage caused by flash flooding in 1564. The second largest bridge forded the river Foss. The bridgemasters were tasked with managing bridge maintenance, collecting revenues from tolls and paying surplus income to the chamberlains, which would be added to the city's coffers.

Each year the parish of St Martin's, Coney Street, made an annual payment of 10d to the bridgemasters. In his role as a churchwarden, one of Henry's tasks was to ensure people like John Clitherow received the right funds at the right time.

It's possible the two men had already done business together, perhaps on a regular basis. John's butcher's shop may have supplied meat and poultry to Henry and Jane's tavern on Davygate. On these occasions, despite their age gap, John may have taken some time out of his busy schedule to stop and talk to Henry's attractive seventeen-year-old stepdaughter, Margaret. Certainly, he must have known and admired her, and been pleased when his intentions towards the young woman were approved by her mother and stepfather.

On 1 July 1571 John Clitherow and Margaret Middleton were married at St Martin's Church in a strictly Protestant Church of England ceremony. The pretty young bride was given away by her stepfather. Nearing the end of his term in office as a sheriff, Henry Maye would have been grandly adorned in official robes and accompanied by a pair of mace-sergeants. It must have been a proud day for Jane, and for Henry especially. What a glorious opportunity to show off to the good people of York just how far he'd come.

Margaret must have been happy too. She'd found a good man to look after her and could now leave the tavern. John had found a new wife. His sons had a mother to care for them. For Jane Maye, this joyous occasion may have been tinged with sadness. Margaret had certainly found a good man with a decent income, but her daughter was no longer the young child who'd followed her around the chandlery.

What did Henry Maye think of all this? Perhaps that he'd found a son-in-law of just the right level of standing. Although John Clitherow was respected and relatively wealthy, and of a similar age to Henry, he could never rise as high or as far as Henry planned to in the Corporation. On a few rare occasions, butchers may be invited to join the Twenty-Four, but they'd never be asked to become an alderman.

As the wedding party left the churchyard for the celebratory feast at the inn on Davygate, did Margaret look up to the heavens or glance down at the grave of poor Thomas Middleton? Did Thomas smile at his daughter from on high as she left the church he'd served so faithfully?

After all, she'd no longer be under the guardianship of Henry Maye, the man who'd taken his place, both in his family and local community.

In the coming days, just as her mother had done decades before, Margaret moved out of a tavern and into a house with adjoining business premises. For her, though, there was to be no sweet smell of melting beeswax and candles. In the Shambles the odours were different. Dead flesh with no refrigeration, and sometimes the stench of waste from the animal pens beyond. Adjacent to the Shambles were the premises of the tallow chandlers. Here, animal fat was melted down to make foul-smelling candles, cheap enough to be used in most people's homes.

Despite this, Margaret set about turning her new household into a happy home. John's first wife, Matilda, had been survived by their two sons, William and Thomas, so as well as a husband, Margaret inherited an instant family to look after. It must have been a daunting prospect for a seventeen-year-old girl.

John's father, Richard Clitherow, had been a tailor, but he'd married the daughter of a butcher. Of all the trades in York, the butchers intermarried more than any other. Close relatives from multiple families and generations often lived together, or alongside each other, in York's narrow streets, especially in the Shambles.

John's rented house and premises, like many others in the street, were owned by the Dean and Chapter of York. Down the years the Clitherows lived alongside many members of their own wider family. This often came in handy. For example, if John was away supervising the other parts of his business, such as the grazing land beyond York, friendly help would be on hand to guide Margaret in her duties, managing the household and supervising the shop. She was also supported by their servants and John's apprentices.

It wasn't all work and no play. John was a man who loved life, food and enjoyment. Often, he'd take his young wife to dine with friends in houses in York and beyond. Sometimes this included ceremonial banquets and dinners hosted by the Butcher' Guild in the Butchers' Hall. This was situated just beyond the animal pens in the direction of Parliament Street. The food at these events was probably particularly good. Over time, though, Margaret tired of these events.

In 1572 Margaret gave birth to a son, Henry. It doesn't appear too far-fetched to believe the boy must have been named after his step-grandfather, particularly as John already had a son called Thomas from his first marriage.

Henry Clitherow was baptised in the parish church which covered the Shambles. Unlike the majority of buildings and places mentioned in this book, Christ's Church, or the Church of the Holy Trinity, and its later replacement, no longer exist. Both have been long since demolished. The little churches were located beyond the Shambles, around the corner in King's Square. If you look carefully today you'll find inscriptions in the paving which mark the place where these churches once stood.

In 1572 John Clitherow became a churchwarden for the parish. One of his assigned duties, of course, was to note down the names of people identified as consistently missing Sunday services without good reason. These lists of names were collected in each parish, before being passed on to be reviewed by the Corporation, the Church's Visitation courts and ultimately the Ecclesiastical High Commission. Some parishes completed the task with more accuracy and diligence than others. Often, men would be reluctant to inform on those around them. After all, these were often their friends, relatives and neighbours.

As the decade wore on, more pressure was placed on the Corporation of York to get this right. Many more people were called before the High Commission, fined and sent to prison for recusancy. Of course, men and women who were good, loyal Protestants, or attended church, had nothing to worry about.

Chapter Six

Conformity or Recusancy (1574–1580)

Elizabeth I – Rise of the Missionary Priests

The Rising of the North and Ridolfi Plot highlighted to Elizabeth's government the threats they were facing from internal rebellions that wished to place a Catholic on the throne. In response, the English authorities accelerated their plans to bring about religious uniformity and address non-conformance.

In contrast, Elizabeth's foreign policy had been relatively conservative. Even with religious strife wreaking havoc across Europe, the Queen had attempted to minimise English military action on the Continent. Official intervention was even being avoided in the ongoing struggle between Catholic Spain and Protestant rebels in the Low Countries. In 1574 England began to trade more regularly with Spain once again, following a major commercial dispute between the two nations.

During Mary's time, many Protestants had lived in exile in Europe. A number of English Catholics now did the same under Elizabeth, including William Allen, a man born in Lancashire who'd studied at Oxford. When Elizabeth became Queen, he'd refused to take the Oath of Supremacy and left the country. Allen's dream was to reconvert his homeland to Catholicism.

In 1567 he visited Rome and developed the idea of creating a series of seminary colleges across Europe. Effectively these would be specialist universities, dedicated to training Englishmen and Welshmen to be Catholic priests. Once ordained, they'd be sent undercover across the Channel to maintain and spread the old faith.

The first of Allen's 'English colleges' was founded at Douai in northern France in 1568. Once up and running, Douai received financial support and protection from King Philip II of Spain. Further colleges were opened in the following years, one each in Rome, Valladolid and Seville in Spain and Lisbon in Portugal.

The clergymen Allen and his associates trained became known as seminary priests. This differentiated them from the more traditional Marian priests, who were generally older Catholic clergy, ordained before or during the reign of Queen Mary. Some of the Marian men had conformed to the revised Church of England. Others had been stripped of their positions, fled to the Continent, or passed away due to illness or old age.

By the 1570s both the Protestant and Catholic Churches in England and Wales were facing staffing and recruitment crises. Much was being done to train and ordain a steady supply of ardent believers for both causes. Whichever Church got this right would have an advantage over the other. Allen was starting from a lower base, but he was determined to make up for lost time.

The first seminary priests began clandestinely to cross the Channel in 1574. It was a hazardous journey. The wording of the 1571 Treason Act marked many of their planned activities down as high treason. If discovered and found guilty, the priests would be facing capital punishment. It would be best if they remained hidden and wore a good disguise. William Allen stated they should arrive in the country wearing a layman's suit of clothes and have six or seven pounds of spending money in their pockets.[1]

The Catholics weren't the only threat to religious uniformity. When Matthew Parker, the Archbishop of Canterbury, died in 1575, Elizabeth promoted Archbishop Grindal from his position in York as his replacement. Archbishop Parker had consistently clamped down on what he considered to be Puritan extremism, particularly in London.

Meanwhile, William Cecil had been keen to bring moderate Puritans on board with the government, to support what he considered to be their shared struggle against Catholicism. With his own Puritanical leanings, Archbishop Grindal supported Cecil's aims. However, Elizabeth was suspicious of the Puritans, and soon fell out with the archbishop. When the Queen demanded Grindal put a stop to some of the more extreme rhetoric being spoken by the more radical Puritan clergy, the archbishop refused. In 1577 Elizabeth suspended him from his position in Canterbury.

In parallel, the seminary priests had begun secretly to enter the country, infiltrating local communities and spreading the word of their mission. Often, these priests were given undercover roles in the households of Catholic-leaning gentry, where they celebrated Mass, provided Bible studies and heard confession.

For many Catholics, this was the first time they'd been able to gain official absolution for a while. Included in many of their confessions was the guilt they felt from attending the state's heretical church services. The priests forgave their new parishioners and attempted to strengthen their resolve to do better in future.

After a dark period, when only a dwindling number of often defrocked Marian priests had been able to support their faith, parts of the Catholic population at last began to receive some encouragement. With the blessing of the Pope, they were being informed that the end of their religion in England wasn't a foregone conclusion. The Reformation had been halted once: it could be stopped again.

Using their network of spies and informers, it became clear to Cecil and Walsingham that the enemy was amongst them. Action had to be taken and it had to be decisive. A series of searches and inquiries were made to seek out and prosecute the invading seminary priests.

In 1576 Cuthbert Mayne left Douai to travel to England. He eventually reached Cornwall, where he posed to the outside world as a rich landowner's steward. Using this disguise, Mayne began to secretly practise as a Catholic priest. In June 1577 a sweep was initiated to seek out and arrest hidden seminary priests. Often, if there was kinship or friendship involved, the priest and their benefactors would remain unmentioned by even some of their Protestant neighbours, but this wasn't always the case. Sometimes there were old scores to settle.

Following a tip-off, Mayne was arrested. Soon after, he was charged and tried. When the senior judge on the bench directed the jury to find him guilty of high treason, they duly complied. However, a stay was placed on Mayne's execution, and an appeal was lodged with the Privy Council. The priest must have paced around his cell with some hope in his heart. Unfortunately for Father Mayne, the appeal was turned down. The Privy Council ordered the local authorities to proceed with the court's sentence. In November 1577 Mayne was executed in Cornwall, by hanging, drawing and quartering.

Prior to his death, Father Mayne gave an indication of just how committed the seminary priests were to their mission. He received an offer from the authorities to commute his sentence from death to imprisonment, but this came with a catch. The priest would have to renounce his Catholicism and confirm Elizabeth as the Supreme Head of the Church of England.

When Father Mayne turned the offer down, he became the first of 158 Catholic priests trained at the English College in Douai to be executed between the years 1577 and 1680. The death toll mounted, and each time word reached Douai of another execution a solemn Mass of thanksgiving was heard for the martyred priest.

Even if he hadn't realised it before, William Allen now understood he was training a stream of idealistic young men to send homewards to their death. One amongst them was John Nelson from York. Originally hailing from the village of Skelton to the north of the city, he'd left his home to train for the priesthood in Douai. Following his return to England, Nelson was arrested and executed in London in 1578.

Around the same time, Allen fell in with another Catholic exile, a Jesuit priest called Robert Persons (sometimes referred to as Robert Parsons). Originally from Somerset, Persons had studied at Oxford and later taught there. However, his Catholic views had led to his resignation. He travelled to Rome and became a Jesuit priest.

Working together, Persons and Allen brought the English colleges under the influence of the Jesuits – the Society of Jesus. The Jesuit order had been created in the 1530s and was approved by the Pope in 1540. The original focus was to train and send missionary priests to all corners of the globe to find people who hadn't heard the Gospel and to convert them to Catholicism. By 1580 the Jesuits had travelled extensively, reaching as far as Japan.

In the meantime, their mission had evolved. It now included attempting to halt the rise of Protestantism in Europe and convert lapsed Europeans back to the Catholic faith. Sharing the same zeal for reconversion of the land of their birth, Allen and Persons got on well with each other. Both men were committed to the same mission. Soon it wasn't only Allen's seminary priests who were being sent to England and Wales; they were joined in their quest by Jesuit missionaries, led by Robert Persons himself.

York – Recusancy and Punishment

The second half of the 1570s saw a major escalation in the persecution and punishment of Catholics in York. Henry Hastings, the Earl of Huntingdon, had established himself as Lord President of the Council of the North. Although he no longer had Archbishop Grindal to work with, he was making steady progress in his mission to root out and punish northern recusants. Often, he was aided in this work by the man who rented out John Clitherow's house, the Dean of York, Matthew Hutton.

In 1575 Edwin Sandys was named as Archbishop of York. Sandys was one of the Protestant clergymen who had married a wife during Edward's reign. When Mary was crowned, he'd been arrested and separated from his family. Imprisonment in the Tower of London and Marshalsea jail had followed, but Sandys had been lucky. He'd narrowly avoided burning at the stake, like so many of his peers, by escaping from prison and taking a boat to the Continent.

Once he'd settled in Strasbourg, his wife, Mary, and young son, James, joined him. Tragically, both died there during an outbreak of plague. There's no known written record of his heartbreak, or whether he blamed Mary or Catholics in general for his loss. Following Elizabeth's coronation, Sandys returned home to England and remarried. By the time of his appointment as Archbishop of York, his second wife, Cicely, had given birth to eight surviving children. Another would follow in 1578.

By all accounts, Edwin Sandys was a difficult man to get on with. During his time in York, he managed to fall out with many people there. This included the Earl of Huntingdon, the Dean of York and many members of the city's Corporation. Sandys was a man with strong views. Using the mantra 'One God, one king, one faith', he saw little differentiation between recusants and traitors. Recusants had to be identified, then they could be punished, that was the law. The two men may have had their differences, but on the subject of recusancy Archbishop Sandys and Lord President Huntingdon were united.

The conflict between the Council of the North and the Corporation continued. In 1577 the Privy Council wrote to the Corporation, via Huntingdon, once again complaining of negligence in the compilation and naming of recusants. Although this was a common complaint, the number of recusancy cases being brought before the Ecclesiastical High Commission was already on the increase.

In November 1574 Dorothy Vavasour's husband, Thomas, a medical doctor, was brought before the High Commission for refusing to attend church and take communion, maintaining Catholic opinions and attempting to convert others to his views. Dr Vavasour was initially sent to jail in York, but later transferred to Hull, a place with a grisly reputation for poor prison conditions. In August 1575 Dr Vavasour was reported to be 'sickly and diseased' and was allowed to move into his brother's house. His future return to prison was covered by a bond.

Often it was the woman, of what might be described today as a 'middle class' household, who was the family's primary recusant. In December 1575 Foxgaile 'wife of Percival' Geldard, Frances 'wife of George' Hall and Isabel 'wife of Peter' Porter were all charged with non-attendance of church services.[2] Of course, when the men were accused, they were never known as the 'husband of …'.

Upon hearing these cases, the commissioners said they were minded to pardon the women, but only if they'd commit themselves to amending their ways and returning to church. When they all refused, they were sent to prison, one to York Castle and the others to the 'kidcote' on Ousebridge. Kidcote is an old Yorkshire word denoting a prison or jail.

These weren't the only prisons in Tudor York. For many years, the Church courts had used their own jails, including Peter's prison next to the Minster. There were two prisons on or next to Ousebridge, positioned on either side of the river. One was sometimes known as the mayor's kidcote (or debtors' prison) and the other the felons' gaol. Additional capacity was added during the rebuilding work of the 1560s, after the bridge's collapse due to flash flooding.

The most important prison in the city was undoubtedly York Castle. This was located around the area where Clifford's Tower stands today. At the time, the castle grounds covered a much wider space. From the mid-1570s onwards, the castle and York's other prisons began to fill up, swiftly populated by male and female recusants.

In 1576 a rare event happened. The lord mayor of York, Edmund Richardson, died part of the way through his term in office. The remaining months were covered by a merchant named Ralph Hall. D.M. Palliser's research indicates Mayor Richardson was one of the last aldermen in York to include openly Catholic wording in his will. This included a request for his soul to be left to God and the saints.

In July 1577, much to his embarrassment, the next lord mayor, John Dyneley, was called before the Ecclesiastical High Commission during his year in office. Dyneley's wife was accused of recusancy. The commissioners weren't impressed by 'a man who is set to govern a city and cannot govern his own household'. In his defence, Lord Mayor Dyneley argued his wife had been ill. In future, he said, if she didn't attend the church, he'd ensure he paid forfeitures on her behalf.

Another alderman was later called forward 'for his wife's like fault'. Robert Cripling would be the lord mayor after next. After hearing the charges read out against him, Cripling assured the commissioners he'd bring his wife to the service at the Minster on Sunday, 'and thereafter as her health will permit'.

On the same day, another York man, George Hall, was called before the High Commission to answer for his own wife. In his defence, Hall claimed he beat her 'now and then' for refusing to go to church. When he was fined for his wife's non-attendance, Hall claimed poverty, although he offered to pay whatever rate was agreed for the lord mayor and the other alderman, probably believing they'd both be let off lightly.

A series of similar cases followed in this hearing and during subsequent sessions. Accused men and women were fined, imprisoned or both. One particular case is of interest to us, but we'll return to that later in the chapter.

Pursuivants were hired to find and return those who refused to attend the court or attempted to escape justice. The Ecclesiastical High Commission made an agreement with one pursuivant, Anthony Durrell, to pay him 3d or 4d for every man or man and wife he apprehended in York and 8d a mile (4d each way) for those he arrested outside the city.

Despite the growing number of cases being heard, the Council of the North and Ecclesiastical High Commission remained unimpressed with the Corporation's ability to create and pass on full and accurate lists of recusants. In their defence, the Corporation could justifiably claim they'd already passed on the names of the wives of a leading alderman and the lord mayor himself.

In October 1577 Lord Mayor Dyneley was informed that things still weren't good enough. He was given five days to return before the High Commission with a fuller list of recusants compiled by the Corporation from individual parish records, along with details of 'what hath been done against each'.

On 29 October John Dyneley stood once again before Archbishop Sandys, Lord President Huntingdon and Dean Hutton. Reluctantly, we must assume, he handed over a longer list of names. Once the list was received, he was given a further dressing down. After receiving a long lecture about doing his duty, he was reminded of his wife's disobedience and continuing non-attendance of church. The lord mayor was ordered to hand over 40s to cover sixteen Sundays and four holidays since July, during which time his wife hadn't attended a single church service.

The 1577 return of recusants presented by Lord Mayor Dyneley to the Ecclesiastical High Commission is fascinating. It includes the names of recusants and reports received from churchwardens in every parish, including many names previously mentioned and others besides.

Some parishes included additional details about issues such as the refusal to pay fines or failed visits to houses. The churchwardens at St Sampson's reported they'd been unable to interview Elizabeth, 'wife of' John Langton, as 'both she and her husband were out, but the young folks locked the doors and would not let the churchwardens in.' It's easy to imagine Mr and Mrs Langton crouching out of sight in a dark corner, wishing not to be interviewed.

At Christ Church, George Hall, the man who'd defended himself by saying he'd beaten his wife 'now and then' told the wardens 'he will submit himself to my Lord Bishop for that he cannot get his wife to go to church.' In the same parish Dorothy Vavasour 'cometh not to church but keepeth the door close'. Her husband was stated as being in prison. The wife of another man, William Cockburn, was 'very sick'.

Many entries listed parishioners' reasons for being unable to pay their fines, which were often described as 'distress'. In St Cuthbert's parish, Helen Williamson, 'wife of' John, had missed church since January, but John 'hath no goods whereof any distress can be levied'. At St Michael le Belfry (the church next to the Minster), Margaret, 'wife of' William Tessimond, a saddler, had also been absent from church since January. She would not let the churchwardens cite 'distress'. Her husband, William, was already in prison for the same offence. You may recall he was the man who'd trimmed the beard from the Earl of Northumberland's severed head.

The Ecclesiastical Commission was now armed with a fuller list of names, and the number of cases began to escalate further. The people brought before the courts included some with central roles in this book.

Margaret's Story – Conversion to Catholicism

The path through the Corporation's hierarchy for a butcher was never a fast or smooth one. Having served his time as a bridgemaster, in

1574 John Clitherow became a chamberlain. The chamberlains were responsible for managing and distributing the city's civic spending, for example, on roads, marketplace improvements, maintenance of Corporation properties, management of poor relief, and so on. The office of chamberlain entitled the bearer to use the title of 'Master' or 'Mr', so Margaret's husband now became Mr John Clitherow.

In 1574, between his business interests and work as a chamberlain, John must have had limited time for his family. His wife, Margaret, was now twenty-one years old. When she gave birth to a daughter, the couple called the girl Anne.

Earlier we mentioned Dr Thomas Vavasour and his wife, Dorothy. Both had been openly Catholic during the early years of Elizabeth's reign. Initially, when York's parishes and Corporation had collected recusancy details with little vigour, the Vavasours had been able to evade scrutiny and punishment, but by the 1570s the situation had changed. As we've examined, both husband and wife had had cases heard by the Ecclesiastical High Commission. Dorothy was fined for recusancy in 1571, while Thomas had been imprisoned in York, and later in Hull. At other times, when he'd fallen ill, he'd been confined to family residences.

Having gained a licence to practice medicine from the Royal College of Physicians in 1556, Thomas was a trained physician. When in York and not in prison, he'd encouraged Dorothy to help the women of the city endure and recover from the rigours of childbirth. The situation created an opportunity to maintain contact with those who shared their faith, and time to work on converting others who, willingly or otherwise, had embraced the state church.

A moment of crisis like childbirth, with its high risk of injury and death, was an ideal time to raise matters spiritual. With no drugs or pain relief, the majority of women went through labour experiencing severe physical pain. In a period when religion, whatever the faith, played a crucial role in people's lives, some women would have looked upwards towards their maker and prayed for their babies and themselves. A soothing word here and there, a few phrases of Latin, a prayer to God spoken softly into the woman's ear while mopping her brow, could have made all the difference to the woman's spirits. For many, this had a lasting effect.

During labour, there were generally no men present, apart from perhaps Dr Vavasour in the background, when he wasn't in prison.

Records from the time show York had a relatively high number of female recusants. We can't be certain, but there's a possibility the Vavasours' maternity clinic was one of the reasons behind this.

When Anne Clitherow was born she became Margaret's second child. Her son, Henry, was around two years old. Margaret's biographer, the Catholic priest Father John Mush, stated it was around this time Margaret converted to Catholicism. Prior to this, Margaret had obeyed the law, attending church services, first at St Martin's, Coney Street, and more recently at the Church of the Holy Trinity next to the Shambles. So, too, had many others in York, despite the fact that not everyone had bought into the changes being made around them.

When Elizabeth ascended to the throne in 1559 Margaret had been six years old. Her father died eight years later in 1567. In between, Thomas Middleton had conformed, at least to a degree. He'd certainly attended the slowly changing St Martin's. If he'd wanted to become a member of the Twenty-Four and fulfil his ambition of becoming an alderman, he'd have felt compelled to. But as we've seen, even in the mid-1570s not every alderman in York walked the Protestant path laid out for them by the Queen, Council and Ecclesiastical High Commission.

It's impossible to say how Protestant or Catholic Thomas Middleton was in his final years. It's quite possible, perhaps even probable, he retained some elements of his Catholic faith. After all, he'd been raised a Catholic. His wax chandlery had flourished under the Catholic Church and dwindled under Protestantism. He lived in York, a city which only begrudgingly, and under orders, was slowly moving in the new direction. Many of the aldermen Thomas had looked up to were certainly Catholics at the time of his death, as was confirmed by the letter of complaint Archbishop Young had written to the Privy Council.

If Thomas Middleton still possessed Catholic leanings, it's likely his family did too. When her mother married Henry Maye in 1567 Margaret may have attended Church of England services to conform, but retained a level of ongoing support for the Catholic faith.

There's no evidence to show Henry Maye was anything other than an adherent to the policy of the day. He'd arrived in York from a less religiously conservative area on the south coast of England. In 1570 as a churchwarden, he'd helped prepare St Martin's church for Archbishop Grindal's visitation. His tasks had included removing the last vestiges of Catholicism. The inspection had gone well.

Henry Maye would have wanted his new family to follow his own example rather than that of his predecessor's. Perhaps Jane, Margaret and George Middleton were instructed to tow the line. If Margaret did so, it may have been reluctantly. Father Mush wrote, 'She had every day a hearty sorrow and humble repentance for her youth spent out of Christ's Catholic Church in vain follies and schism.'

Father Mush wrote these words from the viewpoint of a Catholic missionary priest. As we'll explore, when the seminary priests and Jesuits arrived in England, a debate raged over the rights and wrongs of going to the state church service even reluctantly or being more openly defiant. The Jesuits argued strongly in support of recusancy, making the case that attending Church of England services was heresy.

This was the backdrop to Margaret's conversations with Dorothy Vavasour around the time of Anne Clitherow's birth. Whatever was said between the two women, Margaret was convinced. Whether she'd lapsed towards the new church and converted or been attending Holy Trinity for the sake of her family and a quiet life, things changed. Margaret Clitherow became openly Catholic.

The biggest difference of all was that Margaret was now a recusant, a law breaker. As such, she was joining a sizeable minority of men and women in York at the time. Although not every husband agreed with their wife, many did so. Some attended the state church to limit the financial damage and hardship to their family. Unfortunately for Margaret and the others, this was a time when it was more likely their names would be added to the recusancy lists and they'd be punished for their crimes.

There's no record of the conversation between Margaret and John Clitherow on the first Sunday she refused to walk the few yards down the Shambles to the parish church service at Holy Trinity. It's hard to imagine harsh words weren't spoken. After all, John probably wanted to keep up appearances. The lofty position of alderman may have been beyond him, but he'd been a bridgemaster and a chamberlain. He might still become a sheriff and a member of the Twenty-Four, if he wanted to, and if his family didn't get him into trouble.

Unlike George Hall, John Clitherow didn't beat his wife. Margaret had given birth to their baby, Anne, recently. John may well have used this as an excuse to justify Margaret's non-attendance at church on that Sunday and for many weeks afterwards. He would have argued there was absolutely no reason his wife's name should be added to the list.

But theirs was a small church and a small parish. Everyone lived close to each other in a tightly knit community. People would have talked.

Although John Clitherow remained a Protestant, some members of his family were Catholic. His brother, William, was a Catholic priest, although little information is known about him. At times, a number of adjoining houses in the Shambles were occupied by John's relatives. On one side was Michael Mudd's house and butcher's shop. On the other side lived John's sister and her husband, William Calvert, another butcher. Calvert was either a brother or uncle of John's first wife. The potential religious fervour of those who lived in these houses will be examined later.

As time went by, the pressure applied by the Council on the Corporation of York to maintain fuller and more accurate recusancy lists continued. On 2 August 1577, one month after Lord Mayor Dyneley was forced to defend and excuse his wife's actions to the Ecclesiastical High Commission, John and Margaret Clitherow were summonsed before the commissioners for the very first time.[3]

Many other cases were heard that day. John Weddell's wife, Anne, 'refuseth service sermons and to communicate, she frequenth not the church, the cause whereof is that her conscience will not serve her thereunto.' Anne Weddell was marked down as a conscientious objector for her non-attendance of church services, and was sent to York Castle prison. As he'd failed to make her go to church, her husband, John, was also imprisoned, but not at the castle. Instead, he was committed to the kidcote on Ousebridge.

Next came the Clitherows' case. It had been three years since Margaret had joined York's recusant community. Her absence from the court during this time was presumably down to the Clitherows' parish friends' reluctance to add her name to the list, or perhaps due to the aldermen's reluctance to prosecute every recusant in the city.

By 1577 things had changed. Even the lord mayor could no longer expect his case to go unpunished if his wife didn't attend church. Lord Mayor Dyneley had not yet provided the full and more accurate list of recusants demanded of him by the authorities, but the list the Commission already had appeared to be long enough.

Margaret Clitherow's name had recently been added to York's recusancy roll of shame. She and her husband found themselves facing charges for her non-attendance. 'John's wife refuseth service and summons and also to communicate.' The couple received the same two sentences as the Weddells. Margaret was ordered to attend her first spell in the cells of York Castle.

To his surprise, John was also committed. As with John Weddell, he was despatched to the kidcote on Ousebridge. Other husbands followed; each was found guilty of failing to control their errant wife.

Many of the subsequent cases proceeded in a similar pattern. Next up was Peter Porter 'and wife Isabel'. Their case was followed by Ambrose Cooke 'and wife Anne', and then Perceival and 'wife' Geldard. Although her name wasn't listed, we know from other cases her first name was Janet. After the Geldards came Thomas Tailor 'and wife Margaret'. All were imprisoned separately; the wife sent to York Castle, the husband to Ousebridge. Having had previous cases heard eighteen months earlier, the Geldards and Porters were repeat offenders,

Not everyone summonsed before the High Commission that day was sent to prison. Edward Tesh and 'his wife' (her name was Anne, although it wasn't listed) of Bishopfields were also accused of recusancy. 'He refuseth sermons service and the communion and his wife also.' As the couple didn't appear in court, they couldn't be sent to jail. But they were soon rounded up and their cases heard the following day. Both husband and wife, Tesh, admitted to being unable to 'find it in their consciences' to go to church. After some to-ing and fro-ing it was agreed Edward should attend conferences with church officials at the archbishop's residence to persuade his conscience otherwise. Anne was allowed to return home.

We now come to an interesting case. Unusually for a woman, the High Commission book made a point of recording Elizabeth Hewett's occupation. Elizabeth was described as an 'obstetrix', the Latin word for midwife. This derives from the word '*obstare*' or 'stand before', with Tudor midwives positioning themselves in front of the mother-to-be when preparing for birth.

By detailing Elizabeth Hewett's occupation, the authorities may have been highlighting a connection with Dr Thomas Vavasour and his wife, Dorothy. This adds circumstantial evidence, or at least some grist to the mill, that a significant part of the female half of York's recusancy movement had been born out of conversations held in the Vavasours' house during its time as a makeshift maternity ward for the local community.

Elizabeth Hewett avoided incarceration. Perhaps she was too useful or didn't have a husband to pay her fines. Although she was found guilty of not going to church, Elizabeth was instructed to attend services from that day onwards until Michaelmas (29 September). She was also suspended from working as a midwife until the same date, unless she was given permission to practise by the archbishop. With Cecily Sandys pregnant, perhaps the couple were keen to have an experienced obstetrix available to call upon if needed.

After three miserable nights in prison, John Clitherow, John Weddell, Peter Porter, Ambrose Cooke, Perceival Geldard and Thomas Tailor were all brought back before the High Commission. Each was ordered to take a bond of £20 (a significant sum in those days), and told to return before the commissioners in October, before being released. The men returned before the Commission a number of times during the coming months, while their wives remained locked up in the castle.

Sharing a cold cell in the long winter months may have been intended to try the women's mental fortitude, but it did have its compensations. At least the wives were removed from the worries of their households, their husband's businesses and child-rearing duties. With time on their hands, Margaret and the other women began to enjoy focusing their minds on all things Catholic. Father Mush reports the lasting impact this time in prison had on Margaret. 'They shut her up into close prison, and she learned thereby to forget and despise the world; they separated her from house, children, and husband, and she thereby became familiar with God.'

With little else to occupy her mind, Margaret wouldn't have been the first or last person to be 'radicalised' by a spell in prison. It's likely the women developed a special camaraderie, discussing their religious devotions, praying to God, and setting themselves apart from the heretics outside.

In February 1578 there was a breakthrough in their cases. As a temporary reprieve, the wives were allowed to leave their cells in the castle. Their husbands were ordered to take out new bonds to ensure the women voluntarily returned to prison on the first Tuesday after Low Sunday (the Sunday after Easter). Meanwhile, the wives were ordered 'not to confer with disobedient persons', and told their husbands must pay an additional 2s for any Sunday or holiday church service they missed.

John Clitherow went to the castle, signed for his wife and took her home. Their son, Henry, was almost six; little Anne not quite yet four.

The children must have rushed into their mother's arms. There would have been tears of joy, relief and perhaps sadness too, as the family reflected upon their six months of enforced separation.

For once, John Clitherow probably forgot all about his butcher's shop and business. Hopefully by this time, the servants and apprentices were used to managing the shop without any help from their master or mistress. They were probably guided and directed by John's two elder sons. As John slumped into his chair in the living quarters behind the shop, he may have looked at his second wife and their children embracing and issued a deep sigh of relief. Surely lessons had been learned. This couldn't happen again.

The family would have eaten well that day. No doubt John ensured there was always a good choice of meat, poultry and game on the table. After sharing a hearty meal, Margaret may have put Henry and Anne to bed, kissed them and told them bedtime stories or nursery rhymes. She would have watched their little faces as they drifted off to sleep. Despite the riches of her religion, the risk of permanently losing this must have weighed heavily on her mind.

Afterwards, Margaret may have bathed herself with as much clean water as she could, before going to bed. It's interesting to wonder what she and John said to each other during that cold February night as they lay in each other's arms in their bedchamber. Did John tentatively ask, or even demand, his wife put aside her religious convictions for the good of their family? If so, how did Margaret respond?

On 8 April John Clitherow returned to the High Commission, along with John Weddell and Peter Porter. The trio feared their wives would be taken away again, but this didn't happen. The men were ordered to sign a new bond, stating their wives should return to the castle on 26 June. In the meantime, they were instructed that the women weren't to leave their houses or business premises except to go to church. Once again, the wives were forbidden from conferring or meeting 'known disobedient persons'. The husbands had no choice but to agree to forfeit 2s for every Sunday or holy day church service their wife didn't attend.

Finally, in June 1578, Margaret was released from her bonds. After three months of house arrest, John was told his wife no longer had to return to the castle. Margaret could resume her full life and duties as a married woman, butcher's wife, mother, stepmother, daughter and stepdaughter. The nightmare was seemingly over. John was tasked by the commissioners to see to his wife's future behaviour, and warned he'd be fined more harshly if she misbehaved again.

Once more, conversations must have gone on in the Clitherows' household. Given the Catholicism of some of John's relatives and neighbours, and many of the people he'd grown up with during his life in York, he may have had sympathy for his wife. But surely he told Margaret that times had changed. Lord President Huntingdon, Archbishop Sandys and Dean Hutton were all hellbent on punishing recusants. Missing church was something Margaret could no longer expect to get away with.

Couldn't she see sense and become a Church Catholic (i.e. attend the official service, even if she didn't agree with what was being said)? This would remove her name from the lists and avoid her and her husband having to return to court. John may have said he had no issue with Margaret visiting Dorothy Vavasour's house, or the other places where Mass was celebrated, just as long as she was careful and didn't get caught. However, by this time, even before she'd met a seminary or Jesuit priest, Margaret had caught the bug. Her religious faith, her devotion to God and all things saintly had got the better of her. She no longer had a choice. The Catholic Church had become everything.

If her husband was fined, this was unfortunate, but he could afford it. There were, after all, more important things in life than money. Father Mush reported that Margaret later told him, 'The more folks grew in wealth, the further they were from God, and less disposed to do well.'

But what if Margaret was sent to prison again? She'd miss her family terribly, but so be it. If she was forced to suffer for God, she would gladly do so. Such a stance may be understandable to some today, particularly those with strong religious convictions. To others, it may seem incredible that a woman – anyone – could risk losing everything they had, including the family they loved, for what many non-religious people might think of as an idea or concept.

Of course, her faith was much more important to Margaret Clitherow than this. Her husband, family and friends undoubtedly meant a great deal to her, but as Father Mush outlined in *A True Report*, her religion had become the reason for her life.

Margaret continued to behave 'badly'. When she missed church services and met with 'disobedient persons' her actions didn't go unnoticed. Her name was placed back on the recusancy list. In October 1578 John Clitherow was ordered to pay 30s to the poor and instructed to take out a new bond regarding his wife's behaviour. In April 1579 he was forced to pay out another fine.

At least there was some good news for York's recusant community. Dorothy Vavasour, who'd been charged again, had been released from the kidcote. To enable her freedom, the doctor's wife had promised to remain in her house, except to visit her garden. Additionally, the commissioners had instructed her to 'behave quietly in matters of religion'. The phrase, 'Good luck with that!' comes to mind.

In addition to 'the wife' of John Clitherow, the spouses of John Weddell, Peter Porter, Perceival Geldard and Thomas Tailor had also misbehaved badly following their release. Each husband was forced to pay a series of fines and forfeitures. What happened to Anne and Ambrose Cooke was different. In December 1579 Ambrose was brought before the Ecclesiastical High Commission on charges relating to the birth of a child in his house. We assume Anne was the mother. It was alleged the baby had been baptised by a 'popish priest' rather than a Protestant curate. In his (weak) defence, Ambrose stated 'he could not tell' who had baptised the baby, nor who the child's godparents were. He was quickly despatched to York Castle jail.

It's probable that some of the husbands were Catholics themselves. They may have reluctantly agreed for their wives to demonstrate the family's Catholicism on their behalf, with the wife being less likely to face sterner punishment than the man of the house. However, John Clitherow wasn't a Catholic. Neither was his father-in-law. In 1579 Henry Maye began the second of two three-year terms as a churchwarden at St Martin's. His invitation to join York's aldermen must have seemed tantalisingly close. With the Council of the North and the Ecclesiastical High Commission cracking down on suspected Catholic deviants, even in the Corporation, it was likely anyone identified as a recusant in York would soon be prosecuted.

As a member of the Twenty-Four with high hopes of one day becoming an alderman, having an openly recusant Catholic stepdaughter wouldn't have been an easy pill for Henry Maye to swallow. Surely the more forward-thinking aldermen would focus any future recruitment on members of the Twenty-Four whom they knew to be good Protestants with loyal Protestant families.

In the back rooms of the Davygate tavern Henry must have begun to pull his hair out. When John and Margaret weren't in front of the High

Commission, it's likely they were being summoned to the Mayes' living quarters behind the tap room and lectured about Margaret's behaviour. But if the risk of being separated from her husband and children hadn't deterred her, it seems unlikely a reprimand from Henry Maye would have made much of an impact.

But what was the viewpoint of the person who'd known Margaret longest of all? Did Jane Maye support her husband's stance, or did she stoutly defend her daughter's position and her right to protest? We don't know, but as long as Jane was there to protect her, it's unlikely Margaret would feel the full force of Henry's anger. At Jane's behest, Henry may have even been tempted to use his position on the Twenty-Four to protect his stepdaughter. Certainly, if he became an alderman he'd be in a better position to do this.

Chapter Seven

Schism and Crackdown (1580–1585)

Elizabeth I – Clerical Debates and Legal Changes

Cuthbert Mayne, the priest executed in Cornwall, was one of the first of the seminary priests to cross the Channel and infiltrate the parishes of England and Wales. Others soon followed. It's been estimated around a hundred seminary priests had already arrived in the country by 1580. They would soon be joined by others, including a series of Jesuit missionaries led by Robert Persons and Edmond Campion.

Born in London, like William Allen and Robert Persons, Edmond Campion had studied at Oxford, but his story is different. While in England, Campion had signed the Oath of Supremacy to the Queen. He even gained Elizabeth's personal favour following a public debate in Oxford. Although he retained some Catholic views, Campion was ordained as a deacon in the Church of England. After struggling with his conscience, he travelled to Dublin, but was suspected of retaining dangerous Catholic sympathies. Eventually he fled from Ireland, arriving and studying at William Allen's college in Douai, before travelling to Rome, where he joined the Society of Jesus as a Jesuit priest.

Persons and Campion arrived in England in 1580. They were both painfully aware of how dangerous their mission was. Just as William Allen had ordered his seminary priests to disguise themselves in lay clothes, Persons and Campion were ordered to do the same. The Jesuit leadership instructed the pair were to select garments 'of a modest and sober kind' which offered 'no appearance of levity and vanity'.

Robert Persons crossed the Channel first, reaching Dover in June 1580. Edmond Campion followed a few days later, disguised as a jewel merchant. Assisted by a network of Catholic sympathisers, they made their way separately to London. Walking, riding and sitting atop horse-drawn carts and carriages, they must have fretted about their capture and arrest, and contemplated how their bodies might respond to torture.

The pair were ordered to steer well clear of politics, although it's difficult to see how the Jesuits' mission could be seen as being anything other than political. Despite the Papal Bull, they were instructed not to question or even discuss the Queen's supremacy. Hopes had begun to rise in Rome that Elizabeth might at last marry a Catholic, this time the French Duke of Anjou.

As we've seen, Catholics' responses to the suppression of their faith varied from tacit adherence to recusancy. A major aspect of the Jesuits' mission was to provide clarity on how the country's Catholics should behave. Both Persons and Campion preached, wrote and published demands for stricter observance of Catholic doctrine and the rejection of alternatives. True Catholics didn't associate themselves with, or worship in the company of, heretics. They didn't attend Church of England services. Recusancy wasn't an option: it had to be embraced.

If a significant portion of the country's population had retained Catholic inclinations over the first two decades of Elizabeth's reign, the result of this message could be devastating. If widely adopted, the Jesuits' call for recusancy would result in a mass boycott of the Sunday service. If this happened, the authorities would need a bigger list of recusants, and the courts and jails would be full.

Elizabeth's relationship with the Duke of Anjou was an important factor. Initially believing the royal betrothal was potentially imminent, part of the priests' mission was to demonstrate the considerable weight of Catholic support within the country. Rome believed this might play a decisive role in helping Elizabeth shrug off her doubts and accelerate the couple's union. Once the English Queen was married to a Catholic, who knows what could happen?

The trick was to separate the question of religious faith from loyalty to the Crown. While some people might rebel against the state religion, they could still retain wholehearted support for the Queen. Persons and Campion laid down a difficult challenge for the government. Their call for mass civil disobedience made it difficult for the likes of William Cecil, Francis Walsingham and the Earl of Huntingdon. The English authorities recognised little or no distinction between uniformity with the church and loyalty to the Crown and State.

This was a major test too for the Catholics who'd been attending Church of England services with their fingers crossed, and the surviving Marian priests who'd given them succour. They could argue they'd retained their faith for many years without the help of Rome. With no support forthcoming, they'd had to compromise, including accepting the laws of the land in which they lived. Why were they now being called heretics? Persons' and Campion's messages kicked off a wide-ranging, long-running and heated debate amongst the country's Catholics.

Once in London, Persons worked with his Catholic supporters to establish a set of safe houses designed to allow Campion and himself to travel around the country to spread the word. For the majority of their time in England, the two men remained apart. This meant they could visit twice as many places and meet twice as many people. Equally, their separation reduced the risk of both being captured at the same time, which would bring their clandestine operation to an abrupt and uncomfortable end.

In July 1580, before they headed off on their separate tours of England, Persons and Campion held a major meeting of Catholic clergymen in Southwark on the south bank of the Thames.[1] To their surprise, they weren't welcomed with open arms by everyone. Some attendees suggested they shut up and leave the country. As men who'd lived in exile, they were asked how they could pretend to understand what the country's Catholics had been through to retain their faith and prevent their families from being persecuted. Once discovered by the authorities, the presence of the Jesuits in the country would no doubt result in additional crackdowns and harsher treatment.

After the mini synod in Southwark, the debate for and against the Jesuits' position in terms of out-and-out recusancy raged on. From time to time, both men documented their position and stated the case for non-conformity in a series of pamphlets and papers printed on a hidden illegal printing press.

During 1580 Persons wrote 'A brief discourse containing certain reasons why Catholics refuse to go to church', while Campion published a challenge to the Privy Council, requesting they listen to his arguments. In it, he described the core of his mission as follows: 'My charge is, of free cost to preach the Gospel, to minister the Sacraments, to instruct the simple, to reform sinners, to confute errors – in brief, to cry alarm spiritual against foul vice and proud ignorance, where-with many my dear Countrymen are abused.'

Campion stressed the apolitical nature of his work: 'I am strictly forbidden by our Father that sent me, to deal in any respect with matter of State or Policy of this realm, as things which appertain not to my vocation, and from which I do gladly restrain and sequester my thoughts.'

Campion's document wasn't well received by the English establishment. Amidst claims of his arrogance, the paper was nicknamed 'Campion's Brag'. Well aware that Persons and Campion were in the country, the authorities accelerated their efforts to find them.

Following the meeting in Southwark, Persons and Campion toured their message around England. Persons travelled to the Midlands, visiting Northampton and Derby, and headed west to the cathedral cities of Gloucester and Worcester, near the Welsh border. Campion took the mission further north. It's thought he avoided York, but returned to his native Lancashire, where he attended many meetings and preached the gospel of recusancy.

Both men knew their arrest might be imminent. In one of his reports to their Jesuit leaders, Campion wrote: 'We cannot long escape the hands of the heretics; the enemies have so many eyes, so many tongues, so many traps. I read letters myself that in the first page tell the news that "Campion is captured". This so re-echoes in my ears repeatedly now, wherever I go, that fear itself has driven out all my fear. "My life is ever in my own hands."'

Living and working undercover in an enemy state must have taken a toll on their nerves. As hundreds of officials, spies and informers searched for them, the pair evaded capture for some time. Their network of contacts and safe houses provided adequate support and shelter, and they continued to spread the word to anyone who'd listen, urging those they met to pass their message on.

Although Persons and Campion were the first men to undertake the Jesuits' mission across the Channel, they weren't the last. As the country slowly began to fill with seminary and Jesuit priests, the authorities upped the ante against them. The 1581 Act to 'Retain the Queen's Majesty's subjects in their Due Obedience' was created as a direct reaction to concerns about the activities of the missionary priests. The new act included significant clauses designed to place additional pressure and penalties on the seminaries and the Jesuits, anyone who listened to them and the Catholic population in general.[2]

The act targeted the Catholic priests directly, outlawing persuasion of anyone away from 'their natural obedience to her Majesty', 'withdrawing' people from the religion of the land to 'the Romish religion', or moving people to 'promise obedience to any pretended authority to the See in Rome'.

It became illegal for the Queen's subjects to positively respond to any such action, or to aid, maintain or conceal a Catholic priest in any way. Anyone suspected of the crime could be charged with high treason. Holding a Catholic Mass was to be punished with a 200-mark fine and imprisonment for a year. Anyone attending or hearing Mass would be fined 100 marks and sent to jail for twelve months. (A mark was an amount of money equal to two-thirds of a pound.)

The fines for recusancy were sharply increased to 'twenty pounds of lawful English money', which would be 'forfeit to the Queen's majesty for every month'. For most people, these fines were huge and impossible to pay. While fines could be used to punish and dissuade the gentry from non-conformance, different punishments were needed for the masses. Anyone found guilty could be imprisoned and would 'continue to be bound until such time as the persons so bound do conform themselves and come to the church.'

Some non-conformist Marian priests and seminary men had been disguising themselves as schoolmasters to live undercover in Catholic households. The authorities had grown wise to this. The act included a fine of £10 each month for anyone found guilty of keeping or maintaining a schoolmaster who failed to attend parish church services. The schoolmaster would be barred from being 'a teacher of youth' and 'suffer imprisonment without bail [...] for one year'.

The intention of the act was clear. There were Catholic priests in the country, celebrating Mass, hearing confession and encouraging the nation's Catholics. The Jesuits' leaders, Persons and Campion, were urging the Catholic population to enter a religious general strike of non-attendance of Church of England services. They wanted everyone out, but the government was not for turning. Concessions wouldn't be made. The battle lines were drawn. You were either with the Queen, Her Majesty's religion and the English authorities, or you were against them.

Persons and Campions' mission continued, but their luck couldn't last forever. There were spies and prying eyes almost everywhere. Rewards for the priests' capture became increasingly high. In July 1581 Campion was spotted by an informer at Lyford Grange. This was just a dozen miles south-west of Oxford, where copies of Campion's latest publication, *Ten Reasons*, had been discovered on the benches of a church. Following a brief search of the Grange, Campion was arrested and transported to London.

Campion was imprisoned in the Tower of London, where he was tortured. How much information he revealed about the places he'd been and the people he'd visited isn't fully known. It seems unlikely he could have resisted totally. His body was racked multiple times.

If such extreme torture wasn't enough, Campion was subjected to a series of theological debates with Church of England clergymen. After holding his own in these, he was offered a chance to go free. Of course, there was a condition. Campion would have to renounce his Catholic faith. If he did this, it would be a significant coup for the authorities.

Wholeheartedly convinced in his mission and beliefs, Campion refused. He was placed on trial and found guilty of treason. On 1 December 1581 Edmond Campion was hanged, drawn and quartered with two other priests at Tyburn in London. Eight further priests were executed during the first half of 1582 for their real or alleged links to Campion and Persons.

Following Campion's arrest, the hunt for Robert Persons and the other priests intensified. Although the end looked inevitable, somehow Persons kept his identity secret and managed to evade capture. He escaped to France. Once there, he returned to Douai and met up with William Allen. The two men decided to continue their seminary and Jesuit mission in England and Wales, but from afar. Neither man returned to the land of their birth again.

As the mission continued, so did the crackdown on Catholic priests and the wider Catholic population. In 1582 ten priests were executed. There was a slight lull in 1583 when fewer than five were killed, before the numbers increased again in 1584. The roll count of people identified, fined and imprisoned for non-attendance of church services increased in certain areas. However, there wasn't the massive increase in recusancy numbers which Allen, Persons and Campion had hoped and called for. Higher numbers in some localities could also be attributed to stricter enforcement.

Meanwhile, the possibility of Elizabeth marrying the Duke of Anjou faded. In 1583 the Queen faced another conspiracy: to remove her from the throne and again replace her with Mary Stuart.

Francis Throckmorton hailed from a prominent family of wealthy English Catholics. In 1580 he travelled to Europe and became involved with a group of men who wished to see England returned to Catholicism. Their plans included invading the country with a French Catholic army, backed by Spain, freeing Mary Stuart and crowning her as the Catholic Queen of England.

Although the conspiracy became known as the Throckmorton Plot, Francis Throckmorton's role was a relatively minor one. His main task was to pass secret coded messages between the main conspirators, including the Spanish ambassador to England and Mary Stuart. When Francis Walsingham uncovered the plot, the Spanish ambassador was expelled, and Throckmorton tortured and executed. Once again, Elizabeth refused to heed calls to punish Mary, although she was placed in stricter confinement.

If anything, attitudes in England against Catholics hardened further. It didn't help when intelligence reports were received from Europe claiming leading Catholic exiles, including William Allen and Robert Persons, had begun to advocate military force as the only way to revert England back to Catholicism. As the mission to send priests into the country continued, the two men behind this became increasingly linked with plans to create a Spanish Armada.

York – Aldermen, Priests and Executions

In 1579 Robert Cripling was elected lord mayor of York by his fellow aldermen. Two years had passed since he'd been hauled before the Ecclesiastical High Commission for his wife's non-attendance of church services, alongside the then-lord mayor, John Dyneley. Cripling and Dyneley were members of the Corporation's old guard, York merchants who maintained a level of allegiance to the Catholic Church.

During the first half of Cripling's term in office, he initiated a lull in the Corporation's pursuit of recusants. Enraged by this flagrant disregard for the law and his authority, the Earl of Huntingdon reacted angrily. Cripling was arrested and imprisoned in York Castle prison. Once again, the Council criticised the Corporation for its lack of action against recusants. York's aldermen were told to step up or suffer the consequences. A debate began to rage within the Corporation regarding its future direction. Could the traditionalists win, or would the new guard of Protestant-leaning aldermen begin to hold sway?

The pressure from the Council was unrelenting. At the end of his term in office the aldermen were compelled to disenfranchise Robert Cripling from the Corporation altogether. He was accused by his colleagues of absence from his duties (well, he had been in prison), speaking 'unseemly and foul words' against the clergy and negligence in pursuit of recusants. Although Cripling was forced to stand down, the Earl of Huntingdon hadn't finished with him. Henry Hastings was determined to make an example of Robert Cripling that the other aldermen wouldn't forget.

In November 1580 the ex-lord mayor and 'his wife Lady Cripling' were ordered to stand before the Ecclesiastical High Commission, facing further charges of recusancy. The couple were found guilty and ordered to take out a substantial bond. However, it appears Cripling still had a few friends with influence. Several months later, the case was quietly dismissed. The records stated, 'Mr Cripling has conformed completely'.

The Council's intentions to influence and change the leadership of the Corporation was working. However, if the commissioners believed they'd knocked the stuffing out of Robert Cripling, they were wrong. Freed from the shackles of his Corporation duties, he quickly reconverted to Catholicism. In the coming years, he and Lady Cripling were regular attendees before the High Commission, if not at church services.

Cripling's fall (or push) from grace coincided with the death of the other Catholic-leaning ex-lord mayor John Dyneley. After his death, Dyneley's widow, a long-standing recusant, left York. A short time later she remarried a Catholic.

The early 1580s saw a rapid overhaul in the membership of the Corporation of York's highest tier. Seven new aldermen were elected during the first two years of the decade alone. The last of the remaining aldermen with any significant Catholic sympathies was William Alleyn. Probably under pressure from the Council, he resigned his position in 1581.

Although others may have harboured lingering Catholic affinities or had the odd recusant relative pop up and appear in court now and then, the era of allegiance to Catholicism in the higher echelons of the Corporation was over. The 1580s was a new decade and time for new blood. Among the raft of people vying to be elected as one of the city's new aldermen was Henry Maye.

The Earl of Huntingdon needed men like Henry Maye. Whether he liked it or not, his crusade against York's recusants relied on the Corporation's co-operation. Huntingdon had initiated Robert Cripling's downfall, but he'd needed the aldermen's support to finish the job. A few words here and there would have helped, along with mention of how the Privy Council was watching York and the Corporation closely. In London, suspicions lingered, triggered by the city's role in the Pilgrimage of Grace.

Huntingdon and his fellow members of the Council of the North and the Ecclesiastical High Commission began to receive worrying messages from the Privy Council. William Cecil, Francis Walsingham and others were concerned about the arrival of the seminary priests and the Jesuits' mission in England. As a likely destination for one or both of Campion and Persons, York was placed on high alert.

The Ecclesiastical High Commission was determined to identify, punish and minimise the number of recusants in the city. During 1580–1581, forty-five new names were added to the recusancy lists in York. Facing fines which they couldn't pay and likely imprisonment, a number of them opted to conform. The city was left with a hardcore of less than a hundred recusants. Many of these were women, married to men of middling households. The authorities continued to find it difficult to bring this group around to their way of thinking.

It didn't help that many of them had served time together in York's prisons, with little else to do but discuss and strengthen their religious beliefs. The city's jails had become a place where prisoners of conscience confided in like minds. Many of the religious prisoners found their convictions hardened rather than weakened during their punishment.

The authorities did what they could to convince the captive audience of the errors of their Catholic ways. Archbishop Sandys and Dean Hutton both coerced Catholic prisoners into listening to long and repeated Protestant texts and sermons. Often, the prisoners were challenged to dispute and argue against what they'd heard. The Church authorities believed, due to many of the prisoners' limited levels of education, they'd be unable to do so.

One inmate, Thomas Mudd, was a former monk. He argued a strong and well-made case against the senior churchmen during these debates, to the fury of an increasingly red-faced Archbishop Sandys. The archbishop threatened to have Mudd 'crushed and bruised'. Instead,

Mudd was transferred to Hull prison, punishment enough when he promptly fell ill.

Thomas Mudd wasn't the only Marian clergyman to be placed inside the walls of York Castle. In fact, there was now a steady flow of such men, and they were soon to be joined, albeit briefly for most, by the new breed of Catholic clergy – the seminary and Jesuit priests.

Between the winter of 1581 and the spring of 1582, the missionary priests began arriving in York. Some were returning to the area of their birth. Others were venturing through York's narrow streets for the first time. The Earl of Huntingdon, now supported by the Corporation, was waiting for them. Although Campion claimed the Jesuits' mission was purely a religious one, Huntingdon was of the same mind as William Cecil and Francis Walsingham. There could be no separation between non-uniformity with the Church and treachery to the Crown and State.

In July 1582 a number of seminary priests scheduled an audacious meeting of York's Catholic community. Given that many of its leading members were incarcerated within York Castle prison, this was where the meeting was to be held. No fewer than four missionary priests ventured to the prison. One of their number, Thomas Bell, had famously disagreed with Persons' and Campion's call for recusancy. He argued instead in favour of permitting Catholics to attend church services to avoid punishment, as long as they didn't take communion.[3]

That night, Bell was joined by Fathers William Hart, William Lacy and Anthony Tyrrell. Multiple Masses were celebrated, and many confessions were heard. It seems incredible to believe the castle's authorities could let this go on within their own penitentiary. It is possible money changed hands, or perhaps security was lax. After all, most of the prisoners held in the castle were conscientious objectors rather than hardened felons.

Whatever the reason, Bell and the other priests remained in the castle for many hours until eventually – and inevitably – the meeting was discovered and raided. As the sheriffs' men closed in on them, the Catholics who weren't already locked up frantically attempted to make their escape from the prison grounds. Father Hart had to climb over a high wall and down the other side. After this, he waded through a moat until the water reached up to his chin, but somehow he got away, as did most of the others. In the end, only one of the priests, William Lacy, was apprehended.

The unfortunate Father Lacy was a widower from the West Riding of Yorkshire. He understood what the people locked inside the castle had been going through as he'd spent time in prison for recusancy. After leaving England, Lacy had travelled to Rome, where he'd been given dispensation as a widower to train as a priest. Following his arrest, Lacy was placed in chains and forced to share a dark cell in the castle with another priest, Father Richard Kirkman, who'd been recently arrested.

Also hailing from the West Riding, Father Kirkman had been ordained in France and sent back to England wearing a lay disguise. The priest's good fortune had run out when he'd been spotted near Wakefield. In what sounds like a scene from the film *The Great Escape*, he was stopped and searched. When a chalice and other incriminating items were found in his baggage, Kirkman was arrested and sent to York.

The two men would have known the likely fate awaiting them. Hopefully, they gained a level of solace through not having to face their darkest days alone. Both Lacy and Kirkman were brought before the York assizes court and tried for offences included in the 1581 Disobedience Act. Conveniently, the law was designed for just such an occasion.

Despite the horrific burning of so many Protestants in Tyburn in London, no religious executions had taken place in York during the reign of Queen Mary. Thankfully, the city's population had been spared the sight and smell of such barbarity. Things were changing. On 22 August 1582 William Lacy and Richard Kirkman were transported the short distance up the hill from the castle prison to York's own Tyburn, the Knavesmire, and publicly executed.

During the month of August a further arrest was made. The poor fellow apprehended this time was well known in some local circles, although it had been rumoured he'd been travelling. James Thompson had left York less than a year earlier. In that time he'd visited France, been ordained and returned. He was tasked with officiating Mass for the Catholics of the city, primarily those not already in the castle. Unfortunately for him, it wasn't a long-term assignment. Shortly after his return, Father Thompson was arrested for celebrating Mass in the home of a blacksmith in the parish of St Michael le Belfrey, near the Minster. Under questioning from the Council of the North, Thompson confessed to being a seminary priest.

Father Thompson wasn't the only man to have left York for Douai or Rheims in the early 1580s. For a period, Rheims was used as a temporary home for the Douai seminary. Most who did so stayed away from the city for a much longer time than James Thompson, while others never returned.

With their losses mounting, the seminary colleges needed a steady flow of new recruits. A number of Guy Fawkes' peers from St Peter's School in York[4] left the city to join the Catholic priesthood. The men included Edward Oldcorn, Oswald Tessimond and Robert Middleton. Middleton may have been distantly related to Margaret Clitherow, though if he was, he wasn't a close relation. Other young men leaving York for the seminary colleges around this time included two pairs of brothers, Thomas and William Wright, and Richard and Thomas Cowling.

Following his arrest, Father Thompson was shackled in irons and imprisoned. For a while he was jailed in a more comfortable private prison, but when his funds ran out he was transferred to York Castle. The Council of the North tried him and found him guilty of treason. His case was heard in late November 1582. A few days later he was taken to the Knavesmire.

Before his death, Father Thompson stressed his adherence to the Catholic faith, but denied he was a traitor. He said he'd never plotted, and never would, against the Queen. This might have been the reason his sentence wasn't carried out in the same gruesome manner as many of the others. The priest was hanged until he was dead, but he wasn't disembowelled or quartered. Admittedly, he was still dead.

Despite the significant losses suffered in the locality, the surviving priests didn't go away. Father Hart, one of the men who'd escaped from the Catholic meeting at York Castle by the skin of his teeth, remained at large in York. Hidden in a series of back rooms, he administered Mass, gave communion and heard the confession of the faithful, including Margaret Clitherow.

Like his fellow Catholic clergymen, Father Hart spent each day of liberty knowing it could be his last. By now the authorities knew the priests were among them. The vigilance and rewards offered by the Council for turning in seminary and Jesuit priests were increasing. A wrong word here or there, or being in the wrong place at the wrong time, could lead to a priest's arrest.

There was another more personal risk, betrayal. Christmas time was a busy period for the priests. On Christmas Day in 1582 Father Hart said Mass in the household of William Hutton (no relation to the Dean of York), although the master was himself already in prison. After a good meal, Father Hart fell asleep. Later that night he was roused from his slumber by pursuivants who had arrived to arrest him. The priest's location and identity had been revealed by an informer, an ex-Catholic who'd converted to the Protestant faith.

The next morning Father Hart was dragged before the Earl of Huntingdon. After questioning, he was placed in custody and told his trial would have to wait until the travelling assizes court reached York during Lent. It must have been a cold and miserable way for the priest to spend what he thought would surely be his last winter.

As Father Hart expected, the coming of spring brought no greater cheer. At his trial at York Lent assizes he was found guilty of treason. After two-and-a-half months languishing in his prison cell, he was executed on 15 March 1583.

Still the priests kept on coming. The next one was Richard Kirkeld, a man of Durham. Like the others, he'd been ordained in one of William Allen's English colleges and despatched to England to support the seminary mission of salvation and conversion. During his time in York, he'd said Mass and heard the confession of many Catholics, again including Margaret Clitherow.

Like Father Bell, Father Kirkeld found it difficult to maintain a safe distance from those of his own faith, especially the Catholics locked up in York's prisons. Barely ten days after the savage killing of Father Hart, Richard Kirkeld had attempted to hear the confession of a prisoner inside the kidcote on Ousebridge.

Following the debacle of the mass meeting of Catholics organised by Thomas Bell, the Catholic inmates of York's jails were being watched more closely and their visitors monitored. Before he could leave the kidcote, Father Kirkeld was arrested by the sheriffs' men. Despite his disguise of lay apparel, he confessed under questioning to being a seminary priest.

When he was searched, two keys were discovered in Father Kirkeld's clothing. A local locksmith admitted these were made in his workshop. The sheriffs and some of the aldermen began a search to discover which locks the keys opened. William Hutton's house, where Father Hart was arrested on Christmas night, was searched. A wooden trunk was discovered. It was opened and illegal Catholic books were found inside. In a scene reminiscent of persecution in

Henry VIII, Reign: 1509–1547.

Thomas Cranmer, Archbishop of Canterbury, 1533-1555.

Pilgrimage of Grace, 1536.

Edward VI, Reign: 1547-1553.

Right: Mary I, Reign: 1553–1558.

Below: Thomas Cranmer's Execution, 1556.

Above: Elizabeth I, Reign: 1558-1603.

Left: Mary Stuart.

EDWIN SANDS, Eerts-
bisschop van Jorck.

Right: Edwin Sandys, Archbishop of York, 1577-1588.

Below left: William Allen.

Below right: Robert Persons.

ALANVS CARDINALIS

P. ROBERTVS PERSONIVS
Eersten Missionaris van de Societeyt in Enghelandt.
Obiit Rome Anno 1610 in Seminario Anglicano.

Viri plurimi in Anglia pro fide Catholica retinenda hoc qui expressus est modo coaoq cruciantur donec universi corporis artus singulatim luxentur. Sic Edmundus Campianus Societatis Iesu religiosus, Rodulphus Sheruinus, Alexander Briantus, alij, Sacerdotes summi Pontificis Alumni acerbissime torti fuere Anno Dñi 1581.1582.et 1583.

B.M.
REIMS 31

Jam hiems transiit, imber-
abiit, et recessit: surge, amica
mea, et veni: — Off. Parv.
B. Mariæ ad Vesperas.

Above left: Edmond Campion being tortured on the rack, 1581.

Above right: St Margaret Clitherow.

Left: St Margaret Clitherow.

Above left: Stain glass window, St Margaret Clitherow RC Church, Dulwich Wood Park, photograph courtesy of Steve Pearce.

Above right: Statue, St Margaret Clitherow RC Church, Dulwich Wood Park, photograph courtesy of Steve Pearce.

Right: Stain glass window, The Catholic Church of Corpus Christi, Headington, Oxford.

MARGARET
CLITHEROW ✝ 1586

Above: Stained glass window, Harvington Hall, photograph courtesy of Fr Lawrence Lew OP.

Below: Shrine of St Margaret Clitherow exterior, The Shambles, York.

Right: Statue in Shrine of St Margaret Clitherow, The Shambles, York.

Below: The Shambles, York.

Bottom: King's Manor, York.

THE HOUSE OF
MARGARET CLITHEROW
WHO WAS MARTYRED IN YORK
MARCH 25th 1586
CANONISED OCTOBER 25th 1970

Clifford's Tower (part of York Castle), York.

Above: York Civic Trust Memorial Sign on Ousebridge, York.

Right: Relic of Saint Margaret Clitherow's Hand, Bar Convent, York, photograph courtesy of the Congregation of Jesus.

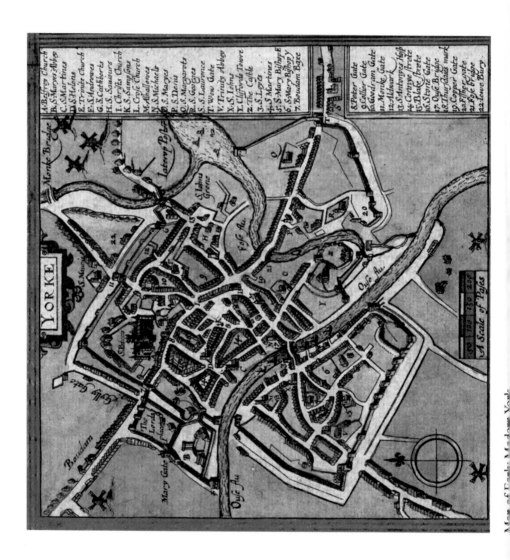

Map of Early Modern York

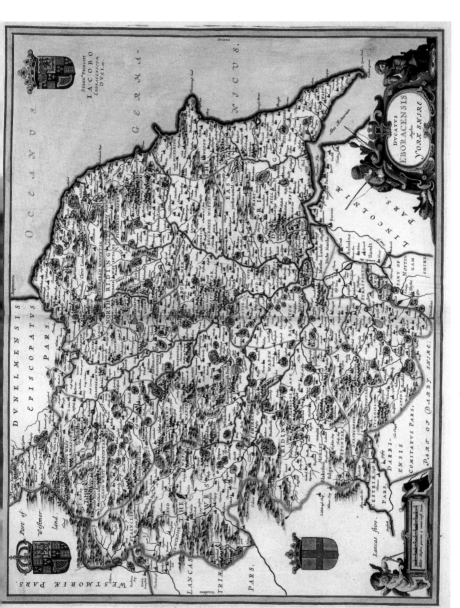

Map of Early Modern Yorkshire.

York City Coat of Arms.

Panorama of York.

Margaret Clitherow's Immediate Family

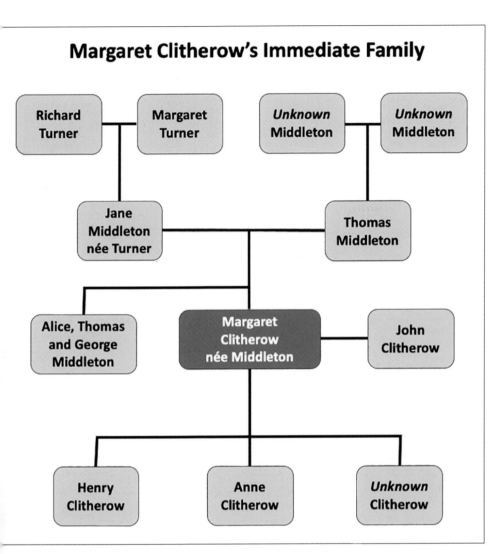

Margaret Clitherow family tree.

Henry VIII	Edward VI	Mary I	Elizabeth I	Elizabeth I continued
1509-1547	1547-1553	1553-1558	1558-1580	1580-1586
Pope awards Henry title of Fidei Defensor for supporting Catholicism	Protestant Reformation accelerates	Repeal of Reformation laws	Second split from Rome as Reformation recommences	Throckmorton Plot
Henry becomes head of the Church of England	Dissolution of the chantries and smaller religious houses	Restoration of Catholic Church in England	Catholics recusants punished for non-attendance of Church of England services	Harsher laws against Catholic priests and lay people
England splits from Catholic Church in Rome	Introduction of English language Book of Common Prayer	Reconciliation with Rome	Pope excommunicates Elizabeth	Arrest and execution of Catholic priests
Dissolution of the larger and medium sized religious houses		Persecution and burning of Protestants	Ridolfi Plot	War begins with Spain
Beginnings of Protestant Reformation			Catholic seminary and Jesuit priests begin secretly entering the country	Mary Stuart implicated in Babington Plot
				First executions of lay Catholics for aiding or harbouring priests...

National timeline.

Henry VIII	Edward VI	Mary I	Elizabeth I	Elizabeth I continued
1509-1547	1547-1553	1553-1558	1558-1580	1580-1586
York in decline	Corporation of York financially challenged	Churches in York restored to Catholicism	Slow economic recovery	Changes in Corporation leadership – closer alignment with Council of the North on religious policy
Pilgrimage of Grace uprising against the Reformation	Closure of York's chantries and smaller religious houses brings hardship to the city	Revenue from many chantries passed back to the city	Council of the North and new Ecclesiastical Commission based in York	Catholic priests at large in York – some arrested, tried and executed
Pilgrimage leader Robert Aske executed in the city	York's churches forced to adopt elements of Protestant worship	Despite events in London, no Protestants executed in York for heresy or treason	York refuses to support Rising of the North	First layman in England executed in York for aiding a Catholic priest
York's larger religious houses closed as part of the Dissolution	Bubonic plague and sweating sickness epidemics	Influenza epidemic with high death rates sweeps across the city	Patchy imprisonment of Catholic recusants	Margaret Clitherow arrested on the same charge...
Council of the North reinstated, with major office in York			Council of the North criticises Corporation for lenient treatment of recusants	

York timeline.

Henry VIII	Edward VI	Mary I	Elizabeth I	Elizabeth I continued
1509-1547	1547-1553	1553-1558	1558-1580	1580-1586
Margaret's mother Jane Turner born in the Angel tavern in Bootham	Parish church of St Martin's Coney Street, forced to adopt elements of Protestant worship	Margaret Middleton born in first year of Queen Mary's reign	Family attend Protestant services at St Martin's	Margaret serves two further prison sentences
Jane marries Margaret's father, the wax chandler Thomas Middleton	Wax chandlery business adversely affected by the Reformation, due to reduced demand for beeswax candles	Thomas Middleton serves as one of the churchwardens at St Martin's, restoring the church to its previous Catholic state	Thomas becomes Sheriff of York but dies	Margaret allows Catholic priests, including John Mush, to secretly say Mass and hide in her home
The couple marry and set up home and wax chandlery business in Davygate	Margaret's brother George born in Davygate	As an infant, Margaret is raised as a Catholic	Jane marries Henry Maye – they open an inn	Margaret sends son Henry to France to train to be a Catholic priest
Margaret's siblings Alice and Thomas born			Margaret marries the butcher John Clitherow and they start a family	Henry Maye becomes an alderman / In 1586 he's elected Lord Mayor
			Margaret converts to Catholicism and serves first spell in prison for recusancy	Margaret is arrested...

Margaret Clitherow timeline

1930s Berlin, the books were taken to the Pavement, where they were publicly burned in the street.

Part of the missionaries' work was to persuade people, including lapsed and Church Catholics, to embrace the Catholic faith. The charges raised against Father Kirkeld included converting one or more of the Queen's subjects from the Queen's Church to the Church of Rome. After two months of providing spiritual advice and hearing confession from the Catholics in the cells around him, his case was heard by the Council of the North's Quarterly Sessions court. The evidence was damning. On 29 May 1583, a day after his trial and sentence, he was put to death.

As previously outlined, not a single Protestant clergyman was executed in York during Queen Mary's reign. In 1582–1583, in less than one year, no fewer than four Catholic priests were put to death in York. The executions of William Lacy, Richard Kirkman, William Hart and Richard Kirkeld were a stark warning to York's hidden Catholic priests and lay people alike.

The authorities in the north of England made no distinction between non-uniformity of religion and supremacy of the Queen. You were either for, or you were against. Laymen and women foolhardy enough to be against were fined huge amounts and imprisoned. Priests found guilty of practicing or professing Catholic worship were hunted down and, following due process, executed. This was the law.

It should be noted, though, that there was a fairly strong level of support for Queen Elizabeth in York at this time. David Palliser's research notes in 1584 that around 1,300 people in York, led by Corporation officials, subscribed to the Association for the Preservation of the Queen. To give this figure context, Coventry, a city with a similar population at the time, had only 200 subscribers.

York's Catholic population, both secret and open, must have been shocked to its core. They'd struggled for a quarter of a century, hoping one day things might change for the better. In recent years things had changed, but only for the worse. It must have been a desperate period for many, sitting in a cell, or at home peeping through small windows wondering when the sheriffs' men and the pursuivants might come to arrest them.

Almost every Catholic in York had attended a Mass hosted by, or had their confession heard by, one of the executed priests. The four fathers weren't mysterious figures clad in robes that existed in stories and fairy tales. They were real people who York's Catholics had known and admired.

The constant pressure facing them forced many recusants to conform. It's difficult to gather evidence about the Church Catholics, but surely many now also stopped attending Catholic Masses, and began to turn the other way when they saw a known Catholic coming towards them in the street. From a modern perspective, it's hard to understand why more didn't do this.

Some historians have argued that Persons' and Campion's intervention was disastrous for the country's Catholics. After examining some of the details of what happened in York, I find it hard to disagree. The Jesuits' mission and their messaging certainly led to the creation of the harsh Disobedience laws. The Marian priests who'd attempted to shout Persons and Campion down in Southwark may have thought they had a point.

Equally, there's little doubt certain Catholics found relief and succour in the messages they'd received from Douai, Rheims and Rome. Their plight hadn't been forgotten. They'd intermittently been able to attend Mass and had their sins absolved. Now, they had to show resolve, turn their cheeks from the heretics, hold onto their faith and survive. The current Queen couldn't last forever. Elizabeth Tudor was fifty years old with no children to succeed her.

In 1584 two new seminary priests arrived in York. The first man was Father Francis Ingleby. His life had begun twenty-five miles to the west in Ripley Castle. He'd studied at Oxford and travelled to France to be trained and ordained as a priest at William Allen's college in Rheims. The second priest came from Yorkshire too. Like Father Ingleby, Father John Mush was in his mid-thirties. He'd soon become the author of the work, *A True Report of the Life and Martyrdom of Mrs Margaret Clitherow*.

Margaret's Story – Recusancy and Imprisonment

In 1580 Margaret Clitherow had not yet heard the messages of support for recusancy being put forward by the Jesuit leaders Persons and Campion. She hadn't met Father Hart, nor any of the other seminary priests; not even her future confessor Father John Mush. However, Margaret's refusal to attend the 'heretical' Church of England services had never been in any doubt.

The Council of the North and Ecclesiastical High Commission were more determined than ever to punish and, if possible, conform York's remaining recusants. October 1580 was a busy month for York's courts. Margaret Clitherow was one of many recusants brought before the Ecclesiastical High Commission.

Margaret's case didn't last long. 'Margaret, wife of John Clitherow butcher […] refused to take an oath or conform […] committed close prisoner to York Castle.' Although Margaret was sent to the castle, this time her husband John avoided a stay in the Ousebridge kidcote. This piece of good news was tempered by the knowledge he would once again be in sole charge of the household, business and family. It was going to be another busy time for the servants and apprentices.

With Margaret sticking rigidly to her position of non-attendance of church, John had been unable, or perhaps unwilling, to persuade her otherwise. This wasn't the case with some of the other butchers' families in York, including some of the Clitherows' nearest neighbours. In the same month Margaret was sent to prison to serve a second term, a number of butchers and their spouses were brought before the High Commission. The results of their cases were as follows:

> Chris Rayne, butcher of York, and wife Margaret – both to certify conformity by 17 January.

> Roger Spence, butcher of York, brought in Millicent, wife of William Calvert, for whose appearance he was surety – she proved she was continuing her conformity, so dismissed.

> Michael Mudd, butcher of York, and wife Ellen – she is sick; he took bond they would both conform and certify.

> Stephen Preston, butcher of York, and wife Jane – took bond to conform themselves and certify.

These cases tell us two things. Long before the arrival of supermarkets, there were a lot of butchers in York. More importantly, the authorities' plans to force York's recusants to conform appeared to be working, even before the harsher penalties introduced by the Disobedience Act. In his book, Father Mush describes Margaret Clitherow as a charitable woman. However, what she thought of her friends and neighbours' promises of conformance as she languished in prison isn't recorded.

It wasn't only the butchers being brought before the court that October. The other recusancy cases included people from a wide range of professions. There were gentlemen, merchants, an apothecary, an armourer, a baker, a cord-wainer (shoemaker), a currier (leather worker), a pewterer, tanner, tapster (weaver) and multiple tailors. What a fascinating insight this gives us into the guilds and trades of Tudor York.

Many of the men appeared with, or on behalf of, their wives. The majority promised the court they would conform. Most were forced to give bonds. Some had their cases dismissed altogether. As always though, a few weren't for turning. Since his previous appearance in these pages, Edward Tesh, gentleman and husband of Anne Tesh, had been sent to Hull jail. The High Commission now fined him a further £50 (a small fortune in those days) for 'obstinate recusancy'. The money was to be collected from 'his land and goods'. In effect, the court was ordering the bailiffs to seize and liquidate Tesh's assets while he was in prison to ensure his fines were paid, despite his absence.

Edward Tesh's hearing was linked to the case of another man. Hugh Manwell is listed in the records as a 'husbandman' (or farmer) from the East Riding. Manwell was told by the justices he would be sent to jail and would remain there until he admitted who'd carried out his marriage service and baptised his child in the Teshs' house in Bishopfields in York.[6]

In addition to being recusants, it appears Edward and Anne Tesh had hosted Catholic priests in their home and allowed them to practise there. As Hugh Manwell's case was heard a little before the first seminary priests arrived in York, the man in question must have been an old-school Marian clergyman.

In another case, Anne Cooke was temporarily released, guaranteed by a bond, to give birth to the child she was imminently expecting. Anne was instructed not to leave her house and ordered to return to the castle within six weeks. A further mandate was passed down from the bench to the Cooke family, warning them to ensure the baby was baptised by a proper Protestant parson.

Although Margaret was in prison, life for the rest of her family went on. In his churchwarden role, Henry Maye continued to work with his colleagues to update the list of recusants in the Coney Street parish. When the Corporation received the list, they added it to the catalogue collected from the city's other parishes. New names were added and others, including those who'd kept promises to conform, were removed.

This was a challenging time for the city's aldermen. Their leader, Robert Cripling, had been forced from office. William Alleyn had resigned, and four others died in quick succession. Interestingly, the deaths of Thomas Appleyard, John Beane, Richard Calom and Catholic sympathiser John Dyneley occurred within a few months of each other. The Earl of Huntingdon and the other members of the Council of the North must have been purring. Their prayers had been answered. Every Catholic sympathiser in the senior echelons of the Corporation had been removed.

To keep their number quorate, the surviving aldermen needed new recruits. A series of replacements had to be elected and sworn in. Having seen what had already happened to Cripling and Dyneley, the aldermen knew the writing was on the wall for any Catholics among them. While casting their eyes over the Twenty-Four for the next generation, they knew they needed to be careful. The aldermen could no longer risk selecting men with known Catholic leanings or unruly recusant wives. Only loyal Protestants would be selected to replace the old guard.

Henry Maye and the other members of the Twenty-Four watched on. Each hoped to get the nod and hear their name being announced. With their dreams and ambitions in the hands of the lord mayor and his fellow aldermen, who would be chosen?

One by one, a series of new aldermen was elected. Robert Brooke was called to replace John Dyneley. Christopher Maltby was announced instead of the now disgraced ex-lord mayor Robert Cripling. Thomas Appleyard was elected to replace another Thomas Appleyard – the new alderman was the previous alderman's son! Finally, Andrew Trew was elected as a replacement for John Beane.

Between March 1580 and January 1581 four new aldermen had been elected but none of them had been called Henry Maye. After everything he'd done, everything he'd gone through, it appeared the aldermen didn't want him. Why, he must have wondered, was he being so cruelly overlooked? Perhaps he looked angrily towards the Shambles, and when Margaret was jailed for a second time, glowered at the walls of the castle prison. Surely, the reason for his non-election was his recusant stepdaughter?

If Margaret Clitherow wouldn't obey Henry Maye's demands to attend church, she didn't listen to her mother either. Equally, Henry may have blamed John Clitherow. After all, one of a man's duties was to ensure his wife behaved herself. Some men, like George Hall, beat their wives to ensure conformance. Although this didn't always work, Henry may have chastised his son-in-law for not doing the same.

From everything we know, largely from Father Mush's *A True Report*, there's no indication that John Clitherow mistreated his wife.[7] Maybe he was tempted, or perhaps he sympathised with her religious cause. Possibly he simply loved her so much that nothing else mattered. Either way, he forgave his wife for her non-conformance, even though he continued to worship in the Protestant church which Margaret refused to enter.

The aldermen, now almost quorate, continued to discuss who should join them. At this stage the Twenty-Four would still have included men with known or suspected Catholic loyalties. These could easily be discounted. A few others, due to their trade or guild, including any butchers, wouldn't even be considered. And then there was Henry Maye. No-one doubted his loyalty and ambition, and St Martin's was a better church for his wardenship. He'd probably made every effort to mask his southern accent. Only one obstacle remained, although some of the aldermen may have even argued against that, reminding the others the recusant woman wasn't his real daughter.

On 1 March 1581 Henry Maye was finally rewarded for his service to the city. At last he was elected as an alderman in place of the deceased draper Richard Calom. A few quiet words may have been spoken to him about his recusant stepdaughter, such as, 'She's not going to be a problem, is she?' and, 'Why don't you get your son-in-law to sort her out?'

Henry Maye's rise from immigrant southerner holding 'the beggar's staff', as Father Mush put it, to the lofty heights of an alderman was complete. There was only one ambition left open to him, to reach the pinnacle of lord mayor of York. How far could he go?

A month-and-a-half later, Henry's stepdaughter gained another temporary reprieve from jail, after Margaret's case was reviewed by the Ecclesiastical High Commission. It transpired that when she'd been sent to prison in October she must have been expecting a child. On 17 April 1581 the court allowed Margaret, like Anne Cooke before her, to be released for a short period under licence. Margaret was instructed to return to the castle no later than six weeks after giving birth. Her husband was instructed to put his hand in his pocket once more to take out yet another bond, this time to ensure his wife's return to prison.

After signing the appropriate papers, John exchanged Margaret's release details with the warders and was given permission to take her home. The couple set off along York's narrow streets on the short journey to the Shambles. Margaret was now twenty-eight years old and heavily pregnant. Wrapped up to protect herself from the inclement April weather, she must have waddled down the street. The couple's joy was tempered by the knowledge that her freedom would be short lived. Afterwards, unless she was allowed to nurse the child in prison, John would be left holding the baby.

Either way, each had their own concerns. What of their other children? John's older sons could fend for themselves, but Henry was nine years old, and Anne was even younger, just seven. They must have once again run to the door with excitement when they heard their parents arriving home. Surrounded by her family's love, did Margaret wonder about the path she was taking?

She hadn't yet met him, but Margaret's biographer, Father John Mush, considered otherwise. The priest's writing indicates the die was cast. By this time Margaret was as much married to God and her religion as she was to her Earthly husband, Mr John Clitherow, the butcher from York.

No doubt when the time for the birth came, Margaret relied heavily on her friend Dorothy Vavasour. In the male-free environment of the makeshift delivery room, the women would have talked freely about their faith, and hopes and fears for the future. Margaret may have mentioned her regret at not being a better mother. In response, Dorothy may have assured her it was obvious to everyone how much Henry and Anne adored her. Both women were determined to ensure the children would never become Protestants.

A baby boy was born. The surviving records don't indicate his name, or when Margaret returned to jail, or when she was released. And of course, there's no mention of who looked after the newborn child. However, there was to be a dramatic twist in the story of Dorothy Vavasour. Probably acting upon a tip-off, the authorities raided the Vavasours' house while an elderly Marian priest was officiating Mass. The raid was supported by a group of aldermen, including the newly elected Henry Maye.

In October 1581 Dorothy's case was brought before the Quarterly Sessions court. By this time, the Act of Disobedience was already in place. In line with the new act, the priest, William Wilkinson, was sentenced to serve a year in jail and fined 200 marks. Dorothy Vavasour and a number of others were found guilty of hearing the Mass. Along with her fellow co-defendants, Dorothy was fined 100 marks and despatched to the kidcote.

The raid and subsequent imprisonment of Dorothy Vavasour was a significant blow to York's underground Catholic community. The Vavasours' house was a place where many of the Marian priests had hidden and said Mass. With the facility removed from them, other premises would be needed to host the priests' secret visits.

If there was any consolation for Dorothy Vavasour and her friends, it came from the increasingly frequent visits to York of the newly arrived seminary priests. She and her cellmates welcomed men like Thomas Bell with open arms. They must have celebrated the night when Bell and the other priests, along with many of the city's Catholics, arrived at the castle to meet and hear Mass. It must have been a great occasion for all of them, right up to the point when the meeting was raided.

Following her own eventual release from prison, Margaret Clitherow started to meet and hear the word of the seminary priests. She heard Mass said by at least two of the earliest missionaries to York, Fathers Hart and Kirkeld. Before long, she was even inviting the priests back to her house in the Shambles. This was a risky business, as Dorothy Vavasour had already found to her cost.

As identified earlier, a number of the seminary priests visiting York as part of their mission were arrested and tried. The aftermath was gruesome. Following the executions of the seminary priests, Margaret began to make secret night-time pilgrimages to pray at the spots where they'd been butchered on the Knavesmire. Having personally known these men, it must have been a harrowing experience. Such a brutal death would certainly be something most parents would wish to ensure their children avoided witnessing, and certainly they'd seek to remove any possibility of their offspring meeting a similar fate.

Margaret was accompanied on these night-time vigils by fellow female recusants, including Anne Tesh, whenever they weren't incarcerated. News of the visitations wouldn't have been well received by the authorities, including the increasingly ambitious Henry Maye, as he eyed the ultimate prize of becoming lord mayor of York.

Although the thought of further separation from her family must have been difficult, Margaret continued to miss the parish services. By March

1583 her name was once again on York's recusancy list, and she was brought to trial. This time, her case was heard before the Quarterly Sessions court.

Along with ten other women and three men, Margaret was indicted and found guilty of recusancy. The group's sentences ranged from two to eleven months. As a repeat offender, Margaret was given one of the longer sentences. She was sent to the castle for a further ten months. The bond her husband had promised against her bad behaviour was also to be forfeited.

Apart from the mental anguish of being separated from his wife, the cost of Margaret's recusant ways didn't come cheaply for John Clitherow. A month later, in April 1583, the Ecclesiastical High Commission heard the case of 'John Clitherow of York' who was asked to forfeit 'a bond of £40'. This time John pleaded poverty, claiming he was unable to pay the full amount due to 'his poor estate'. Upon hearing his plea, the commissioners stated he should be 'allowed to compound for 40s'.

There may have been other causes for John Clitherow's lack of funds, or he could have overstated his case to avoid paying up, but it appears his financial support for his wife's illegal behaviour had been a serious drain on the family's finances. This, of course, was just what the authorities wanted. It was part of the stick they used through their policies to encourage conformance. Once again, words may have been spoken between the Clitherows, although this time it would have been through the prison bars of York Castle.

Margaret wasn't one for languishing in her cell. Father Mush describes her imprisonment and that of her fellow Catholic dissidents as a 'profitable school, where the servants of God (as delivered from all worldly cares and business) might learn most commodiously every Christian virtue.' The priest reported that Margaret learned to read and write, 'I have greatly marvelled oftentimes how she, being an unlearned woman, tossed up and down in worldly business, except only in the times of her imprisonment, wherein she learned to read English and written hand.'

No doubt she set about devouring Catholic publications. We have to assume these documents were smuggled into the prison and kept in a secret hiding place. Any pamphlets, books or papers found would have been confiscated. Perhaps they would have been taken to the Pavement and publicly burned.

Following Margaret's imprisonment and the forfeiture of John's bonds, there's no further mention of the couple in the records of either the Ecclesiastical High Commission or Quarterly Session courts (so meticulously scoured by J.C.H. Aveling) for more than two years. Once her ten-month sentence was served, Margaret was released from prison. After this, she managed to steer clear of the legal system for quite some time.

At last, John Clitherow could rebuild the family's finances, and Henry Maye could curry favour with the Council of the North. In the short term, Henry attempted to make a positive impression with the Corporation aldermen, hoping one day they'd elect him to be their new lord mayor.

When Margaret saw daylight again, early in 1584, she left the castle and trudged back home through the streets of York to the family's house in the Shambles. Little did she or her husband know about the men she'd soon come to meet and who would change their lives forever.

In 1584 two new seminary priests arrived in York. One was called Father Francis Ingleby. His parents were Sir William and Anne Ingleby of Ripley Castle, twenty-five miles west of York. Ripley was a short distance beyond the castle walls of Knaresborough. In between Knaresborough and Ripley lay the village of Scotton, a well-known haunt for recusants. One amongst them, Dionysus Bainbridge, would soon marry Guy Fawkes's widowed mother, Edith.

Francis was the youngest of the Ingleby family's four sons. Their sister, Jane, had married George Wintour of Worcestershire. Two of her sons, Robert and Thomas, would go on to join Guy Fawkes, Robert Catesby and the other conspirators in the Gunpowder Plot, the ultimate Catholic conspiracy against the English Crown.

After leaving England, Francis Ingleby took a similar route to many of the other English Catholics. He studied and was ordained for the priesthood. After leaving Rheims in the spring of 1584, he joined the long line of priests secretly entering the country. He was warmly welcomed, especially in York.

The second seminary priest was called Father John Mush. He arrived a few months after Ingleby. Both were in their mid-thirties at this stage, just a little bit older than Margaret Clitherow. Father Mush had attended William Allen's college in Douai and travelled to Rome. When he returned to England in the summer of 1584 he headed to York.

With Dorothy Vavasour in prison, the men met and became engaged with the newly released Margaret Clitherow. The meeting between Margaret and Father Mush in particular was a momentous one. His book

A True Report of the Life and Martyrdom of Mrs Margaret Clitherow is the reason we know so much about her.

A True Report is a valuable source of information, but as mentioned earlier, like any such record, it's written from a viewpoint and comes with an agenda. Even so, it provides a fascinating insight into Margaret's life, and ultimately her death. With so few texts from the time written about the lives of women who weren't ladies, princesses or queens, it has an even greater impact.

Father Mush was immediately impressed with Margaret. Although most of his book focuses on her spiritual side, the priest describes her appearance around the time of their first meeting. 'As touching her worldly state and condition, she was about thirty years of age, and to her beautiful and gracious soul God gave her a body with comely face and beauty correspondent.'

He was also quick to praise her intelligence and family values, 'She was of sharp and ready wit, with rare discretion in all her actions, a plentiful mother in children.' In contrast, the priest labelled her spouse, John, as a 'husband of competent wealth and ability', which I suppose isn't too bad a description really.

By this time, Margaret wasn't just inviting priests to say Mass in the Shambles. Father Mush, Father Ingleby and others were often staying there secretly during the daytime and sleeping overnight in her house. As Father Mush outlines, Margaret created at least two hidden rooms where she could pray, where Mass could be said to a small congregation and the priests could hide out. The secret rooms were created within the warren of buildings inside, adjacent to and beyond her home in the Shambles.

This is how Father Mush describes the rooms: 'She prepared two chambers, the one adjoining to her own house, whereunto she might resort at any time, without sight or knowledge of any neighbours. In this she served God every day in quiet and calm times, with her children and others. The other was distant a little from her own house, secret and unknown to any but such as she knew to be faithful and discreet.'

Father Mush also reported glowingly about the devout and pious approach Margaret had adopted in her daily life since leaving prison. How much of this pre-dated the priest's arrival, or was shaped and influenced by him, we don't know.

Every morning ordinarily, before she took in hand any worldly matter, she continued secret in her chamber one hour and a half, or most often two hours, praying upon her knees, and meditating upon the Passion of Christ, the benefits of God bestowed upon her, her own sins and present estate of her soul. Immediately after which time (if her husband or some importunate business letted her not) she came to her spiritual Father's chamber to hear the divine mysteries, and with him to offer to God.

After service, when she had committed her and all her works that day to the protection of God, she occupied herself in necessary worldly affairs, endeavouring all the day long to have her mind fixed on God… Her devotions all the rest of the day were as she could get leisure; which almost she never had until four of the clock in the afternoon, about which time she would shake off the world and come to evening-song, where she, praying one hour with her children about her.

Afterward returned again about her care of the household until eight or nine of the clock, at which time she used to resort to her ghostly Father's chamber to pray a little and ask his blessing, which of her own humility she did, and would not slip and forget at morning and night. From thence, going to her chamber, she ordinarily spent an hour at the least in prayer and examining of her conscience, how she had offended God that day.

Margaret's day was exhausting. It didn't help that she often deprived herself of food. At times in prison, Margaret had been forced to fast following a shortage of supplies. Father Mush reports she later adopted a similar level of deprivation for spiritual reasons, before and after leaving jail.

So long as she was in prison she fasted four days every week, (for so did all there, partly for lack of necessary victual, partly to satisfy for their former sins, partly for the greater merit, and the sooner to procure God's grace again to His afflicted Church). The same abstinence she slacked not any time after she was delivered, but kept it still as no less necessary for her spiritual good in the world, than it was in prison. Every Monday, Wednesday, and Saturday she abstained from flesh, and but one meal a day. Every Friday she fasted on bread and drink, afflicting her body with some sharp discipline.

During the winter of 1584 Margaret did something quite extraordinary, something which many of us may struggle to understand. With the help of the priests around her, Margaret Clitherow sent her twelve-year-old son, Henry, the boy who'd been named after her stepfather, away to France to enter one of the seminary colleges. We can only imagine what her husband must have thought of this.

Father Mush explains her actions in *A True Report*: 'She had sent without the knowledge of her husband, more than one year before, her eldest son into France for virtuous education and learning, hoping one day to see him a priest, the which she most desired.'

There's no record of how Henry travelled to France, or who accompanied him. It was agreed that once he arrived he'd eventually be trained for the Catholic priesthood in one of William Allen's English Colleges. Margaret would likely never see her son again, and Henry wouldn't be able to safely return to his family.

Margaret's commitment to the Catholic Church is undoubted. It would, of course, have been impossible for Henry to be ordained as a Catholic priest in England. But for many modern readers her actions appear almost unthinkable. The boy was so young, and Margaret had seen with her own eyes what happened to so many of the missionary priests.

The seminary men were smuggled back into the country, where they administered to the faithful, but many were caught. Once arrested, the priests weren't fined and imprisoned, they were tortured and brutally executed. It's difficult to fathom a parent willingly sending their child into such a situation, with the significant risk they'd meet the same fate.

Margaret Clitherow did this. Although John may have gone through the roof when he found out, it was too late. Their son was gone. There was no way John could find Henry or bring him back. The deed was done. The butcher's only option was to focus on his remaining children. That he continued to stand by his wife appears almost incredible. By then, of course, he was well aware there were more than two people in their relationship. And he knew he couldn't compete.

Chapter Eight

Treason and Plot (1585–1586)

Elizabeth I – Laws, Wars and Executions

Perhaps the most alarming feature of the failed Throckmorton Plot was the involvement of Catholic Spain. Despite pressure from her advisors (although not William Cecil), Elizabeth had wanted to keep England out of the growing conflict in the Low Countries, where local Protestant forces were fighting to gain independence from their Spanish overlords. The Queen was shocked in July 1584 when news arrived of the assassination of the Dutch Protestant leader, William of Orange. If it could happen to William, it could happen to Elizabeth.

In response to the continuing internal plots linked to Mary Stuart and the growing threat from Spain, William Cecil and Francis Walsingham created the Bond of Association. Parliament wasn't in session, so, in October 1584, the bond was initially presented for signature to the Privy Council. The document was designed to bind its signatories to hunt down and execute any persons who attempted to usurp the Crown or assassinate the Queen, including those on whose behalf such an attempt was carried out. The target here was Mary Stuart. A further clause barred the guilty person's successors from taking the Crown, excluding, for example, Mary's son, King James VI of Scotland, from succeeding to the English throne.

The contents of the bond were widely circulated as part of a public information campaign. In parallel, the document morphed into the Parliamentary 'Act for Provision to be made for the Surety of the Queen's Majesty Most Royal Person, and the Continuance of the Realm in Peace'. When the act was finally debated in Parliament in early 1585, the introductory words reflected the mood of the time. 'Sundry wicked Plot and Means have of late been devised and laid as well in foreign Parts beyond the Seas, as also within this Realm, to the great endangering of her Highness's most Royal Person.'

Part of the Parliamentary debate focused on the clause which excluded heirs of the guilty parties from acceding to the throne. The clause was eventually removed. In 1603 the change would be good news for Mary's son, James. Without it, he wouldn't have been able to be crowned King James I of England. The Stuart dynasty would never have existed, with all the historical implications this might hold.

The remaining words of the act included a chilling sentence: 'By all forcible and possible Means, Prosecute to Death all such as shall be found to be Offenders therein, and all their Aiders and Abettors.' If this paragraph was to be exploited, it could, for example, be used to legitimise the execution of Mary Stuart.

While the new act was designed to deter any would-be rebels and potentially entrap Mary, Cecil and Walsingham were well aware of the continuing threat posed by the seminary and Jesuit priests. A second act of Parliament was created to build upon the existing legislation and crack down further on the missionaries. Crucially, the new law included several clauses to severely punish anyone brave or foolhardy enough to support them.

The 1584 'Act Against Jesuits, Seminary Priests and Such Other Like Disobedient Persons' was very clear in its condemnation of the infiltrators. 'Jesuits, Seminary Priests and other Priests […] do come and are sent into this Realm […] not only to withdraw her Highness's Subjects from their due Obedience to Her Majesty, but also to stir up and move Sedition, Rebellion and open Hostility […] to the great endangering of the Safety of her most Royal Person, and to the utter Ruin, Desolation and Overthrow of the whole Realm, if the same be not the sooner by some good Means foreseen and prevented.'

The priests were given forty days to leave the country. Any who remained after this time would be adjudged as having committed high treason. And then came the shockingly punitive clause which addressed the laymen and women who helped or harboured any Catholic priests after the forty days were up. 'Every person […] who shall wittingly and willingly receive, comfort, aid or maintain any such Jesuit, Seminary Priest or other Priest […] knowing him to be a Jesuit, Seminary Priest or other Priest shall also for such Offence be adjudged a Felon, without Benefit of Clergy, and suffer Death, loss and forfeit.'

People living abroad, including men training or planning to train in the seminary colleges, were given six months to return to England.

When they returned home, they would be ordered to swear the oath of allegiance to the Queen's supremacy. If they didn't return, or didn't swear the oath, they would be adjudged to have committed high treason. With no plans for his future return to England in sight, Margaret Clitherow's actions had now placed her son, Henry, in even greater danger.

Sending any type of relief or funding to men in the seminary colleges became illegal. Young Henry and many others were now on their own, unable to receive financial aid from their families, unless, of course, the families placed themselves at risk.

Furthermore, it was made illegal for anyone 'to send his or her Child, or other Person, being under his or her Government' abroad unless a special licence was granted from the Crown, or unless the move was linked to merchant or maritime activities. Fines for breaking this clause were introduced at £100.

While all this was happening, in May 1585 England's relationship with Spain dramatically deteriorated. With a few exceptions, the two countries had managed to trade relatively peacefully for almost ten years, ever since the resolution in 1574 of a previous commercial dispute regarding shipping and raiding. The situation was about to change.

King Philip II of Spain ordered his forces to seize all Protestant-controlled vessels docked in Spanish and Spanish-held ports. This impacted many English ships. The action was met with outrage in England and an on-off war flared up between the two nations. This conflict wouldn't come to a complete end until a new economic pact and treaty, engineered by William Cecil's son Robert, was signed by the two countries in 1604.

In 1585 Elizabeth at last agreed to formally intervene in the Netherlands. The Treaty of Nonsuch promised, 'The Queen of England should send to the United Provinces an aid of five thousand footmen and one thousand horse, under the conduct of a Governor-General who should be a person of quality and rank, well-affected to the true religion, and under other good chiefs and captains, all of whom shall be paid by the Queen as long as the war lasts.'

Elizabeth assigned the Earl of Leicester to lead her English army into the Low Countries. Francis Drake, recently returned from circumnavigating the earth, and other sea captains were given free reign to harry Spanish shipping off the shores of Europe and around the Americas. In response, Spain accelerated plans to create an invading armada, applauded and supported by English Catholic clergymen such as William Allen and Robert Persons.

Once the forty days were over, the hunt for Jesuit, seminary and other Catholic priests began in earnest. The Catholic Church estimates over 600 men and women suffered death in England and Wales for supporting the Catholic Faith between 1535 and 1681. This included many priests.

In 1585, at the time of the passing of the new legislation, a number of priests were already in prison awaiting charge. Additional men were now arrested. Some were subsequently executed;[1] others died in their cells through malnutrition or the effects of torture or illness.

In July 1585 Father Thomas Alfield was tortured in the Tower of London before being charged. He was found guilty of treason and hanged, drawn and quartered at Tyburn in London. His assistant, Thomas Webley, was executed alongside him.

The hardening of the laws against the Catholic priests in 1585 coincided with a sharp increase in the number of deaths amongst seminary men and Jesuits held in prison. Father Thomas Crowther succumbed during his time inside the Marshalsea prison in London. John Jetter, Edward Pole and William Hambledon all died during their own incarcerations, although few details are available about their cases.

Another man, a canon Laurence Vaux, was reported to have starved to death in prison. A layman recusant, Richard Shelley, was imprisoned for his involvement in the creation of a petition to the Queen and Parliament protesting against religious intolerance towards Catholics. Depending on your point of view, Shelley was either courageous or foolhardy. Either way, he lost his life in the Marshalsea.

As 1585 transitioned into 1586, the deaths continued. Edward Stransham, a seminary priest who'd graduated from Rheims, was arrested in London while saying Mass. He was later condemned at an assizes court for being a missionary priest, and, on 21 January 1586, was hanged, drawn and quartered at Tyburn in London.

In addition to their disguises, many seminary priests used one or more aliases. One of the missionaries who'd returned to England was called Nicholas Wheeler. He was sometimes known as Nicholas Woodfen. When he was arrested, he was using another false name, Nicholas Devereux. Father Wheeler, Woodfen or Devereux was executed at Tyburn, alongside Edward Stransham, who was sometimes known as Edward Transham.

A few months later two more Rheims graduates were brought to Tyburn following their arrest, trial and sentencing. Father Richard Sergeant (also known as Richard Lea and Richard Longe) had been born in Gloucestershire. His colleague, Father William Thomson, hailed from Blackburn in Lancashire. Both were hanged, drawn and quartered in April 1586.

The executions weren't limited to London and York. Robert Anderton and William Marsden hailed from the recusancy stronghold of Lancashire. Like so many seminary priests, they studied at Oxford University, before leaving England for Douai or Rheims. Once ordained, the two men set off back to England. While crossing the Channel during the winter of 1585-86, their boat encountered a mighty storm. As waves crashed over the decks, the crew feared all was lost, but somehow they managed to land on the Isle of Wight. The priests must have thanked the Lord for their salvation. Their luck was short lived, however, and both were arrested.

During their court hearing, Fathers Anderson and Marsden were accused of being seminary priests and illegally returning to England. In their defence, the men argued their return was involuntary, and had been forced onto them by the storm. Following the case, the priests were sent to London. Once there, they were instructed to swear the Oath of Supremacy. When they refused, they were found guilty of treason and transported in chains back to the Isle of Wight. Upon their return, the two men were executed by hanging, drawing, and quartering in April 1586.

John Sandys (no relation, or at least not a close one, to Archbishop Sandys) was another Lancastrian. He'd taken the same route through Oxford and Rheims, as Fathers Anderson, Marsden and many others. When he returned to England in 1584, Sandys stuck manfully to his underground religious duty for around two years. Inevitably, he was arrested and placed on trial. He was executed in Gloucester in 1586, in the same gruesome fashion as many other priests.

As 1586 progressed, Francis Walsingham's spies discovered another conspiracy against the Queen. This time, at least one seminary priest was directly involved. Working with an English Catholic gentleman, Anthony Babington, and a number of others, Father John Ballard had set about arranging for Elizabeth's assassination and subsequent replacement as queen of England by Mary Stuart. It was a familiar tale.

Once the conspiracy was uncovered, Francis Walsingham didn't close it down immediately. Instead, he let it play on for a time to ensure its eventual downfall would create the maximum political collateral for himself and his allies in the English government. This included gathering evidence about Mary Stuart's direct involvement. To Walsingham and Cecil, this was gold dust.

Of course, this book isn't about Mary Stuart. The events and aftermath of the Babington Plot took place slightly after the remarkable events in York, which we're now going to focus on for the remainder of the book. The point here is that Elizabeth was in danger and she knew it.

The danger came not only from missionary priests and potential Spanish invaders, but from her own people, including a number of the country's Catholics who wished, and actively conspired, to kill and replace her. Facing this threat, it's hardly surprising she and her government sought to suppress Catholicism, drive uniformity of the state religion and ensure all were committed to her supremacy.

York – Treason and Punishment

By the mid-1580s York was a city of contrasts. With the surplus of baptisms over burials, continued immigration and no major outbreak of disease since before Elizabeth's coronation, the population was rising. In addition, the Council of the North and Ecclesiastical High Commission continued to bring wealth and employment into the city.

Active trade links were in place with the Baltics, France, Spain, some of the German states, the Low Countries and Scotland. Many of the city's aldermen, merchants, gentlemen and tradespeople were more prosperous than they'd been for decades. Of course, this didn't prevent the city from occasionally claiming poverty to the Queen and Privy Council, but this was the natural order of things.

York's growing prosperity was noted in a ballad written by William Elderton, which praised the city above all others in England, with the exception of London. Of course, not everyone in the city prospered. The number of destitute people in York was increasing. With the safety net of the religious houses and hospitals removed, paupers were often reliant on support at a parish level, as set out in the Tudor 'poor laws', or in local rules laid down by the Corporation. Sanitary conditions in many of York's tenement houses were shockingly inadequate, and many dwellings were frequently overcrowded.[2]

And then there was religion. Although the religious laws and crackdowns hadn't impacted everyone in the city, the fines and imprisonment of recusants, and execution of Catholic priests and others, didn't make for a happy backdrop to domestic life.

There were also tensions in relations between the leaders of the city's institutions. Henry Hastings, the Earl of Huntingdon, had been Lord President of the Council of the North since 1572. He was one of the main driving forces behind the clampdown on recusants and missionary priests in York, and across the whole of the north of England. Edwin Sandys, the Archbishop of York and chair of the Ecclesiastical High Commission, had been in position since 1577. The Dean of York, Matthew Hutton, had held his own role even longer, having first been appointed in 1567.

Archbishop Sandys and Dean Hutton worked closely with the Earl of Huntingdon, but their relationship was volatile. Both were committed to rooting out and punishing Catholics, although their views on religion were markedly different. Matthew Hutton was something of a Puritan. Suspicious of Puritan views, Archbishop Sandys made a series of accusations against the Dean, resulting in a long-standing fall out between the two senior clergymen.

Their arguments spilled over into many other matters. With York's combination of wealth and poverty, money lending was rife in the city. Lenders often charged borrowers much higher rates of interest than the ten per cent defined by law. During his inaugural sermon in 1577, Archbishop Sandys raged against this practice and decried the money lenders for charging immoral rates of interest.

In 1585 the archbishop took decisive and divisive action against many of those involved, including York merchants and other leading citizens. In all, forty men were charged. Each was forced to forfeit much of the interest they'd earned. The archbishop subsequently tried to forbid the charging of any interest at all, even at the legal rate, but Dean Hutton and the Council of the North blocked this move.

Another area of focus for the Church in York in 1586 was completion of the merger of a number of the city's parishes. This had been first initiated as a cost-saving measure during Edward VI's reign, when some of the smaller churches in York had been closed. However, the work hadn't been fully completed. Having finally ratified the last few changes, the Church worked with the Corporation to sell off the remaining properties, along with their adjoining land.

We've already examined the leadership structure of the Corporation of York. A freeman in the city could rise from being a chamberlain or a bridgemaster to join the Forty-Eight men of the Common Council. Some would then be appointed to serve as one of York's sheriffs. At the end of their term of office, both sheriffs would traditionally be invited to join the mid-tier council of the Twenty-Four. A smaller number would eventually enter the Corporation's top tier as one of York's thirteen alderman. At the pinnacle, an alderman might be elected by his peers to become lord mayor.

In February 1585 the aldermen elected Andrew Trew as the new lord mayor. Trew was one of the new breed, having been promoted from the Twenty-Four five years earlier as part of the flurry of new recruits at the time. In September, as always, two junior men were elected to be sheriffs.

The city house-books record the result as follows: 'Roland Fawcett and William Gibson were by the most voices of the Lord mayor, aldermen, and Sheriffs, chosen to be Sheriffs of the said city of York for this year next following, according to the ancient charter and custom of this city.'

Only a day after their successful election, there was a debate between the new sheriffs about who should be the more senior. 'Some questions did arise between them, whether of them should be first named and second Sheriffs […] Upon voices secretly taken, the said Roland Fawcett is by most voices elected and chosen to be in the first place.'[3]

Although this was bad news for William Gibson, he was getting used to it. The junior sheriff was still smarting after being named and shamed by Archbishop Sandys for money lending. Following the Archbishop's investigation, Gibson had been instructed to pay back much of the interest he'd earned from his usury activities.

By this time, the bulk of the city's aldermen, including the newcomers, supported the Council of the North and the Ecclesiastical High Commission's views and actions. The listing, trying, fining and imprisonment of recusants continued and, of course, there were priests to catch. The arrest, trial and bloody execution of Fathers Lacy, Kirkman, Hart and Kirkeld had sent shock waves through York's Catholic population. The brutality of their deaths must have also placed fear into the hearts of the missionary priests who remained, and any new ones who came to replace them.

To survive, the priests would need to be more organised. They required even more support from Catholic families, along with better disguises and more secure safe houses to hide in. A small number of senior priests were ordered to take charge, and they began to organise the others. In the north, Catholic clergymen assigned to such leadership roles included Father Richard Holtby, who led the operation around Durham, and Father Thomas Bell, who eventually left York to organise a cell in Lancashire. Bell was succeeded in York by Father John Mush.

A little like the resistance groups in France and other countries during the Second World War, the priests were divided into small groups, with each cell assigned to a geographical area. Most of the priests were ordered never to remain in a single location for very long. Instead, they were told to travel in disguise around their wider circuit area, moving from place to place, staying in a pre-agreed Catholic residence, before moving on to the next one. Working secretly from these houses, they'd offer spiritual advice, celebrate Mass and hear confession.

Sometimes, the priests officiated baptism and wedding services, although this was an even more dangerous game to play. If a lay person was identified as having been recently married, or having had a child baptised but not in the official church, it was a sure sign they'd spent some time in the illegal company of a Catholic priest. A spell in prison would beckon, or worse.

Conditions in the region's prisons were grim. Although many of the recusants were eventually released, some never made it. In May 1585, while his wife was still incarcerated in York, Dorothy Vavasour's husband, the medical doctor Thomas Vavasour who'd been ailing for some time, died in his prison cell in Hull. A month earlier another Catholic prisoner, a Cistercian monk named John Almond, had also died in one of Hull's cells.

Although conditions in Hull were notoriously bad, things weren't much better in York. In the same year, 1585, two Catholics, John Ackbridge and Stephen Hemsworth, died in the city's jails. Few details are available about these men, which suggests they may not have been residents of the city prior to their imprisonment there.

With the Council of the North and Ecclesiastical High Commission based in York, non-York residents were frequently being brought to trial in the city. Two such cases had major reverberations. The 1581 'Disobedience' act had included a clause to punish households for keeping a schoolmaster if they failed to attend church services. This had been written on the basis that many Marian and seminary priests used this role, in conjunction with an alias, to disguise themselves in plain sight.

In autumn 1585 a Catholic schoolmaster was arrested near York. Although not a priest, the man was questioned and tortured. As a result, he promised to renounce his Catholicism and reform. Fearing further punishment, he confessed additional information to the authorities. One of the names he volunteered was Marmaduke Bowes of Angram (or Ingram), a small grange in the countryside north of York. Bowes had employed the schoolmaster to teach his children.

Marmaduke Bowes was a Catholic sympathiser, although 'through fear of losing all his possessions he was an occasional conformist'. There are two differing accounts of why he was arrested. Crucially, both concerned him giving aid to Hugh Taylor, a Catholic priest. One version states he was accused of harbouring the priest in his house. The second claims he was arrested for simply 'having given Taylor a cup of beer at his door'.[4]

Hugh Taylor was known to the authorities, having already been arrested while lodging in another man's house. Father Taylor had been born in Durham. He'd left England and studied, as so many others had, at the English College in Rheims. Once ordained into the priesthood, he'd returned to England, but within eight months he'd been arrested and brought before the Council of the North. They condemned him to death.

Forty-eight hours later, on 26 November 1585, Hugh Taylor became the first priest to be executed under the new Parliamentary act 'Against Jesuits, Seminary Priests and Such Other Like Disobedient Persons'. Chillingly, this law also targeted lay persons who 'Wittingly and willingly receive, comfort, aid or maintain any such Jesuit, Seminary Priest or other Priest'.

Marmaduke Bowes was accused and tried for the new crime by the Council. Although the Earl of Huntingdon was away from York at the time, his deputy, Baron Eure, presided over Bowes's case. Eure was supported by leading members of the Council, including Ralph Hurlestone and Henry Cheke. The prisoner was found guilty and condemned to death.

On 27 November 1585, only twenty-four hours after the execution of Father Taylor, Bowes was hanged, drawn and quartered in York. Upon his death, he became the first lay person in England and Wales to be executed under the new law. The treatment of Marmaduke Bowes didn't bode well for the Catholic citizens of York and beyond. It was especially unpopular with anyone who may have been harbouring Catholic priests. Now, more than ever, they knew their lives were in danger.

Margaret's Story – Hidden Priests and Upheaval

Henry Maye was elected as an alderman on the first day of March 1581. A month later Margaret Clitherow was released on licence to have her third child. After this, she returned to prison and later served an additional sentence of ten months. We assume she was released at the beginning of 1584. During the following two years there are no additional records to indicate she faced further punishment, or that her husband paid any additional forfeitures or fines.

According to the law, Margaret should have been punished. She'd stopped going to church, and from everything Father Mush reports, she didn't return. How did the butcher's wife escape further incarceration?

The cases heard by the Ecclesiastical High Commission and Quarterly Sessions in York during 1584 and 1585 included a number of indictments for recusancy. The case list includes many familiar names, including ex-lord mayor Robert Cripling, but Margaret's name was absent, even in July 1584, when the cases were listed parish by parish.

The only active recusants identified from within Christ's or Trinity parish, which covered the Shambles, were 'William Bachelor, butcher', 'Jane wife of William Phillicekirk, innholder' and 'Dorothy, wife of Thomas Brigham, barber'. Meanwhile in Bishophill, Margaret's friend Anne Tesh and her husband, Edward, were also named once again.

Who or what kept Margaret out of the official records during this time? Surely such an active recusant should have been listed and her case heard by one of the courts? While we may question the efficiency of the process, the Council of the North was placing even more pressure on the Corporation to deliver more accurate returns. By now, the aldermen were committed to the Council's cause.

However, the process of identifying and prosecuting recusants included multiple opportunities to omit, misplace or remove names. The lists were initially created at a parish level by the churchwardens and their helpers. No doubt, some would wish to omit their relatives and friends. The ability to do so would have been largely dependent on the identity of the parish priest, some of whom were more on-message than others.

The parishes passed their lists to the Corporation for compilation and processing. In the Common Hall there were additional opportunities to tinker before the final list was presented to the Council and Commission. Perhaps Alderman Maye removed Margaret's name at his wife's insistence? An ink blot here or a rewritten list there would certainly have secured his stepdaughter's safety. More than that, it would have placated Jane Maye, and critically, kept Henry's slate clean with the Council and aldermen.

In the meantime, Henry Maye's career at the Corporation was blossoming. Aldermen were involved in the city's major decisions and activities. In 1585 the Crown passed ownership and maintenance of 150 properties previously belonging to the chantries and religious houses to the Corporation. In 1586 it converted part of St Anthony's Hall into a House of Correction. It also sold a public lane at a discounted price to Sir Thomas Fairfax so he could extend his property. The details of these actions would have been administered by the chamberlains, but the aldermen would have been involved in their review and approval.

Henry was busy, tirelessly running the tavern in Davygate and carrying out his duties as an alderman. His wife, Jane, was now seventy years old. The couple had been married for nearly twenty years, but Henry was only in his late forties. Around this time he decided to seek physical comfort elsewhere, and didn't go far.

Henry had an affair with Anne Thomson, one of the women working in the Mayes' tavern, but the couple were found out. Unlike others in the city who were publicly humiliated for adultery, Henry Maye avoided punishment, apart from any meted out to him by his family. It appears that certain aldermen could get away with some indiscretions after all.

There's no record of the direct impact that the discovery of her husband's adultery had on Jane Maye, although she fell ill and eventually died. On 12 June 1585 she was buried in St Martin's, the church where both her husbands had served as churchwardens, and where she'd married Henry Maye eighteen years before.

Inside the church, and afterwards in the tavern in Davygate, Jane's family and friends gathered to pay their respects. It's likely the funeral was a fractious affair, filled with tension, anger and accusatory glances. It didn't help much that Anne Thomson hadn't been sent away. Henry had kept her close.

The friction between the Middleton children and Henry due to their stepfather's adultery may not have been the only cause for upset. Margaret was the sole recusant amongst Jane's children. The other members of the family had towed the line. To many in the city, recusants were social outcasts, troublemakers. Animosity may have developed between Margaret and one or more of her siblings. Her younger brother, William, and his wife had four daughters, but not even the youngest girl was christened Margaret, even though the name remained popular and had been passed down the family for generations.

Then there was their father's will. With Jane dead, ownership and control of Thomas Middleton's assets passed to their children. Had Henry been dreading this day, or had he made plans for it? The family property in Davygate was different from the comfortable house and chandlery of Thomas Middleton's time. Through their hard work, Henry and Jane had transformed it into a bustling tavern. The buildings and been improved and extended. Some of the words of Thomas Middleton's will must have haunted Henry: 'I give to Margaret, my daughter, one house lying in Davygate within the city of York, after decease of my wife, to her and to her heirs of her body lawfully begotten.'

As the conversation began to flow more freely during the wake, did Henry gaze across the room at his stepdaughter? Standing in a corner away from the others, Margaret may have wondered how soon she could leave and return home to spend more time with the priests she hid there. She disliked social gatherings at the best of times, and Father Mush reports that she avoided banquets and other similar events.

Henry may have been speculating too. How could he regain control of what he must have considered to be his own property and nobody else's? It was probably a relief to him when Margaret made her excuses and readied to leave, although John was probably disappointed. Father Mush reports that, unlike his wife, he enjoyed company, eating and drinking. Maybe he walked Margaret home, or perhaps he remained at the inn.

Having read Father Mush's *A True Report*, it's difficult not to develop a level of concern about Margaret's state of mind during this time. It appears she had developed, or possibly always possessed, a lack of self esteem. She was constantly considering herself unworthy and highlighting perceived imperfections. In addition, she reacted much more positively to criticism than to praise. These points are highlighted in the following extracts from the priest's book:

> She thought herself nobody but an unprofitable servant to God and man, laden with imperfections, and unworthy of any good, and also (as much as she could without sin and offence to God) desired heartily so to be thought of and accounted in this world: never pleasing herself in the goodness she had already, but continually striving to get that which she perceived in herself to be wanting [...]
>
> Commend or praise her and her doings, and you oppressed her with sorrow; condemn and rebuke her, and seem to despise her, then you filled her heart with joy and inward gladness.

Father Mush described these qualities as Margaret's 'humility', but if she'd lived today I suspect we'd have been concerned about her mental health. Equally, Margaret appears to have wanted her actions not to be driven by the best interests of herself and her family but by God, as directed to her by the seminary priests who visited her house.

In the chapter which describes 'Her Obedience to Her Ghostly Father', Father Mush tells how Margaret was committed to do God's bidding, which on Earth, she considered, was directed by priests like him. 'This golden woman did utterly forsake her own judgment and will in all her actions, to submit herself to the judgment, will, and direction of her ghostly father.'

'Since God of His infinite mercy had sent His priests already to call her to His grace, by delivering her from error in faith and ungracious affections of the will, He would also with like goodness that by their helps she should continue in the same: and as she might offend God in every of her actions, so it seemed to her the only safe way to please God, humbly to submit herself in all things to follow the advice and direction of His priests.'[5]

In this state of mind, and with constant thoughts of her unworthiness, it's hardly surprising Margaret clung to the one thing that mattered most to her, her religious faith, even when this placed her and her family in danger.

A number of Margaret Clitherow's biographers, including Katherine Longley and Jean Olwen Maynard, have highlighted property and land owned by John Clitherow in Cornborough, near Sheriff Hutton. Katherine Longley believes the Clitherows may have considered moving their home from York to Cornborough in 1585.

This view aligns well with Father Mush's comments that Margaret suggested her husband should sell the butcher's shop and focus their business on wholesale trading. Cornborough would have made an ideal base from which to do this. 'And therefore she was in hand often with her husband to give up his shop, and to sell his wares in gross with as much gain and with less unprofitable toil.'

There's little doubt the family's relocation to Cornborough would have made Margaret safer by removing the Clitherows from the line of sight of the Council, Church and Corporation. It would have also helped to obscure the disappearance of the couple's son, Henry, and been a less risky location for harbouring missionary priests as they moved around the Yorkshire circuit.

However, I struggle to believe Margaret wished to leave York. The priests who stayed in her house did so because they needed somewhere secure to hide in the centre of the city. Although Cornborough was a good place for a safe house and an occasional Mass, its location was remote. It's unlikely the priests would have wished to stay there for very long. Given what Father Mush wrote about Margaret's attitude towards him and his colleagues, it appears improbable she'd have wanted to avoid them.

In any case, the family's escape to Cornborough didn't happen. The butcher's shop remained open. The business continued to make a profit, apart from when John was forced to shell out heavy fines and pay forfeits for his wife's misdemeanours. Although John didn't like to be out of pocket, Margaret was less concerned. Father Mush reports, 'In all her husband's losses she would be exceeding merry'. It was an attitude which must have been galling and infuriating for her businessman husband.

Margaret continued to shelter and harbour Catholic priests, particularly Father Mush and his colleague, Father Ingleby. Continuing to flout the law, Margaret also engaged a Catholic schoolteacher, Brian Stapleton, to educate her children. Father Mush describes him as 'a schoolmaster Mr Stapleton, who had escaped a little before out of the Castle, where he had lain almost seven years for the Catholic faith.'

Margaret and Stapleton must have known each other from when they were both inmates in York Castle. After his successful break for freedom, Stapleton had come to Margaret's house in the Shambles, and she'd taken him in. Of course, Margaret Clitherow wasn't the only person in Yorkshire to employ a Catholic schoolmaster to teach her children. Relatively recently, Marmaduke Bowes had done the same thing.

The final months of 1585 had seen Bowes arrested, tried and executed, along with Father Taylor, the priest he'd been accused of aiding. For many in the city, Bowes's death came as a shock, particularly as some believed he'd been executed for simply giving the priest a drink. York's underground Catholics must have wondered if what they were doing was worth risking such a fate. Many would have answered 'No', but Margaret's unequivocal response, supported by the word of God and the priests, would almost certainly have been 'Yes'.

In 1585-86 one of the tasks of the lord mayor, Andrew Trew, was to recommend a successor from his fellow aldermen. It's likely by now the candidates may have been vetted and pre-approved by Henry Hastings, the long-standing Lord President of the Council of the North.

On 15 January 1586 Lord Mayor Trew chaired a meeting of the Corporation's dignitaries in the Common Hall. The agenda included announcing the result of the mayoral election. Henry Maye had known for some time that he was on the shortlist, along with two other aldermen. His rivals were also part of the Corporation's new guard of Council-friendly Protestants.

Ralph Richardson was a merchant who'd been elected as a sheriff in 1577. After this, in 1581, he'd become an alderman, just a few months after Henry Maye. The other challenger was James Birkbie, a wealthy lawyer. Birkbie had succeeded Henry Maye as one of the city sheriffs in 1571. However, he'd only recently been elected to become an alderman in the previous year as a replacement for the deceased Christopher Maltby.

In the city records the election was reported as follows: 'Assembled in the Common Hall of this city, the day and year above said for election of a Mayor according to the charter of election, and upon three elects put in by the Common Council and head searchers of the thirteen and

119

fifteen crafts, that is to say, Mr Henry Maye, Mr Ralph Richardson and Mr James Birkbie, aldermen.'[2]

Of the three contenders, Birkbie was probably the outsider due to his lack of time as an alderman, but there was little to choose between the other two. Both had served for a similar duration on the senior rung of the Corporation ladder. All three would have spent the last few weeks lobbying the electors, making promises and sharing commitments.

Then came the announcement of the result: 'The said Mr Henry Maye is by most voices of the Lord mayor, aldermen and Sheriffs chosen to be Mayor of this city from the feast-day of Saint Blase next coming (3 February) for the year then next ensuing.' Having received more votes than his rivals, Henry Maye was duly elected. The losers wouldn't have been too disappointed as they knew their time would come. In fact, Ralph Richardson became lord mayor a year later, and James Birkbie the year after that. On 3 February 1586 a further meeting was held. This time the Corporation officials gathered in one of the smaller rooms on Ousebridge to swear Henry Maye in as the new lord mayor.

This is how the city's records capture the inauguration, as Lord Mayor Trew passed his solemn duties on to Henry Maye:

> Assembled in the Council Chamber upon Ousebridge, the day and year above said, when and where my Lord mayor delivered to our new master the seals of office of Mayoralty and Statute merchant with six keys thereunto annexed, and one little seal for sealing of passports, and also 40s called Girdlington money, and the basin and ewer of silver parcel gilt of Sir Martin Bowes' gift, and one other basin and one ewer of silver parcel gilt of Mr Thomas Metcalfe's bequest, and two livery pots of silver gilt, one pot of silver gilt, with a cover, of Mr Tankard late Recorder's bequest, and one other pot of silver gilt of Mr Christopher Maltby, late alderman deceased, and one nest of goblets double gilt, and two great salts of silver with a cover double gilt of the gift of Mr John Dyneley, late alderman deceased, and also one silver bowl parcel gilt late brought from St. Thomas' house, and also three scarlet cloaks.

The ceremony included handing over the mayoral keys and a seal, plus a set of gifts. Interestingly, they included one from the troublesome but now deceased Catholic-sympathising alderman John Dyneley. In addition, Henry Maye was now the proud owner of three scarlet cloaks. For the next twelve months he'd wear one of these whenever he carried out his official duties.

Most lord mayors had a lady wife beside them. The widower Henry Maye had no wish to be different. On 15 February 1586, twelve days after his inauguration, Henry married his lover, Anne Thomson, at St Martin's Church. The marriage of the new lord mayor was a grand affair. Donned in one of his scarlet cloaks, Henry would have been accompanied by two esquires and six sergeants-at-mace, the officials adorned in their finest Corporation livery. A number of citizens would have gathered outside St Martin's churchyard to see the spectacle and witness the happy couple arrive and depart.

There's no record of which members of the family attended this ceremony, although it's likely Henry's stepchildren and families would have been there. We don't know if Margaret's refusal to attend Church of England services extended to those that didn't include communion. Father Mush doesn't mention whether she attended her mother's funeral, but we assume she did. Whether she and her husband, John, and some or their children (excluding Henry) attended Henry Maye's second wedding isn't recorded either. Whether they did or not, something was afoot.

Margaret would no longer be afforded protection from her mother. Jane Maye's urgings to her alderman husband, Henry, had fallen silent. Margaret's stepfather was the new lord mayor of York. He'd married a younger bride and his reputation with the Council of the North had to be protected. Lastly, there was a property he wished to gain control of. It was possible Henry could achieve everything he wanted, everything he'd dreamed of and everything he'd worked so hard to achieve. Only his recusant stepdaughter stood in the way.

Chapter Nine

Arrest (1586)

Summons to the King's Manor

In this chapter and the following two we focus solely on the story of Margaret Clitherow. The scene at a national level has been set. England was at war with Spain, in the Low Countries and on the high seas. A small minority of Catholics continued to hatch conspiracies against the Queen and her government. Some of these were supported by the Catholic powers on the Continent. Mary Stuart had been implicated for her role in the Babington Plot, and the English authorities were deciding what to do with her.

As the majority of the country's Catholics kept their heads down, the recusants continued to rebel and were fined and imprisoned for their troubles. The Catholic Church hadn't helped them by excommunicating the Queen. Rome was still sending seminary and Jesuit priests in disguise across the Channel, many of whom were hunted down, caught, tried and executed. In York, a number of priests had already been taken from their castle prison cells to the Knavesmire, where they'd been hanged, drawn and quartered.

The 1585 act 'Against Jesuits, Seminary Priests and Such Other Like Disobedient Persons' had made it a felony to 'wittingly and willingly receive, comfort, aid or maintain any such Jesuit, Seminary Priest or other Priest'. Marmaduke Bowes had become the first lay person to die for this crime.

In York the Council of the North had acted to remove any remaining Catholic sympathisers from the leadership of the city's Corporation. In September 1585 Roland Fawcett had been elected senior sheriff, with William Gibson his junior. In March 1586 the Corporation's newly elected lord mayor was Henry Maye. Although Henry was a loyalist with a friendly disposition towards the Council, he had a recusant stepdaughter and was the step-grandfather of a boy who'd been illegally sent to France to train in the Catholic priesthood.

Such a situation couldn't go on. Henry Hastings, the Earl of Huntingdon and Lord President of the Council of the North, was a committed anti-Catholic. The first few meetings between the Lord President and lord mayor may have been interesting. A direct man, the lord president may have cut to the chase. While he didn't doubt the lord mayor's loyalty, a few things had come up. Apparently, Henry's stepdaughter, the butcher's wife, wasn't going to church. And then there was the grandson. There'd been a whisper the boy was in a seminary college in France. Surely, the lord mayor was aware of what had happened to ex-Lord Mayor Robert Cripling, when his own wife had refused to go to church?

Of course, we can't be sure any such discussion happened, but it's plausible. If it did, perhaps Henry Hastings concluded the meeting with the following words, 'So, you'll do something about it, then? Good. Is there anything we can do to help? There is? Tell me more.'

The details of what happened next were recorded and presented to the world in Father John Mush's *A True Report*.[1] The publication is quoted more extensively in the remaining chapters of the book. Being so closely associated with Margaret Clitherow and many others in her tightly knit community, we must assume the priest researched and developed an excellent knowledge of the events which occurred in York during March 1586.

Many of the detailed happenings recorded by Father Mush must have been relayed to him later, second or third hand, by eyewitnesses or others, rather than captured directly by him. If he'd attended some of the scenes he describes, he'd surely have been arrested. As before, we must be cognisant of the inevitable bias in his writing, but there's little doubt how accurately he captured some of the brutality of the authorities' final dealings towards the butcher's wife.

On Wednesday, 9 March 1586 John Clitherow was called to attend a meeting with a number of representatives from the Council of the North. An appointment like this would only be arranged to deal with a serious matter. Having a son who'd travelled recently overseas to become a seminary priest would certainly fit the bill.

John attended the King's Manor, but the councillors were busy and he managed to leave without seeing them. It's likely he didn't linger long in the Council's offices. Fearing what might happen to him and to his wife, he probably took the first opportunity to creep away quietly, hoping he might slip through the administrative net.

Father Mush explains, 'The Council at York, after a while, had intelligence of it (Henry being sent to France), and greatly stormed thereat, yet lingered to deal in the matter, which caused her husband, as one timorous of their unreasonable cruelty, to be more unwilling to go unto them when they first sent for him, thinking that it was to answer that matter, which, being done without his consent or knowledge.'

However, John's summons hadn't been forgotten. Later that day he received a message ordering him to return the following morning. Tellingly, the men who wanted to see him were Deputy Lord President Lord Eure, Lawrence Meares, Ralph Hurlestone and Henry Cheke. These were the men who'd tried and found Marmaduke Bowes guilty in November. Rather strangely, given his interest in such matters, or perhaps rather conveniently, the lord president was missing from the planned conference.

The next day, Thursday, 10 March 1586, John Clitherow left the butcher's shop and returned to the King's Manor. In his nervous state he probably arrived well ahead of time. When the butcher entered the building he was chastised for missing the previous day's appointment. John explained he had been there but had believed the councillors had been too busy to see him.

This time, they said they weren't ready to see him yet. 'After some few words, they commanded him to return to them again immediately after dinner.' In Tudor times, dinner was a lunchtime meal, eaten around midday, so he was being told to return in the early afternoon.

John left as instructed and returned to the Shambles. Once there, he relayed to Margaret what had happened, explaining he'd been ordered to return before the Council in the afternoon. Upon hearing this, Margaret immediately became suspicious. Once John had left the Shambles for the later meeting, she sought out a priest who'd recently arrived to find shelter with her. This was either Father Ingleby, or more likely, Father Mush.

As Father Mush recounts, 'The martyr, hearing of this, and having good experience of their subtleties, feared the worst; and when her husband was departed, she came to the Father, which came to her but that morning, and said: "The Council hath commanded my husband to be with them again. I pray God they intend no falsehood, and now, whilst they have him, make my house to be searched. They pick quarrels at me," quoth she, "and they will never cease until they have me again, but God's will will be done."'

124

Margaret suspected the Council may have conspired with the Corporation to get her husband out of the way to make it easier for the authorities to raid the family's premises. With the man of the house not there to complain and potentially do something about it, it's more likely the men assigned to the task could do their bidding without obstruction or delay.

Raid on the Shambles

Margaret's supposition proved correct. Roland Fawcett and William Gibson, the senior and junior sheriffs of York, arrived in the Shambles accompanied by 'diverse other heretics'. Their objective was to search the Clitherows' house and root out any priests who might be hiding there. The searchers appeared to be very confident in their task. It was almost as if they knew somebody was secretly hidden in the building, waiting to be found.

This was, of course, accurate. Margaret had spoken to one of the priests less than an hour earlier. There was definitely at least one missionary priest, and perhaps more, sheltering in or around the building. Were they about to be discovered and charged?

Father Mush takes up the story, 'They found the martyr occupied in her household business. The priest was in his chamber, which was in the next neighbour's house, and some other persons with him, and being forthwith certified of the searchers, they were all safely shifted away into a lower chamber of her house.'

What a close call. It appears the priest and a group of lay people had heard the searchers arrive, and managed to slip away to a place where they were confident they wouldn't be found. The Shambles consisted of a warren of interconnected buildings. Many of the dwellings contained multiple rooms, back yards and alleys. Some of the terraced houses and shops had internal doors and hatches to allow the butchers, their families and servants to move freely between the properties.

From Father Mush's description, it appears one of the chambers Margaret had reserved for the priests wasn't inside the Clitherows' house, after all. In fact, the secret room was within a neighbour's house. With so many of the neighbours related to her husband, this may be one of the reasons Margaret had stayed out of prison for so long.

The searchers took to their task. With the priest and his small flock hidden next door, the pursuivants swept through the butcher's shop into the living premises beyond and above. Who or what would they find inside?

'There was a schoolmaster named Mr Stapleton […] Whilst he was quietly teaching his scholars, not knowing what was done in the house below, a ruffian bearing a sword and buckler on his arm, opened the chamber door, and suspecting the schoolmaster to be a priest, he shut again the door, and called his fellows.'

This was the schoolteacher, Brian Stapleton, who Margaret had agreed could stay in her house and teach her children following his escape from jail. It appears he was about to be apprehended and returned to the castle. 'The schoolmaster, thinking him to be a friend, opened the door to call him in; but when he perceived the matter, he shut the door again.'

Brian Stapleton must have been terrified. He'd slammed the door shut in the face of a heavily armed man who'd been approaching him with a sword. He could hear the sound of the heavy boots marching up the stairs as the others rushed to apprehend him. The ruffian with the buckler (a small shield) was already hammering on the door, demanding to be let in.

There was only one way for Stapleton to escape, 'and by that way, which was from the martyr's house to the priest's chamber, escaped their paws.' Leaving behind the children he'd been teaching, Stapleton exited the room through a secret panel that linked Margaret's house to the property next door. The schoolmaster then joined the priest and the others, and they quietly made their way away from the Shambles.

This narrow escape didn't go down well with the sheriffs and other pursuivants. 'The searchers, greedy of a prey, came in great haste to the chamber, and not finding him, they raged like madmen, and as though he had been a priest indeed, took all the children, the servants, and the martyr away with them.'

The searchers must have turned the room upside down but were unable to uncover the man. After this, they took Margaret, the servants and the children into their custody, and set about the rest of the house. 'At this time they searched chests, coffers, and every corner of her house; but, as I learned, they found nothing of any importance.'

By now, the pursuivants were becoming increasingly frustrated. They'd expected things were going to be easy, but so far they'd only spotted one man and he'd got away. The sheriffs must have feared leaving the Shambles empty handed, with nothing to report to their superiors. When their masters received the update, they wouldn't take the news lightly. The sheriffs' automatic invitation to join the Twenty-Four might even be put at risk.

The likely reaction of the lord mayor, aldermen and Council officials focused Sheriff Fawcett's and Gibson's minds. They turned to one of the serving boys, and in desperation, stripped him naked before venting their fury at him.

By now, a small crowd had gathered in the Shambles to see what was going on. Some would have known the Clitherows and been on their side, but probably felt the need to keep quiet for their own safety. Others, perhaps the more Puritanical and loyalist Protestants in the local population, may have egged the searchers on. What happened next was brutal.

'Then they stripped a boy, about ten or twelve years old, and with rods threatened him, standing naked amongst them, unless he would tell them all they asked. The child, fearing that cruelty, yielded, and brought them to the priest's chamber, wherein was a conveyance for books and church stuff, which he revealed.'

The terrified child led the men to one of the hidden chambers. Although there was no priest inside, the pursuivants discovered an amount of Catholic literature, of the type confiscated from William Hutton's house which had been publicly burned in the street. They also found robes belonging to one or more Catholic priests and items used to celebrate Catholic Mass.

With this, the searchers achieved a small victory at least. As the Clitherows were clearly guilty of crimes against the State, the pursuivants began looting their house. 'They took the spoil and conveyed two or three beds away as their own.'

It wasn't quite the result the sheriffs and the other searchers had been hoping for, but it would have to do. At least they'd discovered clear evidence that Margaret kept priests in her house. The children and servants were arrested. Later, they were taken away and incarcerated in 'diverse prisons'.

As Anne and the others watched on helplessly, Margaret was hauled along the Shambles in the direction of the King's Manor. Despite her suspicions that something like this might happen, everything had progressed so quickly. Having been so cruelly separated from her children, she must have been in a state of shock.

Although she would have been relieved that Father Mush, the schoolmaster Stapleton and the others had evaded capture, Margaret must have been horrified at the thought of her children and servants being arrested, questioned and mistreated. The young serving lad had already talked. Given the brutal punishment threatened to him, Margaret may have found it difficult to blame the boy too much for his betrayal.

Margaret was pulled through the streets, past many gawping bystanders. She knew full well where she was going. She knew it would do her no good to break down in front of the Council and plead for mercy. This was a time to be composed. After harbouring fugitive priests for so many months, it's likely she had spent time preparing herself for this moment.

'The martyr was brought before the Council, and being merry and stout for the Catholic cause, thereby moved their fury vehemently against her, especially by her smiling cheerful countenance, and the small esteem she made of their cruel threats and railing.'[2]

Margaret held her ground under interrogation by the panel of gentlemen. During the first encounter, she appeared to be a match for the deputy lord president and his colleagues. In the days that followed, they'd become accustomed to the woman's ability to stand up to their abuse, and the disarming 'smiling cheerful countenance' on her face. Not many men or women brought before the councillors looked them straight in the eye and gave as good as they got.

By now, John Clitherow had been arrested and taken to York Castle. Once there, he was locked in a cell and held separately from his wife. The ruse to get him away from the house in the Shambles had succeeded. Even though he remained a loyal Protestant and had taken no part in Margaret's activities, he must have known about them. He didn't beat her up or put a stop to what she was doing. With so many Catholic items found inside their rented property, John must have known he could expect nothing less than the treatment he was receiving. Worse was likely to follow, particularly for his wife.

Meanwhile on the streets of York, vile rumours began to spread about Margaret. It was said she not only welcomed priests into her husband's house but traded sexual favours with them. One of the traditional punishments for a scold – a woman rightfully or wrongfully accused of cheating on her husband – was to force her head beneath water. The slanderous stories told about Margaret may explain what happened to her during her journey from the King's Manor to York Castle prison.

Margaret must have wondered what was happening as the sheriffs and their entourage made a detour on the way to the castle. When the party reached the banks of the River Ouse, Sheriff Fawcett ordered his men to drag Margaret into the freezing cold water. They pushed her down and held her below the fast-flowing current of the river.

Wet and freezing cold, she was dragged to the castle. Father Mush reports, 'The martyr came to prison in so wet a bath, that she was glad to borrow all kind of apparel to shift her that night.' It's surprising she didn't suffer more from the effects of the dousing, or even catch pneumonia. Some may think it would have been better if she had. Shivering from the cold, Margaret took what comfort she could from the clothing lent to her by her fellow prisoners.

Although she'd kept her head during the harsh questioning from the Council of the North, she must have despaired about her children. She'd been separated from them before, but this time their father, half-brothers and servants weren't there to look after them. The Clitherows had been separated, the children and servants arrested. They'd all been taken away, and neither Margaret nor John had any idea where they were being held.

During the evening the young boy who'd shown the sheriffs to the priests' chamber in the Shambles was questioned further. During his interrogation he agreed with suggestions put to him that the priests had regularly celebrated Mass in Margaret's house. Under duress, the boy divulged further information, including the names of those he claimed had attended the Catholic services. 'The boy accused more that he had seen in the martyr's house at Divine Service; among whom was Mistress Anne Tesh, who was also committed to the Castle the 12th of March, being Saturday, and continued in a chamber with the martyr until Monday following.'[3]

At least Margaret now had a friend to share her cell with. But what crimes was she to be accused of? Clearly the evidence against her given by the young serving boy was going to be crucial. 'A rumour was spread in the town, that the boy had accused her for harbouring and maintaining diverse priests, but especially two by name, that was, Mr Francis Ingleby of Rheims, and Mr John Mush of Rome. It was reported withal that she should suffer for it according to the new law and statute.'

Margaret was formally accused of the same criminal charges that Marmaduke Bowes had faced. The clause in the 'Disobedient Persons' act against lay people had already gained notoriety in York following Bowes' execution. Margaret must have realised that, by the letter of the law, she was guilty. There's little doubt she had 'wittingly and willingly received, comforted, aided or maintained any such Jesuit, Seminary Priest or other Priest.'

Knowing her likely sentence was to be death by hanging, it's reasonable to expect Margaret would have been distraught, but Father Mush reports otherwise. 'When word was brought to her of this, she laughed, and said to the messenger: "I would I had some good thing to give you for these good news. Hold, take this fig, for I have nothing better."'

There was one thing Margaret wanted to do – see her husband. During the immediate period following their arrest the couple were allowed to leave their cells to meet each other, but only on one occasion. 'The martyr was permitted to speak with her husband in the audience of the gaoler and other more, but she never saw him after.'

Despite the relief they may have felt at seeing each other, it must have been a trying occasion. There would have been desperate questions, but very few answers, about the whereabouts and wellbeing of their children. From everything Father Mush tells us, the couple loved each other, although it must have been a strained relationship at times. What impact did Margaret's devotion to God, religion and the priests have on her husband? How did John feel about their enforced separation when she was sent to prison, and the financial burden placed on him from paying her fines and forfeiting bonds?

Surely John Clitherow must have held something against his wife for all this, and for sending their son, Henry, overseas. The butcher must have known how unlikely it was he'd ever see his son again. Even if Henry did manage to come home, he'd have changed. John had lost his wife, and now he'd lost his son to the Catholic Church. His other children had been arrested, and the people of his home city were spreading gossip about his wife sleeping with Catholic priests. John may not have believed this, but what did he think of the priests his wife allowed into their home? What would any of us think if we were in his place?

The final meeting between John and Margaret Clitherow may have been fraught, or tender, or at times both. Afterwards, the husband and wife repeatedly asked their gaolers if they could see their spouse again, but the requests were refused – unless Margaret saw sense and agreed to apostatize. If she'd repent her Catholicism and convert to the new church, she could see her husband, and many other good things would come besides. Of course, Margaret refused.

The timing of the Clitherows' arrest is interesting. Margaret and John were taken into custody on Thursday, 10 March. Four days later, on Monday, 14 March, the annual Lent assizes court would open in York to hear its first cases. The assizes operated as a travelling court, which heard the most serious crimes, such as murder, rape, coining and horse theft. There were six regional assizes circuits in England. York was part of the Northern Circuit. Annual Lent assizes courts were held in March on both sides of the Pennines, in York and Lancaster.

Marmaduke Bowes's trial had been heard by the Council of the North's own court. The harsh sentencing issued to the prisoner had proven unpopular in some circles. Given this, it appears plausible that the Council may have conspired with Henry Maye and the Corporation to choose a suitably convenient date for Margaret's arrest, to coincide with the arrival of the assizes. Any fallout from her subsequent trial and sentencing would fall onto the assizes circuit judges rather than the Council and Corporation officials.

Margaret was informed her case would be the first to be heard by the assizes' judges on the first day of their sitting on Monday. She spent the weekend mentally preparing herself for the challenges ahead, and in religious discussion with her close friend and cellmate, Anne Tesh.

Where was her stepfather, Henry Maye, as all this was happening? It seems inconceivable the sheriffs could have acted in such a brutal manner against the lord mayor's stepdaughter, his son-in-law and family unless the mayor was himself compliant. I strongly believe Henry Maye orchestrated Margaret's arrest. Although there's no direct evidence to corroborate this theory, Henry certainly had a motive. To successfully complete his term of office, it wouldn't do for the lord mayor to have a close family member as a recusant, and certainly not one who harboured Catholic priests. There was also the ownership of the inn in Davygate.

Chapter Ten

Trial (1586)

Day One in Court

On Monday, 14 March 1586 the annual Lent assizes court opened in York. In line with tradition, the judges and officials sat down to a hearty meal before proceedings began. In the meantime, Margaret spent the morning in her cell in York Castle waiting to be called.

Father Mush recounts her state of mind immediately prior to the trial. 'A little before she was called to the judges, she said: "Yet, before I go, I will make all my brethren and sisters on the other side of the hall merry," and looking forth of a window toward them – they were five-and-thirty, and might easily behold her from thence – she made a pair of gallows on her fingers, and pleasantly laughed at them.'

What a revelation. Minutes before she was due to appear in court, Margaret caught the attention of her fellow recusants in the castle and mimicked her own death with her hands. The phrase 'gallows humour' has never been more apt.

Soon it was time to depart. 'The gaoler told her how she must go even then before the judges. "Well," quoth she, "God be thanked, I am ready when you please."'

Margaret was marched through the streets, accompanied by a set of guards carrying halberds, long pikes with a sharpened spikes and axe heads at one end. As they progressed along Coney Street, Margaret would have been able to glimpse towards Davygate, before passing St Martin's church and entering the Corporation's headquarters at the Common Hall where the assizes court hearings were being held.

'The martyr was brought from the Castle to the Common Hall in York, before the two judges, Mr Clench and Mr Rhodes, and diverse of the Council sitting with them on the bench.'

The judges were adorned in their fine scarlet legal robes. John Clench, the more senior of the two men, was from Essex but he did have family connections in Yorkshire, including a grandfather from Leeds. Clench had studied law at Lincoln's Inn from 1556 and been called to the bar in 1568. At the time of Margaret's trial, he was fifty-three-years old, and had served on the Northern Circuit for a number of years.

The second judge, Francis Rhodes, was around the same age as Clench and had been born in Derbyshire. He'd started his career in law earlier than his colleague, having entered Gray's Inn in 1549, before being called to the bar in 1552 while still a young man. In the later months of 1586, Rhodes would play a part in the trial of Mary Stuart. Judge Rhodes was a man with connections, including contacts with the Council of the North.

A number of senior members of the Council were present in the courtroom. They included the men who'd condemned Marmaduke Bowes and questioned the Clitherows, led by Deputy Lord President Lord Eure, Lawrence Meares, Ralph Hurlestone and Henry Cheke, the ex-Member of Parliament for Bedford and more recently Boroughbridge. Lord President Henry Hastings was notably absent.

The lord mayor and many of York's aldermen were also in attendance in the Common Hall. The men sat adorned in their Corporation robes. As lord mayor, Henry Maye was wearing one of the scarlet cloaks he'd been presented with during his inauguration. The arresting sheriffs, their sergeants and mace bearers were also present.

It was an impressive array of dignitaries to bring a butcher's wife to trial. Unfortunately, the Northern Circuit assizes records prior to 1607 have been lost, but it's thought Margaret's charges included harbouring Father Ingleby and possibly Father Mush.

Before we examine the details of Margaret's trial, we should consider two further pieces of information. In Tudor times defendants weren't permitted to have any legal representation in the courtroom. Whatever evidence, witnesses and accusations were brought into play against her, Margaret would have to rebut them herself. The trial pitted together a relatively uneducated woman against the might of England's legal system, enthusiastically supported by the main government body in the north, York's civic authorities and the Church of England.

The second item centres on Father Mush. In *A True Report*, the priest includes a detailed account of the tense courtroom drama, much of which is relayed in the following pages.[1] However, he couldn't have attended the trial in person. Although the seminary priests liked their disguises, unless John

Mush was a master of subterfuge, or made the whole thing up, somebody else must have attended in his stead, observing the events from the public gallery. This person must have acted as the priest's eyes and ears in the courtroom, later passing on to the priest everything that had happened.

Father Mush was probably holed-up in a new hiding place somewhere in the city. He may have received updates and made notes after each session. In my novel, *The Pearl of York, Treason and Plot*, I assign the role of his witness in the courtroom to the youthful Guy Fawkes, who was living in the city at the time. The book was written with a historical novelist's licence to add fiction to fill in the gaps between the facts.[2] The truth is we don't know who played the role but from the amount of detail they captured, we do owe them a debt.

When Margaret was brought into the courtroom, she wasn't dressed like a common felon, but adorned in the attire of a prosperous businessman's wife, including a fine hat. It's reasonable to surmise Margaret had asked one of her friends to fetch her best clothes to the castle. Thankfully, her apparel hadn't been looted by the sheriff's men, unlike some of the family's other possessions. We assume a small amount was paid to the guards to enable the garments to be smuggled into her cell.

As she walked through the public gallery towards the dock cage, flanked by the sergeants of the court, Margaret smiled at the bench and those around her. She then took her place, and the proceedings began.

Over to Father Mush: 'Her indictment was read, that she had harboured and maintained Jesuit and Seminary priests, traitors to the Queen's Majesty and her laws, and that she had heard Mass, and such like. Then Judge Clench stood up, and said: "Margaret Clitherow, how say you? Are you guilty of this indictment, or no?"'

Before Margaret could answer, someone on the bench began shouting at her. She was ordered to remove her fine hat. The wearing of headgear, other than a simple coif to cover a woman's hair, during the court hearing was clearly viewed as being disrespectful to the legal proceedings.

Once she'd taken a moment, unpinned and lowered her hat, Margaret considered her response. When she did speak, her words surprised the judges and everyone else in the courtroom. '"I know no offence whereof I should confess myself guilty."'

Judge Clench looked at her for a moment, before speaking again. 'The judge said: "Yes, you have harboured and maintained Jesuits and priests, enemies to her Majesty."'

'The martyr answered: "I never knew nor have harboured any such persons, or maintained those which are not the Queen's friends. God defend I should."'

Margaret was making an important point here. As we've examined, this was closely linked to one of the major debates of the Elizabethan age. Was it really possible to separate uniformity of the church from loyalty to the Crown?

Judge Clench insisted Margaret must answer the charges facing her by making a plea in the formal manner which the court expected – was she guilty or not guilty? 'The judge said: "How will you be tried?"'

'The martyr answered, "Having made no offence, I need no trial."'

To Margaret's mind, the missionary priests weren't enemies of the Queen. As such, helping and harbouring them wasn't a crime. For the following few minutes the debate continued, both sides repeating 'the same arguments against each other.

Judge Clench asserted, "'You have offended the statutes, and therefore you must be tried;" and often asked her how she would be tried.'

'The martyr answered: "If you say I have offended, and that I must be tried, I will be tried by none but by God and your own consciences."'

'The judge said, "No, you cannot so do, for we sit here," quoth he, "to see justice and law, and therefore you must be tried by the country."'

By the 'country', the judge was referring to the jury. By agreeing the verdict, it would be the jury who would decide Margaret's fate. The men (it was only men) of the jury were selected by the city sheriffs, the same people who'd arrested Margaret in the first place.

The legal system of the sixteenth century was heavily stacked against the defendant. Not every man or woman was found guilty, but without legal defence and with the jury elected often by the same men who'd made the arrest and pressed the case, the odds weighed heavily against them.

The next actions in the courtroom were bizarre. Tiring of the lack of progress, and the prisoner's failure to make a plea, the judges took a different tack. The items found within the secret chamber in Margaret's house were brought into the courtroom.

Father Mush explains what happened: 'They brought forth two chalices, diverse pictures, and in mockery put two vestments and other church gear upon two lewd fellows' backs, and in derision the one began to pull and dally with the other, scoffing on the bench before the judges, and holding up singing breads, said to the martyr: "Behold thy gods in whom thou believest."'

The 'two lewd fellows' were dressed in priests' garments, most likely the ones found in the Shambles, and forced to impersonate Catholic priests. They swung rosary beads in the air and began to verbally taunt Margaret. The prisoner, the gallery and some on the benches looked on with a mixture of derision and bemusement, until the judges turned and spoke to Margaret.

'They asked her how she liked those vestments. The martyr said: "I like them well, if they were on their backs that know to use them to God's honour, as they were made."'

Margaret wasn't impressed with these antics. She considered the men who were wearing the priests' clothing were impersonating God's servants. After this, the fellows were removed from the courtroom.

'Then Judge Clench stood up and asked her: "In whom believe you?"'

'"I believe," quoth the martyr, "in God."'

'"In what God?" quoth the judge.'

'"I believe," quoth the martyr, "in God the Father, in God the Son, and God the Holy Ghost; in these Three Persons and One God I fully believe, and that by the passion, death, and merits of Christ Jesu I must be saved."'

'The judge said: "You say well;" and said no more.'

After this, there was a short gap in proceedings while the judges and the others on the bench conferred. The throng of York citizens packed into the public gallery took in and discussed what they'd witnessed to date. As with the crowd in the Shambles who'd seen Margaret's arrest, it's likely the opinions offered by the public gallery were mixed. Some would have sided with the accused, but felt unable to speak out for their own safety. Others may have come only to watch a Catholic being prosecuted and condemned. A few may have had no connection with the case at all, their real interest being in one of the following cases. Trials at the assizes usually didn't go on for long, and there were quite a few cases scheduled to be heard during the day.

'After a while the judges said to her again: "Margaret Clitherow, how say you yet? Are you content to be tried by God and the country?"'

'The martyr said, "No."'

Judge Clench decided it was time to vary his tactics. 'The judge said: "Good woman, consider well what you do; if you refuse to be tried by the country, you make yourself guilty and accessory to your own death, for we cannot try you," said he, "but by order of law."'

With these words, the judge raised the temperature in the courtroom by several degrees. It's possible many people in the gallery didn't quite understand what he was talking about. We don't even know if Margaret understood his words immediately.

Judge Clench was referring to something called '*peine forte et dure*'. Translated from French into English, the phrase means 'strong and harsh punishment'. It was originally introduced into English common law to prevent people from taking the action Margaret was attempting – refusing to make a plea.

The original punishment focused on starving a defendant into submission. Food and drink would be withheld from them until they made their plea. The law was eventually changed in the early fifteenth century to include pressing the prisoner to death with heavy weights. This was the punishment the assizes judges were now threatening Margaret with.

If she continued to refuse to make a plea it was within the justices' power to order her body be laid down on her back and pressed to death. Increasingly heavy weights would be placed upon her supine, naked torso until her bones were broken and organs crushed. Along with burning at the stake and hanging, drawing and quartering, this was another horrific Tudor means of execution.

Despite this, there was a reason why some prisoners refused to make a plea. This was related to the legal forfeiture and inheritance of property. A defendant who made a plea and was found guilty would be liable to having their assets stripped from their estate and passed to the Crown. Any prisoner who died without making a plea could be assured their estate would be treated as detailed in their will, allowing it to be passed onto their heirs.

As we'll examine, this factor may not have been a major driving force behind Margaret's refusal, but it would have been an area of interest for Henry Maye. Was there a danger he might lose the chance of regaining control over the property in Davygate? Alternatively, had he already done a deal with Henry Hastings to buy the tavern back cheaply from the Crown if – or when – Margaret was convicted and executed? I must stress at this point there's no evidence to confirm such a conspiracy theory, but it's an intriguing thought.

Back in the courtroom, Judge Clench had shown Margaret Clitherow a stick. Now, he offered her a carrot. '"You need not fear this kind of trial, for I think the country cannot find you guilty upon this slender evidence of a child."'

The judge told Margaret that in his view the prosecution's case was flimsy, and he found it hard to believe the jury could find her guilty based upon the evidence of a child. There was something else too. By now, the jury may have been aware of the witness's background. The serving lad, who'd given evidence against Margaret, was an immigrant. 'Born in Flanders of an Englishman and a Dutch woman, and had been brought from thence almost two years before.'

Of course, where the boy came from should not have had any bearing in court, but the local people's suspicion of foreigners, especially those from overseas, would likely have come into play. Margaret considered the judge's words about the 'slender evidence' of the boy. Any slight delay in her reply may have brought hope to the bench that they could finally hear and complete her trial and move on to the backlog of cases behind it.

The judges were disappointed. 'The martyr still refused.' Margaret turned down the carrot.

Judges Clench and Rhodes conferred once more. They shared a few whispers with the representatives of the Council of the North. By now, Eure, Meares, Hurlestone and Cheke were furious. The cat and mouse game playing out in front of them wasn't something they'd been expecting. Perhaps it was time to talk about the accused's relationship with her husband.

'They asked if her husband were not privy to her doings in keeping priests.'

'The martyr said: "God knoweth I could never yet get my husband in that good case that he were worthy to know or come in place where they were to serve God."'

If the bench thought they'd be able to force the defendant onto the defensive by inferring they'd accuse her husband, they had to think twice. In her answer, Margaret made it plain she'd tried to get John involved but he was having none of it. In this case, other than not beating or stopping his wife from doing so, it could be argued there was no evidence John Clitherow had ever aided seminary or Jesuit priests.

Judge Clench returned to the stick-based approach and raised the threat of *'peine forte et dure'* for a second time. 'The judge said:

"We must proceed by law against you, which will condemn you to a sharp death for want of trial.'"

Whether coached by her mentors, Fathers Mush and Ingleby, that she was doing the work of God, or speaking of her own accord, Margaret Clitherow seemed almost glad to receive the threat. 'The martyr said cheerfully: "God's will be done: I think I may suffer any death for this good cause.'"

Now late on into the session, the trial began to turn nasty. A great deal of conversation on the bench and in the gallery appeared to be questioning Margaret's sanity. 'Some of them said, seeing her joy, that she was mad, and possessed with a smiling spirit.'

Judge Rhodes and the representatives of the Council of the North raised their voices and began to shout at Margaret about her heresy and treachery to the country. 'Mr Rhodes also railed against her on the Catholic faith and priests; so did also the other Councillors.'

Tempers began to fray as the powerful men on the bench realised they were getting nowhere. Effectively, they were being given the runaround by a butcher's wife.

Sitting on the official benches, Henry Maye was resplendent in his scarlet cloak. By this time, his face may have been burning a similar colour. The proceedings were taking much longer than he'd expected. The whole thing was difficult enough. He just wanted it to be done.

His first wife, Jane, was dead, Margaret had increasingly become a political embarrassment to him and there was the question of the ownership of the inn. The two most likely outcomes of the trial would each favour Henry. Firstly, if Margaret apostatized, rejected her Catholicism and returned to the state church, one of York's most stubborn recusants would have been converted. This would have been a feather in the cap for the new lord mayor. Perhaps where Margaret led, others would soon follow. Thomas Vavasour was dead. Dorothy Vavasour and Anne Tesh were in prison. Before long, it was possible the city's recusancy problem could be expunged.

In this case, Margaret would probably spend some time in prison, but she'd eventually be released. Henry might even be able to persuade his son-in-law to move the family to Cornborough, where Margaret could be kept out of the way of prying eyes. The problem of the inn would remain, but Henry Maye's status with the Council would be much improved.

The second, and, from what Henry Maye must have known about his stepdaughter, more likely outcome was that Margaret would be found guilty. It didn't matter which way she pleaded. Sheriff Fawcett had chosen the jury, and his future and promotion in the Corporation was dependent on Henry's favour. Of course, the lord mayor would regret his stepdaughter's execution, they all would, but she'd been given a chance to apostatize. The law was the law.

In this case, the defendant's property would pass over to the Crown, which often offered members of the Corporation first refusal when purchasing houses in York at heavily discounted rates. Knowing how hard he'd worked to develop the tavern, surely no one would wish to stand in Henry's way if he offered to buy it back.

This argument takes a dim view of Henry Maye. It makes a case that he was willing to sacrifice his stepdaughter for personal financial gain and to improve his reputation. It's a supposition, a theory, which takes into account inferences about the lord mayor's character in Father Mush's report, but there are no direct accusations.

Whatever the lord mayor's motivations, Margaret's hearing was turning into an awkward situation for him. It was unlikely Henry had anticipated this turn of events. Things became worse a moment later when the vile rumours put around York about Margaret's virtue, or lack of it, entered the courtroom. 'Mr Hurlestone openly before them all said: "It is not for religion that thou harbourest priests, but for harlotry;" and furiously uttered such like slanders, sitting on the bench.'

Having been unable to coerce the prisoner into pleading, the Council members began to make lurid accusations about Margaret's behaviour. If found to be true, there's no doubt they would have brought shame and notoriety to Margaret, her husband and her family. Even if the claims were denied, which they were, Councillor Hurlestone and the others knew mud often sticks.

These claims were designed to incite public outrage against the priests, who, it was alleged, stayed with women like Margaret to 'satisfy their lusts'. These accusations of sexual impropriety between the missionary priests and the women who harboured them were intended to inflame the local population, particularly men with recusant wives who may have aided or spent time with the priests.

Most men would naturally be unhappy, to say the least, if they suspected their wife had been up to no good with a priest. If they could keep their wife's name out of things, some might even decide to turn the priest over to the authorities. This was all part of the thinking behind the claims of the officials.

There would have been uproar in the public gallery at this juncture. Once he'd managed to bring some semblance of order back to the courtroom, Judge Clench took the opportunity to close proceedings for the day. 'The Bench rose that night without pronouncing any sentence against her, and she was brought from the hall with a great troop of men and halberds, with a smiling and most cheerful countenance, dealing money on both sides of the streets.'

Judge Clench left the courtroom, hoping the prisoner would see sense overnight and make a plea in the morning. To help Margaret view things more clearly, he ordered the officials should not return her to the castle, filled as it was with like-minded Catholics. Instead, the judge instructed Margaret was taken to the kidcote on Ousebridge 'where she was shut up in a close parlour'.

Margaret's friend, Dorothy Vavasour, was in the same prison, but the two women were kept apart. Margaret was placed into a small, dark cell. The members of the bench hoped the prisoner would reflect during the long hours of darkness and realise the errors of her ways. They clearly didn't know Margaret Clitherow very well at all. The case would begin again in the morning.

Overnight in the Cell

Margaret Clitherow was barred from seeing any other Catholics, but she wasn't placed in solitary confinement. The authorities forced her into a cell with a Protestant couple in the vain hope their Puritanical company might encourage her apostasy. It's difficult to imagine this happening. Margaret's cellmates, the Yowards, were a married couple who'd been jailed for failing to pay off debts. Father Mush describes the pair as 'evil-disposed persons of their own sect', highlighting the animosity felt between York's religious groups.

Overnight, Margaret received another unexpected visitor. 'The same night came to the martyr, as she was praying upon her knees, Parson Wiggington, a Puritan preacher of notorious qualities, and ministered talk unto her, as their fashion is. The martyr regarded him very little,

141

and desired him not to trouble her, "for your fruits," quoth she, "are correspondent to your doctrine." And so he departed. All that night she remained in that parlour.'

Although Giles Wiggington came to Ousebridge in an attempt to persuade Margaret Clitherow away from her religious views and towards his own, he wasn't acting in an official capacity. Unlike Archbishop Sandys, Wiggington was a Puritan-leaning Calvinist, and one whom Sandys had fallen out with. The archbishop had written a letter about the parson to a fellow bishop complaining, 'He laboureth not to build, but to pull down, and by what means he can to overthrow the state ecclesiastical.'[4]

Some in the higher echelons of the Elizabethan Church of England feared the radical Puritans almost as much as the Catholics. In 1584, having arrived in London, Parson Wiggington was hoping to preach in the capital, but the Church authorities intercepted him. After he'd been questioned and refused to take an oath, the parson was imprisoned for a number of weeks. Giles Wiggington was clearly no friend of Archbishop Sandys, and it's unlikely the north's most senior clergyman would have been happy to discover the preacher had returned to York.

After the failed attempt to make Margaret 'see sense', she settled down in her cell, but it's unlikely she slept much that night. The proximity and sleeping sounds of the other prisoners wouldn't have bothered her. She was used to this from her previous spells in jail, but it's only natural her mind would have played back the events of the day and looked ahead towards the morning.

One thing that most likely dominated her thoughts was her refusal to make a plea. With the senior judge arguing the prosecution's case was weak, with insufficient evidence to sway a jury, would she consider changing her mind?

Why did Margaret take such an exceptional stance in the first place? Father Mush puts forward two possible explanations. The first, he said, was developed from Margaret's sympathy for the members of the jury. Given her position, this seems a selfless act of kindness. 'But well you know for what reason the martyr, of her own discretion, after her apprehension (not having any counsel in this or any other point), refused to be tried by the country, as they willed her. Not thereby she meaning to favour or save her life, but only pitying to cast her blood into the hands of man; whereas, by her refusal, it should in that case principally rest in the judge's bosom, although also many more were guilty of it.'

Father Mush argues that Margaret was concerned in case her death would fall onto the consciences of the 'country', the men of the jury. Believing they'd likely be forced into finding her guilty, irrespective of the evidence and most possibly under duress, Margaret had no wish to dilute the judges' guilt with their own.

Father Mush reinforces this argument near the end of *A True Report* by quoting Margaret directly. 'Said she, "I knew well the country must needs have found me guilty to please the Council, which earnestly seek my blood; and then all they had been accessory to my death, and damnably offended God. I thought it therefore in the way of charity on [my] part to hinder the country from such a sin; and since it must needs be done, to cause as few to do it as might be; and that was the judge himself."'

The second explanation Father Mush gave for Margaret's obstinance in the matter also came from words he attributed to her. '"Alas!" quoth she, "if I should have put myself to the country, evidence must needs have come against me, which I know none could give but only my children and servants. And it would have been more grievous to me than a thousand deaths, if I should have seen any of them brought forth before me to give evidence against me."'

For me, this argument sounds the more convincing. Margaret's concerns were understandable. Having seen how Sheriff Fawcett had treated the terrified half-Flemish boy in the Shambles, she feared force might be used to persuade her children and servants to testify against her in court. Anne and the others might even be tortured to ensure they did as they were told.

While this may be a compelling argument, there could have also been other factors at play. Father Mush describes the beginning of the infamous raid on the Shambles as follows. 'They found the martyr occupied in her household business. The priest was in his chamber, which was in the *next neighbour's* house.'

Only the Clitherows' property was searched. When the Catholic vestments and artefacts were discovered in the hidden chamber inside her house, the searchers ransacked and looted Margaret's property, before moving on. Critically, they failed to investigate the houses adjoining the Clitherows' shop.

For some reason (perhaps because he was braver than history gives him credit for), the terrified boy didn't lead his tormentors to the room next door. He only showed them into the secret chamber in Margaret's house, which he would have known by then was empty. Although this was enough to have his mistress arrested and charged, the boy's actions gave the priest and the lay people hiding next door time to escape.

Perhaps one of the reasons Margaret feared the greater scrutiny of a trial, with scant evidence against her, was the risk that the pursuivants might return and search the adjoining properties. This may have led to the arrest and prosecution of one or more of Margaret's friends and neighbours, perhaps even her husband's relatives. Again, this seems a plausible argument for her refusal to make a plea.

We now come to Margaret's understandable belief the jury was rigged against her. Some of the jurors might have been keen to play their part in ensuring a Catholic recusant who harboured priests was punished. Others may have had lingering sympathies for Margaret's plight, but the deliberations of this particular jury wouldn't have been a good time to share them.

Sheriff Fawcett had arrested Margaret, and he had chosen the jury. The men of the jury would make their verdict under the observation of the powerful men who controlled their lives. The Church, the Council and Corporation were all watching them. There seems little doubt which way their votes would have been swayed.

Even then, there was a potential benefit, if we can call it that, to Margaret of being found guilty, rather than refusing to make a plea. As a guilty woman, Margaret would be hanged. It was a quicker death than being crushed beneath heavy weights with a sharp stone beneath her back.

There was also the matter of the inheritance. Under the terms of Thomas Middleton's will, Margaret, unlike most women, was the legal owner of substantial property. In 1585 she'd inherited the house and buildings on Davygate, much to her stepfather's dismay. However, I believe we can discount this as a factor in Margaret's refusal to plead. The rules of '*peine forte et dure*' would have allowed her children to inherit her estate, but as we've heard from Father Mush, Margaret had little time for worldly goods. She had no desire to set up her children financially, preferring instead for them to join a religious order. Evidence of this can be seen from the enforced exile of her son, Henry.

I have a personal view to add, which I acknowledge is purely supposition. There's no evidence behind this theory, although it's difficult to see how there could be. We know from *A True Report* that Margaret spent many months in close personal contact with Father Mush. I'm not suggesting there was a physical relationship between them, and John Clitherow's behaviour and his constancy towards his wife suggests otherwise. I also have no wish to upset anyone who might understandably hold this remarkable woman in high regard.

From what we know, the relationship between Margaret Clitherow and Father Mush was a spiritual one. They talked many times of religious matters and, of course, the terrible, but lawful, treatment of Catholics in England. Margaret spent many evenings visiting the places where the Catholic priests she'd personally known, had befriended and worshipped with, had been slain.

In the chapters of *A True Report* leading up to her arrest, Father Mush provides many details about Margaret's state of mind. In particular, he highlights how much the butcher's wife was willing to suffer for her faith. 'She never feared nor once shrunk at any worldly affliction or pain sustained for the Catholic faith and her conscience; but was most desirous and as willing to suffer as the enemy was to afflict her [...] It was her daily prayer that she might be worthy to suffer anything for God's sake.'

The priest was well aware that Margaret was willing to endure 'anything for God's sake'. Given she was now on trial and fighting for her life, these were chilling words. Father Mush freely admits that he and Margaret had discussed the idea and possibility of her martyrdom, quoting Margaret's own words. '"I see not in myself any worthiness of martyrdom; yet, if it be His will, I pray Him that I may be constant and persevere to the end."'

When John Clitherow set off to the King's Manor for the third time in two days, Margaret was half-expecting to be arrested. She entered the trial in a forthright manner. Her decision not to make a plea may have already been made ahead of time. Of course, it might have also been swayed by some of the factors examined above.

There's a possibility that Margaret's discussions with Father Mush went further than he reported. Could the priest have used his position, and Margaret's willingness to do his bidding as God's servant on Earth, to persuade her towards martyrdom?

If this was the case, the only course of action that could guarantee her death and speedy ascent to heaven would be refusing to make a plea.

There was a possibility, albeit a slim one, that the jury might find her innocent.

If Father Mush acted in this way, what were his motivations? Certainly, he'd lose one of his favourite hiding places in York, but there would be others. He may not have been expecting Anne Tesh's arrest, for example. Although we don't know where he hid next, he certainly found somewhere. He wasn't arrested around the time of Margaret's trial.

The arrest and execution of the Jesuit and seminary priests had become almost commonplace in York and beyond. Many people no longer blinked an eye when it happened. Even the authorised slaying of the layman Marmaduke Bowes had had little impact. To cause a public outcry perhaps what was needed was the brutal execution of a woman in the prime of her life, a pretty, 'comely' woman with a family and young children.

Is it possible Father Mush used Margaret Clitherow to further his own, and the Catholic Church's, propaganda agenda? We don't know, but it's plausible. Interestingly, the word 'propaganda' came into common use in the English language not long afterwards. It was associated with the Catholic Church's proposals to counter the Reformation as it spread like wildfire across Europe.

Day Two in Court

The next morning was the second day of York Lent assizes. The proceedings started early. Margaret was taken from her prison cell on Ousebridge. Her hands were tied, and she was led back along Coney Street, flanked by halberdiers. By eight o'clock she was standing before the bench in the Common Hall.

Father Mush describes how once again the judges attempted to persuade her to make a plea and have her case heard by the jury. 'She standing at the Bar, the judge said to her: "Margaret Clitherow, how say you yet? Yesternight we passed you over without judgment, which we might have then pronounced against you if we would: we did it not, hoping you would be something more conformable, and put yourself to the country, for otherwise you must needs have the law. We see nothing why you should refuse; here be but small witness against you, and the country will consider your case."'

There was nothing new in Judge Clench's opening statement. Nevertheless, those in the courtroom must have looked on at the accused expectantly. Had the woman come to her senses? Was she ready to make a plea?

"'Indeed," said the martyr, "I think you have no witnesses against me but children, which with an apple and a rod you may make to say what you will.'"

Margaret began the second day in court by deriding the prosecution's case. Specifically, she highlighted how easy it was for the authorities to tempt or torture young witnesses into mouthing whatever they were told to say.

Her words caused Judge Rhodes to break immediately with the previous line from the bench. Instead, he claimed she was guilty. "'It is plain that you had priests in your house by these things which were found.'"

Rather than deny these accusations, Margaret went out of her way to admit she had harboured priests. 'The martyr said, "As for good Catholic priests, I know no cause why I should refuse them as long as I live; they come only to do me good and others."'

Facing a capital crime, this was an astounding admission. Any supporters she may have had in the public gallery must have wondered what she was doing.

The response from the judges and Councillors was an angry one. 'Rhodes, Hurlestone, and others said, "They are all traitors, rascals, and deceivers of the Queen's subjects."'

'The martyr said, "God forgive you. You would not say so of them if you knew them."'

'They said, "You would detest them yourself if you knew their treason and wickedness as we do."'

'The martyr said, "I know them for virtuous men, sent by God only to save our souls."'

Father Mush concludes this part of the conversation with a summary of Margaret's attitude and delivery. 'These speeches and the like she uttered very boldly and with great modesty.'

As we've examined, as a fugitive missionary priest, Father Mush must have been working from second- or third-hand memories and descriptions of the words and actions in the courtroom. However, his court reports are compelling reading. He outlined next how the senior justice, Judge Clench, gave Margaret another opportunity to make a plea. '"What say you? Will you put yourself to the country, yea or no?"'

'The martyr said, "I see no cause why I should do so in this matter: I refer my cause only to God and your own consciences. Do what you think good."'

With this response, Margaret appeared to be saying she didn't recognise the jurisdiction of the court. She was digging her heels in. The judges, with many cases still to hear, and others in the courtroom, were beginning to lose their patience. 'All the people about her condemned her of great obstinacy and folly, that she would not yield; and on every hand persuaded her to refer her trial to the country, which could not find her guilty, as they said, upon such slender evidence; but she would not.'

Father Mush's next words give the impression that even Judge Clench, who'd given Margaret so many opportunities to make a plea, was preparing to move on: '"Well," said Judge Clench, "we must pronounce a sentence against you. Mercy lieth in our hands, in the country's also, if you put your trial to them; otherwise you must have the law."'

Sensing what was about to happen, there was a hubbub of conversation and speculation in the gallery. Would Margaret be sentenced and suffer *'peine forte et dure'*? At this stage of the proceedings, with the writing on the wall, there was a dramatic intervention from within the court room.

'The Puritan preacher, called Wiggington, stood up and called to the judge on the bench, saying, "My lord, give me leave to speak;" but the murmuring and noise in the Hall would not suffer him to be heard: yet he continued still calling that he might speak, and the judge commanded silence to hear him.'

Finally, the gallery grew quiet. Giles Wiggington addressed the bench. '"My lord, take heed what you do. You sit here to do justice; this woman's case is touching life and death. You ought not, either by God's laws or man's, to judge her to die upon the slender witness of a boy; nor unless you have two or three sufficient men of very good credit to give evidence against her. Therefore, look to it, my lord, this gear goeth sore."'

Parson Wiggington, the man who'd visited Margaret in her cell to urge her apostasy, was a Calvinist Puritan. As such, he was on the opposite side of the religious divide to Margaret. Both probably considered the other to be a deluded heretic, hellbent on damnation. But here he was, speaking on her behalf in the courtroom, potentially risking arrest and punishment from the Church of England.

With Father Mush so diametrically opposed to the parson's views, the inclusion of Wiggington's intervention in *A True Report* indicates there may have been a level of grudging respect between the two renegade clerics. Despite Parson Wiggington's demand for the judges to discontinue their case, or at least postpone the proceedings until they'd found 'two or three sufficient men of very good credit [i.e., Protestants] to give evidence against her', Judge Clench pressed on:

'The judge answered, "I may do it by law."'

'"By what law?" quoth Wiggington.'

'"By the Queen's law," said the judge.'

'"That may well be," quoth Wiggington, "but you cannot do it by God's law" and he said no more.'

The parson sat down, defeated. After a few moments, Judge Clench addressed the prisoner once more. 'The judge, yet desirous to shift the thorn out of his own conscience into the whole country, and falsely thinking that if the jury found her guilty his hand should be clear from her blood, said again, "Good woman, I pray you put yourself to the country. There is no evidence but a boy against you, and whatsoever they do, yet we may show mercy afterward."'

With these words, Judge Clench was attempting to provide Margaret with one more opportunity to avoid the painful death of '*peine forte et dure*' by having her case heard by the jury. Even if she was found guilty, she'd die more quickly from hanging than by being crushed to death.

Why would such an experienced circuit judge go to so much trouble on Margaret's behalf? Judge Clench would have been well used to condemning prisoners to death for a range of crimes, both men and women. It wasn't just Catholic priests who were executed in York.

In 1582 George Foster of Tadcaster was executed at the Knavesmire for coining. In the following year, Peter Clark suffered a similar fate for murdering Hannah Thompson in Pocklington, as did Rinion Foster, after being convicted of horse theft and raping Mary Thompson, a servant of William Johnson of Dunnington. In August 1585 George de Kirwan of Ripon and Thomas de Alasco of Penistone were condemned to death and executed at the Knavesmire for their role in coining guineas at a local silversmith's house in York.

Father Mush believed Judge Clench did what he did for selfish reasons, rather than for any desire to see justice done. The judge would have been aware how likely it was that the Council and Corporation had conspired over the timing of Margaret's arrest. In some ways he'd been stitched up. The authorities in York wanted to ensure Margaret's case was heard by the assizes court rather than by the Council's Quarterly Sessions. This would make the assizes judges responsible for her case and any repercussions afterwards.

The priest believed Judge Clench was now seeking to shift the blame – from himself to the jury. If Margaret pleaded not guilty, and the jury found otherwise, it would be they, not he, who were responsible for her death.

There may have been an additional factor in his thinking. What would Queen Elizabeth make of executing the woman? A senior justice like himself, without a blot on his record, could expect to be knighted by Her Majesty in future. However, despite a long and worthy career in the law, before and after this case, Judge Clench never did get asked to kneel before the Queen or feel the touch of her sword on his shoulder.

Margaret's response to the latest offer of a partial reprieve was the one that the court had, by now, come to expect. 'The martyr still refused.'

According to Father Mush, following this latest setback, Judge Rhodes made his frustrations clear to his senior colleague. '"Why stand we all the day about this naughty, wilful woman. Let us despatch her."'

When Judge Clench spoke again to Margaret, it was with a solemn voice. The courtroom listened intently. '"If you will not put yourself to the country, this must be your judgment. You must return from whence you came, and there, in the lowest part of the prison, be stripped naked, laid down, your back upon the ground, and as much weight laid upon you as you are able to bear, and so to continue three days without meat or drink, except a little barley bread and puddle water, and the third day to be pressed to death, your hands and feet tied to posts, and a sharp stone under your back."'

It's likely there would have been gasps around the courtroom at finally hearing the chilling sentence. Despite everything that Father Mush has informed us about Margaret's faith, her conviction and state of mind, she must have been struck for a moment by the judge's words, which condemned her to such an awful and painful death.

Judge Clench had been describing the traditional method of execution, where the prisoner was forced to suffer for several days before they were finally killed. In the enlightened times of Elizabeth I, the punishment was usually accelerated by placing heavier weights more quickly onto the accused's body. Often, death occurred within twenty minutes, albeit of agonising pain.

Knowing this full well, Margaret looked at the bench. She caught the senior judge's eye. "'If this judgment be according to your own conscience, I pray God send you better judgment before Him. I thank God heartily for this.'"

Margaret's words seemed to affect Judge Clench deeply. In his response, he attempted to defend himself and justify his actions. "'Nay," said the judge, "I do it according to law.'"

But he couldn't help himself. Once again, he gave Margaret a chance to yield to the wishes of the court. "'This must be your judgment, unless you put yourself to be tried by the country [...] Consider of it, you have husband and children to care for; cast not yourself away.'"

If the sentence wasn't upsetting enough, Margaret's response to the judge's offer made things even worse. It certainly shocked the public gallery. 'The martyr answered, "I would to God my husband and children might suffer with me for so good a cause."'

There was uproar in the courtroom. Margaret appeared to be saying she wanted John and their children to be executed alongside her. 'Upon which words the heretics reported after, that she would have hanged her husband and children if she could.'

Men in the Common Hall must have thought of their own wives and wondered if they'd wish the same about them. Judge Clench, perhaps mindful of the Queen's likely reaction, and by now desperate to pass on responsibility for what might happen to the jury, tried once again.

"'How say you, Margaret Clitherow? Are you content to put yourself to the trial of the country? Although we have given sentence against you according to the law, yet will we show mercy, if you will do anything yourself.'"

Of course, it didn't work. Although Margaret was happy to die for God, she had no wish for Judge Clench and Judge Rhodes to salve their consciences by blaming the law.

'The martyr, lifting up her eyes towards heaven, said with a cheerful countenance, "God be thanked, all that He shall send me shall be welcome;

I am not worthy of so good a death as this is: I have deserved death for mine offences to God, but not for anything that I am accused of."'

The outcome of the case was clear enough. Judge Clench wouldn't ask again. The murder, horse theft, coining and other trials could now be heard. Margaret would be taken away and brutally executed, not for being found guilty of committing the crimes she'd come accused of, but for refusing to make a plea in court.

'Then the judge bade the Sheriff look to her, who pinioned her arms with a cord. The martyr first beholding the one arm and then the other, smiled to herself and was joyful to be bound for Christ's sake; at which they all raged against her.'

Sheriff Fawcett, the man who'd arrested Margaret Clitherow in the Shambles less than a week earlier, tied her arms together and led her off towards Coney Street. The details of her indictment, sentencing and reaction became the talk of the city.

'So the Sheriff brought her with halberts to the bridge again, where she was before. Some of the Bench were sent to mark her countenance as she was carried forth of the Hall, but she departed from thence through the streets with joyful countenance, whereat some said, "It must needs be that she received comfort from the Holy Ghost," for all were astonished to see her of so good cheer. Some said it was not so, but that she was possessed with a merry devil, and that she sought her own death.'

This final claim that Margaret had gone to court to seek her own suicide would be put to her again in her prison cell in the days to come.

Chapter Eleven

Punishment (1586)

A Chance to Live

Margaret returned to the cell on Ousebridge and was barred from speaking to the other prisoners, apart from her Puritan cellmates. No visitors were allowed, unless first sanctioned by the Council of the North. Despite her brave words and smiles at the end of her hearing, the reality of what lay ahead must have been a daunting prospect, especially to face alone.

John Clitherow was also locked up, across the way in York Castle. His reaction upon discovering his wife's sentence demonstrates the love he felt for her. 'He fared like a man out of his wits and wept so vehemently that the blood gushed out of his nose in great quantity, and said, "Alas! Will they kill my wife? Let them take all I have and save her, for she is the best wife in all England, and the best Catholic also."'

We only have Father Mush's account of John's reaction, but it appears to be tenable. It certainly wasn't the response of a man who believed his wife had been sleeping behind his back with Catholic priests, or had done anything else to upset him, apart from committing herself to the faith she so fervently believed in.

Despite the fact that she'd already been sentenced, Margaret's apostasy would be a major coup for York's Protestant authorities. Isolated from her friends and family and facing death, they believed there was still a strong possibility she could be brought around to their way of thinking.

Father Mush outlines the Council's attempts to engage her. 'Two days after, as I remember, came to her Mr Meares, Sir Thomas Fairfax, and others of the Council, and secretly asked her many things, the certainty whereof I cannot as yet learn in particular. I cannot learn more than that they asked her if she would go to the church with them, if it were but to one sermon, and she should have favour.'

153

Father Mush's admission that he didn't know exactly what was said during these meetings adds credence to the contents of *A True Report*. When the priest found information to be lacking, or not available, he didn't make things up. While there's bias in his writing, more often than not Father Mush appears to have attempted to tell the truth as he understood it.

The priest continues by outlining Margaret's response. 'She answered that she would, if it pleased them to let her choose the preacher, and grant him safe conduct to come and go.'

The Protestant councillors and clergymen must have loved that. While they wanted Margaret to hear a sermon, she insisted she'd do so, but only if she could listen to a priest of her own choice, no doubt a Catholic, with a promise of his safety. Of course, Margaret knew there was no way the Council would agree.

The Council's next attempt was an interesting one. Margaret had been sent to prison once before during the early stages of pregnancy. An unbeknown (to us at least) source raised a suspicion this may have happened again. 'They asked her also if she thought in her conscience that she were with child.'

This is one of the most incredible parts of Margaret's whole story. Here was an opportunity for everyone, Margaret and the authorities included, to prevent her death. Executing a woman who was known to be pregnant was against the law. At the very least, the execution would have to be placed on hold until the baby was born.

If Margaret claimed she was pregnant and this was found to be true, there'd be a significant delay in the execution of her sentence. In the meantime, perhaps her case might be reviewed by the Privy Council in London, or a message passed to Queen Elizabeth asking for clemency.

Surprisingly, Margaret made the following response. 'She said she knew not certainly, and would not for all the world take it on her conscience that she was or she was not but, as she thought rather she was than otherwise.'

Margaret Clitherow was a remarkable woman. Virtually anyone else in her situation would surely have answered that they were quite certain they were pregnant. The Council members who'd been assigned to question her must have felt perplexed, wondering why she hadn't made more of this opportunity to attempt to save her life.

'They asked her why she would not so much as desire to be reprieved for some time. She said, "I require no favour in this matter; you may do your pleasures."'

It's easy to imagine the representatives of the Council catching each other's eyes and wondering at some of the responses they were hearing. From the answers Margaret gave to some of their questions, it was almost as if she wished to die a martyr instead of choosing life.

The councillors remembered it wasn't only Margaret they wished to apprehend and punish. 'They asked her if she knew not Ingleby and Mush, the two traitor priests.'

'She answered, "I know none such."'

'They replied, "Will you say so? Beware of lying."'

'She said, "I have not to accuse any man; you have me now, do your wills."'

Having admitted in court that she had harboured Catholic priests, it's interesting to hear Margaret deny knowing her two most recent missionary visitors. This was presumably an attempt to protect them.

Once again Father Mush makes it plain that he hadn't been able to find out everything that had been said during Margaret's questioning. 'Thus much have I heard, and no more, that the Council should say unto her. After this they went to the judge, and told him what she had said.'

The news of Margaret's potential pregnancy spread very quickly. 'Her kinsfolks and friends laboured much all that week to cause her to say directly that she was with child, but she would never affirm it of any certainty, but said she would not dissemble with God and the world, for that she could not tell certainly whether she was or no.'

Quite how these members of her family and her friends communicated with Margaret when she wasn't allowed to see unsanctioned visitors, we don't know. The jail guards weren't well paid, and York's Catholics were familiar with them. Palms may have been greased to permit short visits, or the people bringing Margaret's food may have been allowed to linger in her cell doorway to talk to her.

With no date set for Margaret's execution, a debate began between the authorities. Judge Clench found himself in a tricky position. 'Upon Wednesday the Sheriff of York came to the judge, Clench, and demanded what he should do with her. The judge answered, "She may not be executed, for they say she is with child."'

Once again, the senior justice appeared to grab at an opportunity to ensure Margaret's death wouldn't be placed upon his shoulders. However, his fellow judge and the senior representatives of the Council disagreed with him. 'Rhodes, Meares, Hurleston, Cheke, and the rest urged sore that she might be executed according to judgment and law. And Mr Rhodes said, "Brother Clench, you are too merciful in these cases; if she had not law she would undo a great many."'

'Then Judge Clench said, "If she be with child, I will not consent that she shall die."'

'"Then," quoth the Sheriff, "my lord, I shall make a quest of women to go upon her."'

'Quote the judge, "Call four honest women, which know her well, and let them try it."'

There's no record of which women were tasked with confirming whether Margaret was pregnant. They may have included one or more of Dorothy Vavasour's obstetrix friends, at least if they'd been able to hide their Catholicism. The next day the 'four honest women' visited Margaret in her cell. Afterwards, they presented their findings to Judge Clench. 'The four women upon the Thursday came to the martyr, and returned answer to the judge, that she was with child as far as they could perceive or gather by her own words.'

Although their findings weren't conclusive, the women stated they believed Margaret was probably pregnant. It would have been a harsh-minded woman, or one with strong dislike of Catholics, to judge otherwise. Such a verdict would surely condemn the prisoner to an awful death.

Over in the King's Manor sides had been taken. Judge Clench took one position, while Judge Rhodes, the officials of the Council of the North and the Church took the other. Sheriff Fawcett and the Corporation's officials were probably more than happy to let the circuit judges and the councillors argue the matter out amongst themselves.

'That night, or the next day, Hurlestone, the Councillors, and ministers, who most greedily thirsted after her blood, came to Clench in his chamber and said, "My lord, this woman is not to have the benefit of her condition, for that she hath refused trial by the country, and the sentence of death is passed against her."'

'The judge answered, "Mr Hurlestone, God defend she should die, if she be with child; although she hath offended, yet hath not the infant in her womb. I will not for a thousand pounds, therefore, give my consent until she be further tried.'"

'Hurlestone urged still and said, "She is the only woman in the north parts, and if she be suffered to live, there will be more of her order without any fear of law. And therefore, my lord, consider with yourself," quoth he, "and let her have law according to judgment passed."'

Councillor Hurlestone and the others heaped as much pressure as they could onto Judge Clench, claiming Margaret was the most notorious female recusant and harbourer of priests in the north. If she wasn't executed, others with Catholic leanings would follow her example. The clampdown on the missionary priests would suffer, and Judge Clench would be to blame.

As we've seen, the judge was minded to place a stay on Margaret's execution. If she was pregnant, the baby wouldn't be born for many months. Even if not, weeks would pass before the pregnancy could be fully disproven. If this was the case, the sentence could continue, but the assizes court would have moved on. Judge Clench wasn't due to return to York until the assizes' second annual sitting in the city during the summer.

However, Ralph Hurlestone was a clever man. With his next words, he offered the judge a way out. He and, by extension, the Council of the North, would, '"take it upon my conscience that she is not with child."'

Offered this compromise, Judge Clench believed he might be able to extract himself from what happened next. 'The judge would by no means consent; but, thinking to wash his hands with Pilate, referred all to the Council, and willed them to do their own discretions; and at his departure he commanded to stay the execution till Friday after, which was the twenty-fifth of March and the feast of our Lady, and then to do as they should think good, if in the meantime they heard not from him to the contrary.'

The senior justice instructed Margaret's execution should be delayed until the assizes court left York. After this, the Council of the North could take whatever action it saw fit, based upon the councillors' 'own discretions'. Judge Clench had been unable to transfer responsibility for Margaret's fate to the jury. Now, he passed it on to the consciences of the councillors.

When word of the decision reached the prison on Ousebridge, 'The martyr, after her judgment, with much prayer and fasting prepared herself to die, fearing still that she was not worthy to suffer such a death for God His sake.'

Upon hearing the news, Margaret smuggled out a heartfelt message to Father Mush, urging the priest to pray for her soul. 'In this time she sent word to her ghostly Father, desiring him to pray earnestly for her.' Whoever passed this message on must have been someone they both trusted.

Words and Fears

With the bump in progress caused by Margaret's potential pregnancy seemingly over, the authorities returned to question her. One of Margaret's main interrogators was Edmund Bunny. Like Parson Wiggington, Bunny was a man with Calvinist leanings. He was also a prolific writer.[1] The previous Puritan-leaning Archbishop of York, Grindal, had appointed Bunny as the rector for Bolton Percy near Tadcaster, ten miles from York.

> The second day after her condemnation came Bunny, a notorious minister, Pease and Cotterill, arrogant heretics, with others, and said, "Mrs Clitherow, we are sent by the Council to confer with you touching three points, and to see if you will be any whit tractable or no. First, we must know why you refuse to be tried by the country, according to the order of law, wherein you show yourself wilful in seeking your own death contrary to God's law, and damnable to your own soul, as making yourself guilty of your own death without trial, forcing the law to proceed by order, which could not be abridged in such a case; where otherwise, upon trial, you might have been saved upon so simple evidence, yet notwithstanding," said they, "it was well known and proved that you maintained and harboured traitors, contrary to the Queen's Majesty's laws."

'To this the martyr answered, "I am a woman, and not skilful in the temporal laws. If I have offended, I ask God mercy, and I know not whether I have offended against them or no; but in my conscience I have not. As for traitors, I never kept nor harboured any in my house."'

The discussion returned to the recurring theme of the day. In Margaret's view, non-uniformity with the Church didn't turn a man or a woman into a traitor against their Queen and country. As this was the case, she may have sheltered priests, but she'd never harboured a traitor.

Then came another question, followed by Margaret's answer. 'Secondly, they asked, "Do you know yourself to be with child or no? Although," quoth the minister, "you cannot have the benefit of your condition."'

'The martyr said, "I can neither say that I am nor that I am not, having been deceived heretofore in this, and therefore I cannot directly answer you, but of the two I rather think that I am than otherwise."'

The authorities were attempting to salve their own consciences and clear their path from any blame in the future. By saying it didn't matter how she replied, as she'd be executed anyway, they hoped Margaret would admit she wasn't with child. If she did, things would go easier for them, if not for her. The answer she gave didn't help them. If Margaret really was pregnant, her execution would be illegal, and the death of her unborn child would be placed at the Council's door.

With the first questions out of the way, Bunny and the others moved on to ecclesiastical matters. 'Thirdly, they asked, "Why refuse you to come to our church, we having so plain and sure testimonies to show on our side for the truth?" And to this end they brought forth many texts of Scriptures.'

'The martyr answered, "I am not minded to your Church, God defend I should, for I have been within the Catholic faith twelve years."'

Working backwards in time, this infers Margaret converted to Catholicism a dozen years earlier, around 1574. However, as we've explored, it's possible she was attending Church of England services but had always retained a level of support for the faith she'd been born to.

At this point, one of the other ministers, Robert Pease, joined the debate. 'Pease said, "Then what is the Church? You know it not: you have been led away by blind guides, making you believe in stocks and stones, and tradition of men contrary to the word of the Lord. Answer me," quoth he, "what is the Church?"'

'The martyr said, "it is that wherein the true Word of God is preached, which Christ left to His Apostles, and to their successors ministering the Seven Sacraments, which the same Church hath always observed, the Doctors preached, and Martyrs and Confessors witnessed. This is the Church I believe to be true."'

Bunny began quoting verses of scripture at Margaret, until she interrupted him, hoping to make the men desist and leave. She reiterated her position to the trio of Protestant clergymen. 'The martyr said, "I beseech you trouble me not; I am no divine, neither can answer you to these hard questions. I am according to the Queen's Majesty's laws to die, and my spirit is very willing, although my flesh may repine."'

With this statement of how her 'flesh may repine', Father Mush gives us a first glimpse into the fear and anguish Margaret must have felt inside, although she continued her short speech to the ministers: '"I say, as I have said heretofore, my desire is to die a member of the Catholic Church. My cause is God's, and it is a great comfort for me to die in His quarrel: flesh is frail, but I trust in my Lord Jesu, that He will give me strength to bear all troubles and torments which shall be laid upon me for His sake."'

'After that, Pease railed and blasphemed a while, they departed for that day.'

Margaret had faced down three more Protestant priests. They'd questioned her and quoted scripture at her, but as always, she'd given as good as she got. What a remarkable show of fortitude, for someone so alone, in such a desperate position.

When the clerics had failed, a less official visitor returned. It appears little wonder Father Thomas Bell and the others had been able to organise their Catholic meeting in York Castle years before. The security in the city's prisons appears to have been remarkably lax.

'The third day came Wiggington, the Puritan, and, as they say, he began in this manner: "Mrs Clitherow, I pity your case [...] Cast not yourself away; lose not both body and soul. Possibly you think you shall have martyrdom, but you are foully deceived, for it cometh but one way. Not death, but the cause maketh a martyr."'

Parson Wiggington's motivation appears to have been genuine, as does his wish for Margaret to save herself. His point about Margaret being 'foully deceived' is enlightening. Did he believe someone like Father Mush had put her up to this?

The parson continued, '"In the time of Queen Mary were many put to death, and now also in this Queen's time, for two several opinions; both these cannot be martyrs. Therefore, good Mistress Clitherow, take pity on yourself. Christ Himself fled His persecutors, so did His Apostles; and why should not you then favour your own life?"'

Suggesting Margaret could take a similar action as Christ and the Apostles to save herself was a good angle to take with such a devout woman, but Margaret continued to toe the line. 'The martyr answered, "God defend I should favour my life in this point. As for my martyrdom, I am not yet assured of it, for that I am yet living; but if I persevere to the end, I verily believe I shall be saved."'

'"Are not you assured?" quoth he.'

'"No," quoth the martyr, "so long as I am living, because I know not what I may do."'

'"How think you," quoth Wiggington, "Mrs Clitherow, to be saved?"'

'The martyr answered and said, "Through Christ Jesus. His bitter passion and death."'

The discussion continued for a while, but Parson Wiggington realised he was getting nowhere. Reluctantly, he brought the meeting to an end. '"Well, Mrs Clitherow," said Wiggington, "I am sorry that I cannot persuade you," and so departed for that day.'

Although John Clitherow was forbidden from seeing his wife, the rules about other visitors appear to have become more relaxed. The clergymen continued to return, but other people also came to visit. It's likely some of these callers met up later with Father Mush and shared what they'd discovered for him to record in *A True Report*.

'Every day after there came to her either minister or some of her kinsfolks, both men and women, to desire her to consider of her husband and children; but the martyr answered them with great courage and constancy.'

Margaret had many visitors, yet one of the men most central to her story had not yet been to see her. In fact, the last time Henry Maye had gazed at his stepdaughter was when she was having her hands tied and being led away from the courtroom, having just been condemned to death in the Common Hall. What Henry had been doing since then, we don't know. The lord mayor's name didn't crop up when Father Mush described the Council of the North's lobbying of Judge Clench. Nor was it mentioned when Sheriff Fawcett was ordered to find four honest women to verify if Margaret was pregnant.

Henry Maye's stepdaughter had been condemned and sent to prison. A stay had been placed on her execution, after which time she'd been condemned again. What did her stepfather think of all this? How did he feel? At last, Henry Maye arrived to visit Margaret in her Ousebridge cell. 'Amongst whom also came the Lord Mayor, and by all means persuaded her to yield in something, and he would not doubt yet to get her pardon.'

Henry may have held out a slight hope of his stepdaughter's apostasy. Had he not learned anything about her character? Understandably, Father Mush didn't consider the lord mayor very favourably. 'He kneeling down on his knees, as they say, with great show of sorrow and affection, by all flattery allured her to do something against her conscience, but she valiantly resisted.'

From everything we know about Henry Maye, it must have taken something for him to crouch on his knees in a dirty prison cell and plead with his stepdaughter to change her mind. When this inevitably failed, Henry attempted to take something else from her. 'And when he perceived that nothing would serve, he desired her to give him her eldest daughter. She thanked him, and refused his courtesy, because that she was loathe her child should be infected with his heresy.'

Henry's failed attempt to adopt Anne Clitherow is interesting. Did he really care about the girl? Did he believe it better for Anne to be raised as a wealthy Protestant's stepdaughter rather than a persecuted Catholic? Why did Margaret refuse him? Was this for religious reasons, or was there something else in their family background which prevented her from handing her daughter over? Either way, Henry Maye left the kidcote empty-handed, without either an apostasy or a new ward.

During the following days there were further visits to Margaret's cell. On Saturday, this included the return of Minister Bunny. His visit ran much like the previous one. Nearing the end of his second failed attempt to sway Margaret's mind, he became angry. 'Bunny said: "Alas! Mrs Clitherow, I am sorry you are so wilful: I would to God you would see the danger for your soul. The Lord illuminate the eyes of your heart, that you may see how blindly you have been seduced by these Romish Jesuits and priests."'

On the Monday, Parson Wiggington returned once more to the kidcote. As always, he did his best but was sadly unable to change Margaret's mind. He left her cell, disappointed rather than angry, for a final time.[2]

Wiggington was soon followed by another preacher called Harwood. This visit began with an attempt to persuade Margaret to face the jury and confess she'd offended God and the Queen. Harwood said if she did this, 'she might possibly find mercy'. After receiving another polite refusal, the preacher lost his temper and began to 'rail and blaspheme against Jesuits and priests'.

Bunny, Wiggington and Harwood weren't Margaret's only visitors. 'Others also came to her at diverse times, and said she died desperately, and had no care on her husband and children, but would spoil them, and make all people to exclaim against her; and how mercifully the Queen's laws were, and how the Council were willing to deal with her, and show favour upon her submission.'

Of course, Margaret was never tempted, not even for a moment. Instead, Father Mush attributes the following long and touching speech to her, during which she attempted to address some of the arguments raised against her.

> The martyr said: "You charge me wrongfully. I die not desperately nor willingly procure mine own death: for not being found guilty of such crimes as were laid against me, and yet condemned to die, I could but rejoice; my cause also being God's quarrel."
>
> "Neither did I fear the terror [of the] sentence of death, but was ashamed on their behalves to have such shameful words uttered in the audience as to strip me naked, and press me to death among men, which methought for womanhood they might have concealed."
>
> "As for my husband, know you that I love him next unto God in this world, and I have care over my children as a mother ought to have; I trust I have done my duty to them to bring them up in the fear of God, and so I trust now I am discharged of them. And for this cause I am willing to offer them freely to God that sent them me, rather than I will yield one jot from my faith."

For the second time, she admitted her growing fear at what was to come. '"I confess death is fearful, and flesh is frail, yet I mind by God's assistance to spend my blood in this faith."'

Despite this, the ministers and the Council officials kept on appearing in Margaret's cell. With so many visitors, some of the councillors must have been desperate to hear Margaret's apostasy. Surely, it must have dawned on them by this time what Judge Clench had so skilfully done.

163

The responsibility for Margaret's fate and potentially that of her unborn child was in their hands.

As they had in court, when Margaret's accusers failed to gain her agreement to be tried by the jury, they turned to slander. 'When they saw that they could not persuade her, nor make her yield in anything, they brought in ridiculous slanders against her, and told her how the boy had confessed that she had sinned with priests, and that the priests and she would have delicate cheer, when she would set her husband with bread and butter and a red herring.'

Knowing her family and friends were aware she'd been accused of committing adultery with the Catholic priests must have been difficult for Margaret. The good name of her family was being dragged through the gutter.

Father Mush describes Margaret's diet during this time in prison as 'water pottage, rye bread, and small ale, which she took but once a day, and that in little quantity.' Although on this diet she must have been physically weakening, her mental resolve against the ongoing onslaught was remarkably strong. Despite being locked in a dark cell with a Puritan couple and facing repeated rants and threats from the councillors and preachers, Margaret batted back everything thrown at her.

'When she heard these words, she smiled and said: "God forgive you for these forged tales; and if the boy said so, I warrant you he will say as much more for a pound of figs."'

The visitors kept chipping away at her, believing Margaret's relationship with her husband was a weak link. 'But principally they urged her to confess she had offended her husband. The martyr said, "If I have offended my husband in anything but for my conscience, I ask God and him forgiveness." Still they urged her to confess some fault against him, thereby to slander herself.'

'The martyr said, "I trust my husband will not accuse me that I have offended him at any time, unless in such small matters as are commonly incident to man and wife; and I beseech you," said she, "let me speak with him before I die."'

Once again, Margaret's request to see her husband before her execution appears to highlight the strength of the Clitherows' relationship. What she was asking for was reasonable enough, but it would only be permitted if Margaret co-operated. 'They said she should not, unless she would yield unto something. The martyr said, "God's will be done, for I will not offend God and my conscience to speak with him."'

By this stage, Margaret probably knew she'd never see her husband again, and John probably expected the same about his wife. This was one of the final attempts made to convert Margaret to the Church and Council's will. Afterwards, the Council met with the Corporation's leaders, and a date was set for her execution.

Over in the castle, John Clitherow received a visit from the representatives of the Council of the North. He was told he would be released, but only on condition he left the city for a number of days. If he was found within York's walls during this time, he'd be arrested.

As he left the prison, John must have known what was planned. The Council had lured him to the King's Manor to arrest Margaret. Now they were sending him away. It could only mean one thing. As he left the city, he passed word on of what was to happen. 'Her husband was set at liberty, and commanded by the Council to depart the city for five days, whereby the martyr and all others first gathered that they intended indeed to suck her blood.'

Official confirmation of what was planned soon reached Ousebridge. The Corporation Sheriffs Fawcett and Gibson visited Margaret in her cell. 'Two days before her martyrdom, the Sheriffs of York came to her and told her what day was appointed for her death.'

If Margaret ever doubted this might happen, she now knew that in two days she'd be crushed to death. Unsurprisingly, the knowledge affected her deeply. 'After the Sheriffs were departed, the martyr said to a friend of hers, "The Sheriffs have told me that I shall die on Friday next; and now I feel the frailty of mine own flesh, which trembleth at this news."'

Margaret was human after all. Shaking with fear, but also determined, she mentally prepared herself for the trials ahead. '"My spirit greatly rejoiceth. Therefore for God's sake pray for me, and desire all good folks to do the same." And she kneeling down praying a little, the fear and horror of death presently departed.'

In addition to her mental and spiritual preparations, Margaret made some other arrangements. She requested the hat she'd worn when entering the courtroom on the first day of her trial be passed on to her husband, 'in sign of her loving duty to him, as to her head', and requested her hose and shoes be saved and passed to her daughter, Anne, 'signifying that she should serve God and follow her steps of virtue'.

There wasn't much else Margaret could do. She spent the final hours of her life praying and fasting. From the moment she received the awful news from the sheriffs, 'She took no food at all.'

Father Mush completes the lengthy chapter covering her final days of imprisonment by describing her thoughts and feelings immediately prior to her execution. 'Her mind was always on her end, craving all good prayers for perseverance and for ghostly strength to overcome all combats, and joyfully to depart from this world to the glory of God and advancement of the Catholic Church.'

Execution

Late into the evening of Thursday, 24 March 1586, Margaret Clitherow prepared herself for death. She'd taken no food or liquid for the best part of two days. The steady stream of visitors to her cell, the ministers, the councillors, her stepfather, had dried up. Margaret was alone, apart from her two Puritan cellmates, Mr and Mrs Yoward. Any hope the authorities may have had that their presence would make a difference had long since passed.

Indeed, Mrs Yoward had become Margaret's loyal friend. We assume she later shared some of the details of their final hours together with Father Mush. By this stage Margaret was finding it difficult to conceal the depth of her fear and loneliness. 'She said to Yoward's wife, "I would gladly have one of the maids to bear me company this night, not for any fear of death, for it is my comfort, but the flesh is frail."'

'The woman said, "Alas! Mrs Clitherow, the gaoler is gone, the door is locked, and none can be had."'

Despite their religious differences, the two women had by this time developed a close relationship. 'Then the said Yoward's wife, being ready to go to bed, clasped again her clothes, and sitting beside the martyr almost till midnight, after went to bed.'

Over the past few days, Mrs Yoward had watched Margaret sew together a simple white shawl or smock. She hoped the sheriffs would allow her to wear this the next morning, to prevent the men who would be at her execution from seeing her naked.

Father Mush describes Mrs Yoward's observations of Margaret's last night in the cell:

> At twelve of the clock she saw the martyr rise from her knees, and put off all her apparel, putting on a linen habit, like to an albino, which she had made with her own hands three days before to suffer martyrdom in. Then she kneeled down again, without anything upon her saving that linen cloth, from twelve of the clock until three, at which time she arose and came to the fireside. There she laid her down flat upon the stones one quarter of an hour. After that she arose and went to her bed, covering herself with clothes, and so continued until six in the morning. Then she arose and put on her apparel, and made herself ready against the Sheriffs' coming.

In addition to wearing the shawl, Margaret wanted to die in the company of her friends and people of a similar faith. 'She desired Yoward's wife to see her die, and wished her that some good Catholics were by, in her last agony and pangs of death, to put her in remembrance of God.'

'Yoward's wife said she would not see her die so cruel a death for all York; but quoth she, "I will procure some friends to lay weight on you that you may be quickly despatched from your pain."'

The kind offer to minimise Margaret's pain by accelerating her death was rejected. 'The martyr said, "No, good Mrs Yoward, not so. God defend that I should procure any to be guilty of my death and blood."' In the same way she'd acted to protect the consciences of the jury, Margaret had no wish to place any burden from her death onto anyone other than the judges who'd condemned her.

Margaret denied herself the opportunity of a final meal. As she waited for what would happen next, a sizeable crowd built up outside. People lined the roads on both sides of the bridge. In addition to the material and a needle to make the simple shawl, Margaret had asked her friends to bring a length of inkle (linen tape or cord). She readied this now, along with a purse of coins to give alms to the poor.

'About eight of the clock the Sheriffs came to her, and she being ready expecting them, having trimmed up her head with new inkle and carrying on her arm the new habit of linen with inkle strings, which she had prepared to bind her hands, went cheerfully to her marriage, as she called it; dealing her alms in the street, which was so full of people that she could scarce pass by them. She went barefoot and barelegged, her gown loose about her.'

With the crowd around them, the task to execute this potentially pregnant woman couldn't have been easy. The sheriffs and their men were nervous. Sheriff Fawcett wanted to get the deed over as quickly as possible. 'Fawcett, the Sheriff, made haste and said, "Come away, Mrs Clitherow."'

'The martyr answered merrily, "Good Master Sheriff, let me deal my poor alms before I now go, for my time is but short." They marvelled all to see her joyful countenance.'

Despite the trepidation and fear she'd felt overnight in her cell, Margaret smiled at the crowd. As she handed out coins to them, she was unaware there'd been a final missed opportunity to prevent her death. The city's sergeants, the men tasked with laying the weights on her body, had refused to go through with their orders.

Unfortunately, the sheriffs had found an alternative solution, as Father Mush outlines: 'The place of execution was the tollbooth, six or seven yards distant from the prison. There were present at her martyrdom the two Sheriffs of York, Fawcett and Gibson, Frost, a minister, Fox, Mr Cheke's kinsman, with another of his men, the four sergeants, which had hired certain beggars to do the murder, three or four men, and four women.'

The group entered the tollbooth. Which of the occupants reported to Father Mush the details of what happened next, we can't know for certain. Perhaps it was one of the unfortunate beggars.

'The martyr coming to the place, kneeled her down, and prayed to herself. The tormentors bade her pray with them, and they would pray with her. The martyr denied, and said, "I will not pray with you, and you shall not pray with me; neither will I say Amen to your prayers, nor shall you to mine."'

'Then they willed her to pray for the Queen's majesty. The martyr began in this order. First, in the hearing of them all, she prayed for the Catholic Church, then for the Pope's Holiness, Cardinals, and other Fathers which have charge of souls, and then for all Christian princes.'

'At which words the tormentors interrupted her, and willed her not to put her majesty among that company; yet the martyr proceeded in this order, "and especially for Elizabeth, Queen of England, that God turn her to the Catholic faith, and that after this mortal life she may receive the blessed joys of heaven. For I wish as much good," quoth she, "to her majesty's soul as to mine own."'

At this point, despite his previous money-lending misdemeanours, junior Sheriff Gibson could take no more. 'Sheriff Gibson, abhorring the cruel fact, stood weeping at the door.'

The man who'd been elected above him as senior sheriff of York wasn't so easily deterred. 'Then said Fawcett, "Mrs Clitherow, you must remember and confess that you die for treason."'

Additional commentary of what happened next is not really needed. I'll let Father Mush describe the events in his own words:

> The martyr answered, "No, no, Mr Sheriff, I die for the love of my Lord Jesu," which last words she spake with a loud voice.
>
> Then Fawcett commanded her to put off her apparel; "For you must die," said he, "naked, as judgment was given and pronounced against you."
>
> The martyr with the other women requested him on their knees that she might die in her smock, and that for the honour of womanhood they would not see her naked; but that would not be granted. Then she requested that women might un-apparel her, and that they would turn their faces from her for that time.
>
> The women took off her clothes, and put upon her the long habit of linen. Then very quietly she laid her down upon the ground, her face covered with a handkerchief, the linen habit being placed over her as far as it would reach, all the rest of her body being naked. The door was laid upon her, her hands she joined towards her face.
>
> Then the Sheriff said, "Nay, you must have your hands bound." The martyr put forth her hands over the door still joined. Then two sergeants parted them, and with the inkle strings, which she had prepared for that purpose bound them to two posts, so that her body and her arms made a perfect cross. They willed her again to ask the Queen's Majesty's forgiveness, and to pray for her.
>
> The martyr said she had prayed for her. They also willed her to ask her husband's forgiveness.
>
> The martyr said, "If ever I have offended him, but for my conscience, I ask him forgiveness."

I'll intervene at this stage. If you are of a nervous disposition, you may wish to skip past the next two paragraphs, as they describe Margaret's death.

'After this they laid weight upon her, which when she first felt, she said, "Jesu! Jesu! Jesu! have mercy upon me!" which were the last words she was heard to speak.'

'She was in dying one quarter of an hour. A sharp stone, as much as a man's fist, put under her back; upon her was laid to the quantity of seven or eight hundredweight at the least, which, breaking her ribs, caused them to burst forth of the skin.'

Some time between eight and nine o'clock on the morning of 25 March 1586, Margaret Clitherow died. Having so graphically described her death, Father Mush moved to happier thoughts, as he described his belief that Margaret's soul had passed over to a better place. 'Thus most victoriously this gracious martyr overcame all her enemies, passing [from] this mortal life with marvellous triumph into the peaceable city of God, there to receive a worthy crown of endless immortality and joy.'

Margaret's crushed body was kept in the press until three in the afternoon. After removing it, the Corporation's officials took the corpse away for burial in a secret location to avoid Catholics from holding a vigil and praying there, or removing her corpse, locks of hair, or other body parts to use as relics.

Chapter Twelve

Post-mortem (1586 and Beyond)

Margaret's Story – Impact on her Family

The closing section of the book reviews the aftermath of Margaret Clitherow's execution by examining what happened next to her family and friends, and by exploring events in York and at a national level.

Father Mush reports that Margaret's body remained in the press in the tollbooth until three in the afternoon. Afterwards, her crushed corpse was taken away and secretly buried in an unmarked grave. Having lost one of their leading players, York's underground Catholic community began a quest to discover Margaret's resting place.

In his book *The Troubles of the Catholic Forefathers Related by Themselves*, the nineteenth-century Jesuit priest John Morris transcribes a number works from earlier Catholic writers. The contents include Father Mush's *A True Report* and works attributed to Father Christopher Grene, a seventeenth-century Catholic priest. Grene details what happened to Margaret's body after its removal from the tollbooth.[1] 'Mrs Clitherow's body was buried beside a dunghill in the town, where it lay full six weeks without putrefaction.'

Grene also describes what happened when the body was finally retrieved. 'It was secretly taken up by Catholics and carried on horseback a long journey, to a place where it rested six days [...] and after was laid up as a worthy treasure until God redeem us out of the servitude and tyranny of these furious blood-suckers.'

There's no lasting record of where Margaret was subsequently buried. The people who'd dug her second grave were as wary of its discovery as those who'd created her first. Some claim her remains were eventually interred beneath Stydd Chapel in the Ribble Valley in Lancashire. In those days, travelling by horseback from York to Stydd would have represented a 'long journey'. Whether this specific claim is true, we don't know.

A second theory states Margaret's body is buried in the chapel at Hazlewood Castle between York and Leeds. An attendee at one of my local history talks once told me this was common knowledge in the area when she was growing up. Although not a 'long journey' from York, in the sixteenth century Hazlewood Castle was owned by the wealthy Vavasour family. No definitive relationship has been identified between the Vavasours of Hazlewood Castle and Thomas and Dorothy Vavasour of York, but they were all Catholics and there could be a connection.[2]

Another fascinating aspect of Margaret's burial, particularly for anyone planning to visit York, is what may have happened to one of her hands. In addition to seeing the shrine of St Margaret Clitherow in the Shambles (probably on the opposite side of the street from her own house), I'd recommend attending the Bar Convent on Blossom Street. Established a century after Margaret's death in 1686, the convent's exhibits include a relic which is said to be one of Margaret's hands.

Following her brutal execution, Father Mush reports that the authorities sought to justify themselves. 'Next day the heretics railed against her out of their pulpits with most shameful lies and slanders. The Lord Mayor, called Mr Maye, to show his gentle mind to the martyr's mother, which had taken him from the beggar's staff, made this his honourable table talk among his heretical brethren, that she died desperately, and that she had been an unhonest woman, with many such like and false heretical slanders.'

Whatever his previous motives may have been, Henry Maye sought to ensure all blame for his stepdaughter's death was placed at her door. The lord mayor put forward the case that Margaret had gone to the court seeking her own suicide, having disgraced herself and her family through the sexual relationships she'd had with the priests she kept in her house.

Father Mush includes a lengthy diatribe against the lord mayor and his colleagues in the Corporation and Council.

> But what shall I need to speak against the vicious murderers in defence of this chaste martyr whose honesty and other virtues are well known to her neighbours, as well heretics as others, who can witness that as she was not once suspected of any dishonest behaviour in all her life, so it will be

impossible after so glorious a death for heretics to persuade any but such as wallow in the same abominable puddle of uncleanness with them that their slanders be true. For who seeth not this, that these are the ordinary fruits of their heretical humour, then chiefly to heap up most untrue and detestable slanders, without all proof or likelihood, when they would contrive or have committed some shameful fact, thinking thereby to cover their horrible practices and barbarous cruelty.

At this point in his own book, Father Morris makes a decision not to write everything included in the previous transcriptions of Father Mush's work. Instead, he includes a footnote stating, 'Six pages of declamation to the same effect are here omitted.'

Towards the end of *A True Report*, Father Mush makes a lengthy and stout defence of Margaret's actions, as well as defending himself and the other priests, to address the 'shameful lies and slanders' made by the authorities. Most of all, he contrasts the accusers' actions with Margaret's innate goodness.

Behold how God hath wrought by His servant all things to her immortal honour, and your endless confusion and shame. She, a woman, with invincible courage, entered combat against you all, to defend that most ancient faith, wherein she and you were baptized, and gave your promise to God to keep the same to death; where you, men, cowardish in the quarrel, and faithless in your promise, laboured all at once against her, to make her partaker of your turpitude and dishonesty.

She in everything simple and innocent, you in everything deceitful and mischievous; she patient and joyful, you furious and fretting; she victorious, you conquered; she exalted, and you confounded.

Father Mush derides both the Council and the judges, arguing that Margaret's martyrdom had exposed their laws as being badly flawed. 'Where is now the force of your tyranny and impious law? Hath she not weakened both them and your statute?'

The priest also questioned the new law for harbouring priests and the court's right to use the punishment of *peine forte et dure* in Margaret's case. He closes his work with a personal message to Margaret, herself:

> But now, O sacred martyr, letting go thy enemies, I turn to thee. Remember me, I beseech thy perfect charity, whom thou hast left miserable behind thee, in times past thine unworthy Father, and now thy most unworthy servant, made ever joyful by thy virtuous life, and comfortable by lamenting thy death, lamenting thy absence, and yet rejoicing in thy glory [...]
>
> Be not wanting, therefore, my glorious mother, in the perfection of thy charity, which was not little towards me in thy mortality, to obtain mercy and procure the plenties of such graces for me, thy miserable son, as thou knowest to be most needful for me, and acceptable in the sight of our Lord, which hath thus glorified thee; that I may honour Him by imitation of thy happy life, and by any death, which He will give me, to be partaker with thee and all holy saints of His kingdom, to whom be all glory and honour, now and for ever. Amen.

Before he'd finished writing these final words, what did Father Mush do? In addition to taking part in the search for Margaret's body, the priest made the decision to create a lasting record of what happened to her. Whether he did this to ensure her sacrifice wouldn't be forgotten, or to gain maximum political capital from her martyrdom for the Catholic Church, we can only speculate.

Where did he source the information to write such a detailed account? In terms of the aspects he covered about Margaret's earlier life, and her state of mind and behaviour in the months leading to her arrest, we must assume he learned these directly from Margaret herself.

After Margaret's arrest, things became more difficult. The pair didn't meet or speak again. The priest must have received various details second or third hand. Many of the potential witnesses were serving time in York's prisons, including Margaret's cellmates Anne Tesh and Mrs Yoward.

There had, of course, been many other prisoners and visitors to York Castle and the kidcote on Ousebridge during Margaret's time there.

In terms of her court case, it appears inconceivable that Father Mush could have smuggled himself inside the Common Hall. The priest must have received reports on the court's proceedings from one or more people who'd found their way into the public gallery.

Lastly, there was the execution itself. Neither of the sheriffs (not even Gibson who'd been upset), nor the sergeants, minister or Council officials would have been likely to have any contact with the priest. If he didn't invent the scene, it appears Father Mush may have later interviewed one or more of the beggars who'd been forced to place the weights onto Margaret's supine body. Some of them may have been Catholics and approached the priest for confession and absolution.

Father Mush continued to gather witness statements and reports as he compiled the first edition of *A True Report* during the following weeks. After this, he remained in York for several months as it lay at the centre of his 'northern circuit'. We'll return to examine what happened to Father Mush and Father Ingleby in the following section.

As previously outlined, John Clitherow was released from prison prior to Margaret's execution. Following his wife's death, he returned to York to pick up the pieces of his shattered life and business. One of his first tasks was to replace the items which had been looted by the pursuivants who'd raided his house. A widower twice over, he couldn't replace Margaret directly, but he did marry again. This time, the butcher sought to ensure his third wife remained a Protestant.

He also appears to have somehow rebuilt his relationship with his father-in-law. John Clitherow must have been a forgiving man, or perhaps he didn't believe Henry Maye was capable of plotting Margaret's downfall. Either way, when Alderman Maye died a decade later he bequeathed John the gold signet ring he wore on his little finger.

No records remain of what happened regarding the ownership of Thomas Middleton's property on Davygate. We don't know if the buildings ever passed from Margaret to her offspring. Perhaps a deal was done; perhaps not. Henry Maye appears to have suffered financial difficulty following Margaret's death. Although he was an alderman until the day he died in 1596, he was called before the city's courts in 1591 on charges relating to unpaid bills and debts.

Young Henry Clitherow never returned to York. He studied at the English college in Rheims and later at the English college in Rome, before spending some time with the Capuchin and Dominican orders. The date of Henry's death isn't recorded, but it's understood he may have suffered from mental problems, or perhaps changed his mind about the religious path his mother had chosen for him. Despite the primitive communications of the time, it's likely Henry was aware of Margaret's death.

Following their mother's arrest, Henry's younger sister, Anne, suffered very badly. Father Mush states, 'The little girl was at the first committed to ward because she would not betray her mother, and there extremely used for that she would not go to the church; but when her mother was martyred, the heretics came up to her and said, that unless she would go to the church and hear a sermon, her mother should be put to death. The child, thereby thinking to save her mother's life, went to a sermon, and thus they deceived her.'

To discover that she'd been lied to in such a vile way, and her mother had been so brutally and painfully executed, must have been an awful thing for a young girl. In 1589 Anne ran away from York. She was eventually arrested and imprisoned in Lancaster for 'causes ecclesiastical'. In 1593 her father discovered her whereabouts and set about persuading the then lord mayor of York, Robert Askwith, to write a letter on his behalf to the Earl of Derby, requesting Anne's release.

Extracts from the letter are quite revealing:

He [John Clitherow] hath had three wives, by the second of which he hath a daughter born within this city Anne Clitherow […] The which daughter, as he informeth me, did about four years ago depart from him without his consent or knowledge, and at this present is in Lancaster gaol by your honour's commandment for causes ecclesiastical. His humble suit unto your honourable lordship is, that it would please the same to grant that he may have his said daughter delivered unto him upon his bond to bring her to this city with him to remain here to be conferred withal by some learned and godly preachers for such reasonable time as to your honour shall seem convenient, and if within the same time she cannot be conformed, then to make her appearance before her Majesty's Commissioners for causes ecclesiastical in these parts.

John had suffered sorely for his second wife's non-conformance, but he'd continued to support her. It appears he would do the same to ensure the safety of their daughter, even though she'd defied him and run away from home. The butcher put his new wife and business aside and travelled across the country to Lancaster to negotiate Anne's release. He was also prepared to pay a bond to vouch for her good behaviour.

John Clitherow wasn't a lord or a king. We don't know that much about him really, but I think the letter says a lot. Some parents might not think so. Surely we'd all travel across the Pennines to help one of our children, but we should consider the times John lived in, and the events that had occurred around him. His second wife had been ostracised and executed as an enemy of the State. His daughter appeared to be going the same way. To support Anne wouldn't have done John any favours, but neither had being a loving and dependable husband to Margaret, despite the problems and scandal she'd brought to their house.

Although John may have managed to get Anne back to York, she didn't stay long. This was a city with bad memories, the place where her mother had been humiliated and executed, and where the Protestants had lied to her to get her to their church.

Even if John hadn't enforced his promise that Anne would listen to 'learned and godly preachers', it's no surprise she ran away from home again. This time she wasn't caught, arrested or brought back. Like her brother, Henry, Anne Clitherow left England and travelled to Europe. Most probably, she secured a passage on a ship from Hull. Once on the Continent, Anne travelled to Louvain (now in modern-day Belgium), where she entered a convent and became a nun. She remained in Louvain, serving God and the Catholic Church, until her death in 1622. Her mother would have been pleased.

Margaret's stepsons, William and Thomas, from John's first marriage, eventually became recusants themselves. It appears their stepmother still had some influence on the family. What poor John Clitherow thought of all this, having lost his second wife, one of his younger sons and latterly his daughter to the Catholic Church, we can only imagine.

Following her death, Margaret Clitherow became known as the 'Pearl of York'. The detailed records of her life, faith and martyrdom in *A True Report* provide a fascinating, if somewhat gruesome, insight into the religious struggles of the time. In more recent years, Margaret's life and martyrdom have been widely recognised and celebrated by the Catholic

Church. She was beatified by Pope Pius XI in 1929 and canonised as Saint Margaret Clitherow by Pope Paul VI in 1970, becoming one of the 'Forty Martyrs of England and Wales'.

York – The Struggle Continues

Despite the shock of Margaret's execution to some of York's population, the authorities continued to pursue the missionary Catholic priests who visited the city and the lay people who were brave or foolish enough to aid them. Rather than describe every case, we shall examine a sample with connections to the Clitherow family.

After Margaret was arrested for harbouring a pair of priests, the Council of the North determined to track the men down. The first suspect, Francis Ingleby, was described by another priest, Father Warford, as being, 'most highly esteemed by all Catholics on account of his great zeal for souls, and especially for his remarkable prudence.'[3]

Operating undercover in a city in a country with laws written specifically to hunt down men like himself, Father Ingleby's 'remarkable prudence' could only get him so far. Luck and good fortune would also be needed. Shortly after Margaret Clitherow's execution, the priest's luck ran out.

Father Warford describes Father Ingleby's arrest:

> On a certain day he left York on foot and in the dress of a poor man without a cloak, and was courteously accompanied beyond the gates by a certain Catholic of that city. The gentleman, though intending to return at once, stayed for a few moments' conversation with the priest on an open spot, which, unknown to the priest, was overlooked by the windows of the Bishop's Palace.
>
> It happened that two chaplains of the pseudo-bishop, idly talking there, espied them, and noticed that the Catholic as he was taking leave, frequently uncovered to Ingleby, and showed him, while saying good-bye, greater marks of respect than were fitting towards a common person meanly dressed. They ran therefore and made inquiries, and finding he was a priest they apprehended him.

Once again, this sounds like the scene from *The Great Escape*, in which the escaped prisoners of war, played by Richard Attenborough and Gordon Jackson, climb onto a bus wearing civilian clothes. When a Gestapo officer says, 'Good luck!' to them, Gordon Jackson's character can't help but reply, 'Thank you,' in English, and the two men are arrested. I find it hard not to imagine the archbishop's chaplains uttering something similar to Father Ingleby in Latin and waiting eagerly for his reply.

In *A Yorkshire Recusant's Relation*, Father Grene, perhaps transcribing Father Mush, describes what happened next. 'Sir Thomas Fairfax, vice-president, Henry Cheke, Ralph Hurlestone and the rest, arraigned Mr Francis Ingleby, condemned and murdered him as a traitor, because he was a priest of Rheims.'

It wasn't just Father Ingleby they were looking for. Through a combination of torture and trickery, the authorities attempted to get the priest to inform on his colleagues and the lay people who'd been helping him. 'With him they used much guileful dealing, that they might entangle him with an oath to disclose in what Catholic men's houses he had been harboured, but they could not deceive him.'

To his immense credit, Father Ingleby remained silent. He didn't give up the whereabouts of the other priests, or the identity of the lay Catholics who'd sheltered them since Margaret's arrest. After what had happened to Mrs Clitherow and Marmaduke Bowes, these people must have been very brave and committed. On 3 June 1586, still retaining his silence on the matter, Father Ingleby was taken to the Knavesmire, where he was executed by hanging, drawing and quartering.

One of the men involved in the trials of Marmaduke Bowes, Margaret Clitherow and Francis Ingleby was Henry Cheke. A few weeks after Father Ingleby's execution, on 23 June 1586, Cheke died in mysterious circumstances. He was reported to have made disparaging remarks about the recently executed priest. A few hours later he was found dead at the bottom of a stairwell in the King's Manor, with his neck broken.[4] He was buried in York Minster.

Around this time, Father Mush remained at large in the city, working on *A True Report*. Ingleby's arrest and execution must have been a bitter blow for him. Each day he must have worried and suspected his turn would be next. In October 1586 his fears proved to be well-founded.

Volume one of the second series of the *Lives of the English Martyrs* (published in 1914) covers the period between 1583 and 1588. The contents include a chapter about a layman, Richard Langley, who most likely harboured Father Ingleby. He certainly provided shelter for Father Mush and a number of other priests.

'Richard Langley, a man of great soul and remarkable piety, spent all his estate in succouring priests. He built a very well hidden house underground, which was a great place of refuge for priests during the persecution.'

Acting on a tip-off, the Council of the North uncovered Langley's operation. 'The Earl of Huntingdon, then Lord President of the North, a ruthless persecutor, often referred to simply as "the tyrant", sent a band of justices and ministers to search the houses on 27 October 1586 [...] These were accompanied by a large band of soldiers.'

The raid was remarkably successful. Henry Hastings, the Earl of Huntingdon, must have been delighted. He'd not only closed down one of the best hiding places for priests in York and the whole of the north, but he'd also arrested the key man he was looking for, the priest who controlled the missionaries' movements around Yorkshire, Father John Mush.

'Mr Langley was taken together with two priests, John Mush, the biographer of Margaret Clitherow, and Mr Johnson. All three were carried before the Lord President at York, who railed at them in his furious and heretical arrogance awhile and then committed them to York Castle.'

Richard Langley was questioned harshly and placed on trial. 'He said that he would never repent that he had harboured priests, and that they were the messengers of God, but rather was sorry that he had not harboured more and oftener than he had done; also that he thanked God that he might die for so good a cause.'

Despite making a response that Margaret Clitherow would have been proud of, the Council offered Langley a deal. If he apostatized and informed on others who aided priests, his life would be spared. Like so many of the renegade Catholics, Richard Langley was a brave man. He rejected the offer.

As a result, the composition of his jury was altered to ensure the verdict would go against him. 'He would not make suit to the tyrant nor the Privy Council for his life in this cause, which sentence grieved the tyrant and his complices exceedingly, insomuch that they altered the jury, which was first impaneled of his honest neighbours, fearing these would deal favourably and justly, and instead of them appointed such as they knew would work their desire to murder him, as they did.'

During a series of hearings, Father Mush and Father Johnson were also found guilty. Along with Langley, they were given the death sentence. 'He [Richard Langley] was condemned to death with the two priests.'

When the Council was ready, they planned to transport the trio to the Knavesmire to execute them. Langley and the priests were placed into separate cells. With nothing to lose, Father Mush and two of his colleagues made an audacious attempt to break free. We don't know if they dug their way out, went over a wall or bribed the warders, but somehow, they managed to get away: 'that very night, they being confined in another part of the prison, were enabled to make their escape with a third priest.'

After the priests made their daring escape, the Earl of Huntingdon was furious. Although he'd promised the layman Langley wouldn't be executed before the Lent assizes in the spring, he went back on his word. Richard Langley was hanged in York on 1 December 1586.

Father Mush lived on. He completed and published *A True Report* and several other works. Later, he became a controversial figure in the English Catholic community. At one stage he travelled to Rome and spoke to the Pope about the leadership and state of the Catholic Church in England following William Allen's death, during the so-called 'Archpriest Controversy'. We'll return to this topic shortly.

Father Mush continued operating undercover as a Catholic priest in England until he died from natural causes in around 1612 in Buckinghamshire. At this stage, he was acting as a chaplain for Lady Dormer, a woman with family connections to the Gunpowder Plot.

Henry Maye served the full term as lord mayor of York. A few months after Margaret's execution, Henry Hastings, the Earl Huntingdon, was formally renewed as Lord President of the Council of the North. During a grand ceremony, Henry Maye presented Hastings with a ceremonial sword on behalf of the city.

Crucially, he passed the weapon to Hastings with its blade facing downwards. This action broke with a tradition created as far back as 1396 as part of York's royal charter. The sword was only to be lowered for the King or Queen of the day, or their direct heirs. With Hastings being a distant cousin of the Queen, Henry may have considered him to be a legitimate heir to the throne, or perhaps he was showing undue deference. Maybe he simply didn't know the rules!

In February 1587 Henry Maye handed over his title of lord mayor to his successor, Ralph Richardson, one of the men he'd competed with for the appointment a year earlier. Perhaps if Richardson had won Margaret Clitherow may still have been alive.

Henry's second wife, Anne Maye (née Thompson), gave birth to several sons. When Henry died in July 1596 he was 'buried under a white stone' in the nave of the Church of St Martin's in Coney Street. His widow was still a relatively young woman. Like her husband before her, she remarried quickly. Whether through treachery, irony or poetic justice, her second husband was a Catholic.

It was now Henry's turn to turn in his grave. In 1598, two years after their marriage, Anne's new husband, Gabriel Thwaites, was listed as a recusant in the St Martin's, Coney Street, parish. This was the same church where Thomas Middleton and Henry Maye had been churchwardens and were buried beneath.

Thwaites must have also made an impact on his stepsons. It wasn't long before Edward Maye and Henry Maye junior were both being cited for failing to partake in communion and for non-attendance of church. In 1615 Henry was accused, along with his stepfather, of recusancy. The recusant community in York had been impacted by Margaret's execution and other events, but it hadn't gone away.

Margaret's friend, the midwife Dorothy Vavasour, remained in prison on Ousebridge throughout 1586, sharing her cell with several fellow recusants. Unfortunately, she never left the place. Father John Morris's book *The Troubles of Our Catholic Forefathers Related by Themselves* contains a section entitled 'Notes by a Prisoner in Ousebridge Kidcote'. A short paragraph describes Dorothy's fate. 'Mrs Vavasour, Mary Hutton and Alice Oldcorne [...] being shut down on a cold winter night without their bedding into a low, filthy prison, where they took their death with cold, and coming up sick, they all died within three days.'

In October 1587 Dorothy Vavasour and two other women were placed in a dank, low-lying cell adjacent to the river. This was their punishment for refusing to confess what they knew about the removal of several heads of executed Catholic priests. The heads had been placed on display in the city but had recently vanished. As key members of the city's Catholic community, it was assumed the women knew the names of the culprits.

Unfortunately, the damp conditions of the temporary cell brought about a sudden illness, resulting in the deaths of all three women. It must have been an embarrassment for the gaolers, although there are no reports that anyone was punished.

Margaret's other friend, Anne Tesh, had been arrested on the testimony of the half-Flemish boy who'd led the sheriffs to the hidden room in Margaret's house. Under duress, the lad had claimed Anne had celebrated Mass in the secret chamber. Anne was brought before the assizes court in York when it next returned to the city in August 1586.

In 'A Yorkshire Recusant's Relation' (transcribed by Father Morris in *The Troubles of Our Catholic Forefathers*), Father Grene provides details of Anne's case. 'The Flemish boy accused her [...] to have heard Mass in Mrs Clitherow's house [...] At this arraignment Hurlestone, Rhodes and the rest railed shamefully against her with many dishonest speeches, charged her that she had harboured priests, and openly said to the jury, "Find her guilty"; which yet they did not for harbouring any priest, but upon the boy's words [...] they condemned her a hundred marks for hearing Mass.'

Surprisingly then, given the pressure placed upon them, the jury held firm. They adjudged Anne Tesh to be not guilty of the capital charge of aiding a priest. Their verdict is an interesting one. Perhaps not all juries in York could be swayed by the Council. Should Margaret Clitherow have placed her trust in the 'country' and made a plea of not guilty?

Of course, the evidence against Margaret was much stronger than in Anne Tesh's case. We may not like these laws, and certainly the vast majority of us will disagree with the punishment, but, on balance, Margaret Clitherow was guilty of harbouring priests, whereas it's possible that Anne Tesh wasn't.

However, the jury found Mrs Tesh guilty of the lesser charge of celebrating Mass in Margaret's house. She was fined according to the law. Father Grene reports the furious reaction of the judges at the main not guilty verdict. 'And the bench said, "If we live to the next assizes, we will have thee found guilty of harbouring priests."'

A footnote written by Father Morris beneath the text describes what happened to Anne Tesh a dozen years later. It appears the Council of the North were willing to wait for their revenge, even if took more than a decade. A Protestant minister imprisoned in York Castle had pretended to be interested in being converted to the Catholic faith. The man had encouraged a group of Catholic prisoners, including Mrs Tesh, to have lengthy discussions to persuade him around to their point of view. Once these talks were complete, he contacted his superiors in the Church and the prisoners were accused of attempting to convert him, a treasonous offence.

At the ensuing trial, all six prisoners were found guilty. 'In 1598, Mrs Anne Tesh and Mrs Bridget Maskew were condemned to be burnt alive – the punishment of high treason in the case of a woman.'

The two women must have waited in their cells filled with fear and anguish, just as Margaret Clitherow had. What awaited them was perhaps an even more horrific death than the one Margaret had suffered. Thankfully, for some reason, the authorities had a change of heart. 'They were reprieved and remained in York Castle, as long as Queen Elizabeth lived.'

Why were Anne Tesh and Bridget Maskew allowed to survive? It's likely the authorities feared creating two additional female martyrs. It's also possible Queen Elizabeth had made it clear the disgust she had felt following Margaret's death. There are reports that the Queen wrote a letter to the people of York stating Margaret shouldn't have been executed, due to her gender.

Unfortunately, the two women's reprieve didn't extend as far as the men who'd been charged alongside them. Three Catholic laymen, George Errington, William Knight and William Gibson, were all condemned and executed by hanging, drawing and quartering. This took place in York in November 1596. A stay was placed on the execution of the fourth man, Henry Abbot, although his luck didn't hold out for long. He was executed in York in July 1597.

Back in 1586, Margaret Clitherow, Francis Ingleby and Robert Langley weren't the only Catholics executed in York. Robert Bickerdike was a layman from near Knaresborough. He was arrested in 1585 and brought to the court in the Common Hall following reports he'd been seen drinking with a priest. It was claimed Bickerdike had bought the priest a drink. Evidence enough, the judges argued, to find him guilty and condemn him.

Thankfully, the jury disagreed. Robert Bickerdike was acquitted due to the lack of evidence against him. This was perhaps another sign the Council didn't always get their way. To some degree, English justice was working, although to many of us the laws will appear to be extremely flawed.

A year later, in June 1586, Bickerdike was back in York on the day of Francis Ingleby's execution. When a witness claimed he overheard the man speak out in support of the priest, Bickerdike was immediately arrested. It appears that someone in the Council had been keeping an eye on him. After this, he was retried for treason and, much to the relief of Judge Rhodes, Robert Bickerdike was found guilty and executed.

John Finglow was another missionary priest. Ordained in Rheims, he'd spent four or five years in England before being discovered by the authorities and arrested. He was placed inside the Church's own St Peter's prison next to York Minster. We know he was executed in 1586 in York, but few details are available about his case.

And so it went on: the clampdowns on recusants in York, the arrests and the executions continued. The number of recusants ebbed and flowed. Sometimes new names appeared on the list; for example, Henry Maye's sons. It's impossible to say how many others in the city retained a more discreet level of Catholicism as Church Catholics, hoping one day for a change of monarch and state religion.

Despite the ongoing religious battles in the city, York continued to recover economically throughout Elizabeth's reign. Perhaps it was this relative prosperity and the lack of any deadly epidemic which allowed some of the city's people and the northern authorities to expend so much of their time and energy on preserving or persecuting Catholicism.

There's an additional factor worth mentioning which links together events in York with those at a national level. Like Margaret Clitherow, Guy Fawkes was born and raised in the city. In his youth, he converted to Catholicism, and was almost sixteen years old at the time of Margaret's execution. Was the brutal slaying of the Pearl of York the incendiary event that radicalised the young man and transformed him into a future terrorist, willing to sacrifice his life for the Catholic cause in the Gunpowder Plot?[5]

Elizabeth I, James I and Beyond

In 1586, two decades before Guy Fawkes joined Robert Catesby and the other conspirators in the Gunpowder Treason, a dozen Catholics were executed for their role in the Babington Plot. The scheme had proved to be equally disastrous for Mary Stuart. Having been placed on trial, Mary was found guilty of conspiring to assassinate her cousin Queen Elizabeth.

Despite Elizabeth's reluctance to sign Mary's death warrant, eventually she did put quill to paper. Even if, as some believe, the Queen's intention was to delay a final decision, a chain of actions was set in motion. On 8 February 1587, Mary was beheaded.

However, not everyone implicated in the Babington Plot was apprehended. The escapees included one David Ingleby, brother of the executed priest, Francis. Known as 'the fox', David eventually managed to escape to Spanish-held territory in the Low Countries, where he lived in exile until his death in 1600. The 'fox' left behind a strong reputation – many a spy sent from England to Scotland was warned to 'beware of David Ingleby'.

The real and perceived threats from Catholic plots and foreign powers continued throughout the remainder of Elizabeth's reign. Although Francis Walsingham died in 1590 and William Cecil passed away in 1598, others were quick to take their place. The most notable amongst them was Cecil's second son, Robert.

The year 1588 saw the greatest threat of all to Elizabeth's reign, the Spanish Armada. The intention was to carry an invading force across the Channel from Flanders to England. In 1940 the Germans fought to gain control of the skies over Britain to enable their planned invasion: in 1588 the Spanish knew they needed to control the waves. When this failed, and the Armada was defeated, the threat of invasion waned. Although war with Spain continued, the danger to Elizabeth's crown from external Catholic forces was never as great again.

The missionary priests didn't stop coming. As before, some survived, while others were arrested and executed. The country's lay Catholics continued to be split between those who defied the state and those who preferred a quieter and less risky life. The execution of lay people, including Marmaduke Bowes, Margaret Clitherow and Richard Langley in York, following the 1585 act, had increased the stakes and risks of defiance.

The law continued to harden against Catholics. In 1587 the fines for recusancy were sharply increased. Those who couldn't pay became liable to having two-thirds of their assets seized by the Crown. The 1593

'Act for Restraining Recusants to some certain Places of Abode' forbade convicted recusants above the age of sixteen from travelling more than five miles from their home. Anyone found guilty of failing to comply with this order could suffer 'loss and forfeit all his and their Goods and Chattels, and shall also forfeit to the Queen's Majesty all the Lands, Tenements and Hereditaments, and all the Rents and Annuities'.

As the authorities sought to strip remaining Catholics of their wealth, the Catholic cause wasn't helped by the continuing lack of consensus amongst their clergy. This manifested itself in a number of ways. Many surviving Marian priests and even some of the seminary men became increasingly concerned by Jesuit support for Spain's plans to invade England. This would clearly be treason against the state and was very different to non-uniformity with the church.

The main prison set aside for Catholic clergy was Wisbech Castle in Cambridgeshire, which held Jesuit and traditional priests. The inmates then separated into two factions, the Jesuits and the other priests, which fell out with each other in a series of altercations known as the 'Wisbech Stirs'. A number of senior priests, including Father Henry Garnet and Father John Mush, visited Wisbech in an attempt to intervene and bring an end to the squabbling.

Father Mush was also involved in the 'Archpriest Controversy', prompted by the death of William Allen, the man who'd created the English seminary colleges. Despite living in exile, Allen had been the de facto leader of the Catholic Church in England. Upon his death in 1594, a power vacuum was created. Robert Persons wished to succeed Allen but was deemed by many as too divisive a figure. Even the man chosen for the role, George Blackwell, was accused of being too close to the Jesuits.

A long and bitter argument developed. Many English and Welsh Catholic priests argued against Blackwell's appointment. Some of these became known as the 'Appellants'. A few, including Father Mush, travelled to Rome to make their case.

Elizabeth and her government saw an opportunity to exploit the situation. Printing presses were made available to the Appellants to create anti-Jesuit propaganda. There was even an informal discussion about a move towards religious tolerance in return for a declaration of allegiance to the Queen and the formation of a joint alliance against the Jesuits. Some of the Appellants, including Father Mush, swore an oath of loyalty to Elizabeth, but nothing was achieved in terms of reduced intolerance.

The Pope opted to keep Blackwell in position but made a number of concessions to address some of the Appellants' demands. Blackwell was instructed to no longer consult with the Jesuits, and some positions on his staff were allocated to Appellant priests. It sounds like a very modern political compromise. At a time when their congregation had needed them most, the Catholic clergy had been split and spent years arguing amongst themselves, much to the government's delight.

As Elizabeth's reign began to draw to a close, there was one further uprising. Although the Essex Rebellion wasn't motivated by religion, a number of the Earl of Essex's supporters were Catholics. Men like Robert Catesby and John Wright had given Essex their backing in the hope that removing the Queen from the throne might lead to religious tolerance. However, the insurrection was over almost as soon as it had started. Essex and several of his supporters were beheaded. Catesby was wounded, imprisoned and heavily fined.

In 1603 Elizabeth died, aged sixty-nine. Her long reign and the Tudor dynasty had come to an end. Wishing for a Protestant successor, Robert Cecil and the Privy Council arranged for King James VI of Scotland to become King James I of England. Although James was Mary Stuart's son, they'd been separated when he was an infant and James had been raised as a Protestant.

As James Stuart travelled south from Edinburgh to accept the English crown, he promised a greater degree of religious tolerance towards the Catholic population, famously telling Robert Cecil, 'I will never allow in my conscience that the blood of any man shall be shed for diversity of opinions in religion.'

There were even rumours that James's wife, Anne of Denmark, the new Queen of England, was secretly Catholic. For once, the Catholics of England and Wales seemed to be justified in their optimism. Unfortunately, this didn't last for long. King James may have meant to keep his promises, but events took a different turn.

A number of Catholic priests, including one of the Appellants, Father William Watson, supported by several other men, hatched a plot to kidnap the King and hold him captive until he agreed with their demands for immediate religious tolerance and the removal of some of his key advisers, including Robert Cecil. This plan became known as the 'Bye Plot'.

The plotters attempted to recruit a prominent Jesuit priest, John Gerard, to support their cause, but Gerard declined. Instead, he informed Father Garnet and Archpriest Blackwell. It's believed Garnet and Blackwell may have then secretly tipped off the authorities.

It was claimed by the government that a second conspiracy, known as the 'Main Plot', had also been hatched. The intention here was not to kidnap King James but to remove him from the throne and replace him with his cousin Lady Arbella Stuart. It was alleged this conspiracy was supported by Spain, and one of the Englishmen involved was Sir Walter Raleigh.

A number of arrests were made and many of those accused of involvement in one, or both, plots were brought to trial. A number of the men, including Father Watson, were executed. Others, including Raleigh, were imprisoned.

Despite the intervention of Garnet and Blackwell, the plots resulted in desperation in Catholic circles. The hopes for change following the death of Queen Elizabeth evaporated. King James's policies hardened, until they were little different from his predecessor's.

A small group of men led by the charismatic but by now increasingly bitter Robert Catesby developed a major conspiracy not only to kill the King, but to blow up Parliament, slaughter most of the government and begin an uprising in the Midlands, Wales and the north of England. The King's daughter was to be kidnapped, converted to Catholicism and crowned Queen Elizabeth II. Support would be expected and welcomed from Catholic Spain.

Of course, these plans did not come to fruition. Guy Fawkes was discovered with his gunpowder beneath Parliament in the early hours of 5 November 1605, and tortured. Robert Catesby and many of his followers were cornered and killed in a shoot-out in the Midlands. The eight surviving conspirators, including Fawkes who was still suffering terribly from his torture, were placed on trial and convicted of high treason. All were hanged, drawn and quartered in late January 1606.

Robert Cecil ensured a number of Jesuit priests were also implicated for their alleged role in the Gunpowder Plot. Arrest warrants were issued for several Jesuits, including Fathers Garnet and Gerard. Although Father Gerard managed to escape, Father Garnet was caught and tortured. He was tried and executed in May 1606.

As during Elizabeth's reign, the government under James I introduced new laws to punish and further reduce the Catholic population.

189

Following the failed Gunpowder Plot, Parliament passed the 'Act for Public Thanksgiving to Almighty God every year on the Fifth Day of November'. This kicked off the nation's annual Guy Fawkes bonfire night and firework celebrations.

More seriously, the 'Act for the better discovering of Popish Recusants' and 'Act to prevent and avoid Dangers which may grow by Popish Recusants' introduced further harsh penalties against recusants. Rewards were introduced for churchwardens and others to identify recusants and inform on missionary priests. Recusants were disbarred from holding 'Certain Offices and Functions', including law, medicine, the military and public office. Between them, the two new laws were lengthy and included many detailed restrictions and punishments.

The new laws also addressed the thorny issue of bringing to heel married female recusants such as Margaret Clitherow. A specific clause was included, detailing how their husbands could be forced to forfeit most of their assets as a punishment for their wives' behaviour. In the event of their spouse's death, recusant women were barred from benefiting from their husband's estate.

Chapter Thirteen

Closing Thoughts

I began this book with a view that the majority of people in most societies obeyed their governments. Some have done so willingly, others have not, and a minority have rebelled. The reign of the last Tudor monarch, Elizabeth I, was marked by a desire to combine uniformity in religion with the supremacy of the Crown.

During this time, the Catholic population of England and Wales became the minority. Some converted to the slowly reforming Protestant Church of England. Others conformed, reluctantly and publicly, but retained their earlier faith as Church Catholics. Only the recusants (apart from a small number of Puritans on the opposite side of the Reformation) openly rebelled. Over time, the recusants became marginalised and severely punished as enemies of the State.

The Catholics' plight wasn't helped by repeated attempts to replace the Queen with one of their own. The most notable of the would-be monarchs was Mary Stuart, the former Queen of Scots. A series of external interventions also proved disastrous for the country's Catholic population. The Pope labelled Elizabeth a heretic, fit only for assassination and replacement. Seminary and Jesuit priests crossed the Channel to provide succour to their congregation and spread the word, but drove fear into the hearts of the establishment. Spain's antagonism with England led to war and a failed invasion. Each of these actions resulted in additional suspicion, prejudice and laws which clamped down on Catholics.

Both Catholic priests and lay people were punished. As Elizabeth's reign continued, the body count mounted. We don't know exactly how many Catholics died in prison, but approximately 200 were executed between her rise to the throne in 1558 and James's I accession in 1603.

It's only right we should compare and contrast this number with the equivalent during Mary I's reign, when nearly 300 Protestants were killed in less than six years. They included fifty-six women. During Elizabeth's reign, Catholics were mistreated and harshly punished. A number were executed, but there was no religious genocide.

During Elizabeth's reign, many Catholic females, including Anne Tesh, came close to execution, but ultimately only three suffered such a terrible fate for religious reasons. Each of the trio was charged with harbouring or helping Catholic priests, but only two were found guilty of the crime.

Margaret Ward was hanged at Tyburn in London in 1588. She died alongside five Catholic laymen. Ann Line suffered the same awful fate at the same location in 1601. The two priests accompanying her were hanged, drawn and quartered.

As we know, the third woman, and the first to die, was Margaret Clitherow. She refused to enter a plea, and so could not be found guilty of the charges brought against her. Instead, she suffered *peine forte et dure*. From Father Mush's *A True Report*, we know the senior justice at her trial, Judge Clench, made repeated attempts to persuade her to have her case heard by the jury, but Margaret refused.

We've examined a range of reasons why Margaret may have considered such a drastic course of action. This includes two theories advanced by Father Mush. Of these, the defence of her family, servants and neighbours appears to be the more compelling argument. However, I can't help but harbour a doubt in my mind about whether Father Mush may have subtly persuaded Margaret towards martyrdom. If so, his motivation would likely have been to garner support and 'publicity' for their shared cause. Of course, I may be wrong. Each of us must form our own opinions, based upon the evidence available.

Whatever our views about Margaret Clitherow, her family, neighbours and the wider population of York and England and Wales, there's little doubt religious persecution damaged and devastated the lives of many people during this time. Whole families were torn apart. In some cases, the new laws were used as a lever or an excuse for personal gain.

Once again, we may have our own views about the actions of Margaret's stepfather, Henry Maye. Having such an obstinate and law-breaking stepdaughter couldn't have been easy for such an ambitious man, but to my mind history doesn't look favourably upon him.

The persecution and punishment of the country's Catholics continued. The laws and restrictions introduced under Elizabeth I and James I remained in place through the following centuries. Emancipation began only slowly, beginning with the Roman Catholic Relief Acts of 1778, 1791 and 1829. Even these stretched out across half a century.

Personal prejudice and sections of the law took much longer to change. Members of the royal family have only been permitted to marry Catholics and remain in line for the royal succession since 2015. Having said that, Catholics (and all other non-Protestants) are still excluded from succession to the throne. The king or queen of the land must 'be in communion with the Church of England and swear to preserve the established Church of England and the established Church of Scotland. The Sovereign must also promise to uphold the Protestant succession.'

The *peine forte et dure* law, which Margaret Clitherow suffered so horribly from, remained unchanged for almost another 200 years. Finally, in 1772, the law was changed. After this date, refusing to make a plea became the equivalent of pleading guilty. In 1827 the law was amended for a second time. Since then, failing to issue a plea has been considered the same as pleading not guilty. This seems to make more sense. We can only wonder how this amendment might have affected Margaret Clitherow's case.

Bibliography

Aveling, J.C.H., *Catholic Recusancy in the City of York 1558 - 1791* (Catholic Record Society, 1970)

Bede, Camm, *Lives of the English Martyrs: Under Henry VIII* (Longmans, Green and Co., 1904|)

Burton, Edwin H. and Pollen J.H., *Lives of the English Martyrs: 1583 - 1588* (Longmans, Green and Co., 1914|)

Challoner, Richard, *Memoirs of Missionary Priests and other Catholics of both sexes, that have suffered death in England on religious accounts, from the year 1577 to 1684* (John T Green, 1839)

D'Ewes, Simmonds, 'Journal of the House of Lords: January 1559', in *The Journals of All the Parliaments During the Reign of Queen Elizabeth* (Irish University Press, 1682),

Dodds, Charles and Tierney, M.A., *Dodd's Church History of England from the Commencement of the Sixteenth Century to the Revolution in 1688* (Charles Dolman, 1840)

Dickens, A.G., *The Yorkshire Submissions to Henry VIII, 1541* (English Historical Review, Volume 53, 1938)

Gee, Henry, *The Elizabethan Clergy and the Settlement of Religion, 1558 - 1564* (Clarendon Press, 1898)

Haigh, Christopher, *English Reformations, Religion, Politics and Society Under the Tudors* (Clarendon Press, 1993)

Hildyard, Christopher and Torr, James, *The Antiquities of York City, and the Civil Government Thereof* (Hildyard, 1719)

Holcomb, Justin S. and Johnson, David A., *Christian Theologies of the Sacraments: A Comparative Introduction* (NYU Press, 2017)

Holmes, Peter, *Resistance and Compromise, The Political Thought of the Elizabethan Catholics* (Cambridge University Press, 1982)

Johansen, Sarah, *'That silken Priest': Catholic disguise and anti-popery on the English Mission (1569–1640)* (Historical Research, Volume 93, 2020)

Lake, Peter and Questier, Michael, *The Trials of Margaret Clitherow: Persecution, Martyrdom and Politics of Sanctity in Elizabethan England* (Bloomsbury, 2019)

Longley, Katharine, *Saint Margaret Clitherow, Her Trial on Trial, Reply by Katherine Longley* (Ampleforth Journal, Spring 1971)

Longley, Katharine, *Saint Margaret Clitherow* (Anthony Clarke, 1986)

Maynard, Jean Olwen, *Margaret Clitherow* (Catholic Truth Society, 2003)

Monro, Margaret T., *Blessed Margaret Clitherow* (Burns Oates & Washbourne, 1948)

Morey, Adrian, *The Catholic Subjects of Elizabeth I* (George Allen & Unwin, 1978)

Morgan, Tony, *The Pearl of York, Treason and Plot* (Kindle Direct Publishing, 2020)

Morris, John (Editor), *The Troubles of Our Catholic Forefathers Related by Themselves* (Burns and Oates, 1872 - 1877)

Mush, John *A True Report of the Life and Martyrdom of Mrs Margaret Clitherow* (Published and transcribed several times, firstly in 1619)

Nicholson, William (Editor), *Life and Death of Margaret Clitherow, The Martyr of York* (Richardson & Son, 1849)

Pallen, Conde B. and Wynne, John J, *The New Catholic Dictionary – Martyrs* (Universal Knowledge Foundation, 1929)

Palliser, D.M., *Tudor York* (Oxford University Press, 1979)

Palliser, D.M., *The Reformation in York 1534 - 1553* (Borthwick Papers No. 40, 1971)

Raithby, John (Editor), *The Statutes at Large of England and of Great Britain, Volume IV From 1553 to 1640* (G. Eyre, 1811)

Sapoznik, Alexandra, *Bees in the Medieval Economy: Religious Observance and the Production, Trade, and Consumption of Wax in England, C. 1300–1555* (Economic History Review, Vol. 72, Issue 4, 2019)

Tillott, P.M. (Editor), *A History of the County of York: the City of York* (Victoria County History, 1961)

Wadham, Juliana, *Saint Margaret Clitherow, Her Trial on Trial, The Case Against Her* (Ampleforth Journal, Spring 1971)

Walsham, Alexandra, *Church Papists: Catholicism, Conformity and Confessional Polemic in Early Modern England* (The Royal Historical Society, 1993)

Wabuda, Susan, *Marian Martyrs* (Online Oxford Dictionary of National Biography, 2008)

Notes

Chapter One

1. This figure is included in the *New Catholic Diary* of 1929.
2. For example, a copy of William Nicholson's 1849 version of Father Mush's *A True Report* is held in York Minster's Archives.
3. Father Morris's *The Troubles of the Catholic Forefathers Related by Themselves* was published in 1877.

Chapter Two

1. Details of the Laws in Wales Acts can be found at www.legislation.gov.uk administered by The National Archives.
2. A copy of *Assertio Septem Sacramentorum*, signed by Henry VIII is held by the Royal Collection Trust – www.rct.uk.
3. Thomas Cromwell was to be the Church of England's only 'Vice-Gerent in spirituals'. The role didn't survive his death.
4. To find out more about differing belief and the Sacraments, the *Christian Theologies of the Sacraments* book included in the bibliography provides comprehensive analysis and comparison.
5. D.M. Palliser's *Tudor York* provides an excellently researched and presented overview of governance in the city.
6. A dozen miles from York, Towton remains the bloodiest battle ever fought on the British mainland.
7. The text of the full submission is captured in the 'The Yorkshire Submissions to Henry VIII, 1541' in Volume 53 of the *English Historical Review*.
8. Details of Margaret Clitherow's family are included in Katharine Longley's book *Saint Margaret Clitherow*.
9. There's an interesting 2019 article about wax production and religion before 1555 in Volume 72 of the *Economic History Review*.

Chapter Three

1. *Marian Martyrs* written by Susan Wabuda provides a fascinating insight into the positions, occupations and locations of Protestants executed during Mary's reign.
2. The sale of these churches is detailed in D.M. Palliser's booklet on the *Reformation in York 1534 - 1553*.
3. D.M. Palliser's *Tudor York* provides an excellent insight into such events.
4. There's some debate about the year of Margaret Clitherow's birth in her biographies. From the information available, 1553 seems most plausible, but nobody knows for sure.
5. The History of Parliament website is a great source of information concerning former MP's. For example, here is John Beane's entry: http://historyofparliamentonline.org/volume/1509-1558/member/beane-john-1503-80.

Chapter Four

1. The text of Bacon's speech, taken from the *Journal of the House of Lords: January 1559*, can be freely accessed over the internet from the British History Online website.
2. There's a very good summary of the impact of the falling clergy numbers in Christopher Haigh's *English Reformations*.
3. D.M. Palliser's *Tudor York* provides a wealth of information about York at this time.
4. Details are included in Henry Gee's *Elizabethan Clergy*.
5. Katherine Longley's *Saint Margaret Clitherow* provides further details of John Clitherow's background and family.
6. These records from the city's house-books are detailed in Father Morris's *The Troubles of the Catholic Forefathers Related by Themselves*.

Chapter Five

1. The Thirty-Nine articles are documented on the Church of England's website: https://www.churchofengland.org/prayer-and-worship/worship-texts-and-resources/book-common-prayer/articles-religion.

2. Raithby's *The Statutes at Large of England and of Great Britain* includes the full text of the 1571 Treason Act.
3. J.C.H. Aveling's in depth research for his book *Catholic Recusancy in the City of York 1558 - 1791* is an invaluable resource in this area.
4. Edward Besley's record in The History of Parliament website can be found here: https://www.historyofparliamentonline.org/volume/1509-1558/member/beseley-edward-1532-1613-or-later.

Chapter Six

1. Sarah Johansen's article 'That silken Priest: Catholic disguise and anti-popery on the English Mission' offers a fascinating insight into this area.
2. Once again, we are indebted to the research of J.C.H. Aveling and his book *Catholic Recusancy in the City of York 1558 - 1791*.
3. Aveling's research indicates Margaret Clitherow was charged with and imprisoned at least three times for recusancy.

Chapter Seven

1. Persons' and Campion's mission and the resulting debate is very well covered in Lake and Questier's *The Trials of Margaret Clitherow*.
2. Raithby's *The Statutes at Large of England and of Great Britain* includes the full text of the 1581 'Disobedience' Act.
3. Thomas Bell features heavily in Lake and Questier's *The Trials of Margaret Clitherow*.
4. St Peter's (first established in 627 AD) is reputed to be the fourth oldest school in the world. In addition to a number of future Catholic priests and Guy Fawkes, other pupils at the time included two more Gunpowder Plotters, John and Christopher Wright.
5. Accounts of many of the executed priests' stories are contained in Burton and Pollen's *Lives of the English Martyrs: 1583 - 1588*.
6. The amount of research Aveling must have carried out when writing *Catholic Recusancy in the City of York 1558 - 1791* is quite remarkable.

7. Although Father Mush wasn't gushing in his praise for John Clitherow in *A True Report*, neither was he ever overly critical of Margaret's husband.

Chapter Eight

1. Details of many of these men are included in Burton's and Pollen's *Lives of the English Martyrs: 1583 - 1588.*
2. Palliser's *Tudor York* provides a good summary of the Corporation's actions to support York's least fortunate citizens.
3. Details of these meetings and others are included in John Morris's *The Troubles of Our Catholic Forefathers Related by Themselves* as part of the foreword to Father Mush's *A True Report.*
4. Details of Marmaduke Bowes' arrest and execution are included in Burton and Pollen's *Lives of the English Martyrs: 1583 - 1588.*
5. Father Mush's *A True Report* includes many other similar comments with regards to Margaret Clitherow's state of mind and devotion.

Chapter Nine

1. Father Mush includes a detailed description of events leading up to Margaret's arrest.
2. Father Mush, *A True Report.*
3. Father Mush, *A True Report.*
4. The records from the city's house-books are detailed in Father Morris's *The Troubles of the Catholic Forefathers Related by Themselves.*

Chapter Ten

1. Father Mush includes a very detailed description of events in court.
2. Guy Fawkes did live in York at the time. He was probably in his final days at St Peter's School. His family home was either on Stonegate or High Petergate, a few hundred yards from Davygate and the Shambles.
3. The Oxford Dictionary of National Biography includes a good summary of Giles Wiggington's life: https://doi.org/10.1093/ref:odnb/29368.

Chapter Eleven

1. Edmund Bunny's works include *A Book of Christian Exercise*, part of which is an edited version of a work by the Jesuit Robert Persons. See Lake and Questier's *The Trials of Margaret Clitherow* for more details.
2. After the trial, Wiggington left York for London, where he was once more arrested.

Chapter Twelve

1. Father Christopher Grene's account of Margaret Clitherow's burial is detailed in a work entitled 'A Yorkshire Recusant's Relation' within Father Morris's book. It's possible the actual text was originally written by Father Mush.
2. The Vavasours of Hazlewood Castle were a prominent Catholic family but remained loyal to the Crown.
3. Father Warford's comments are described in Burton and Pollen's *Lives of the English Martyrs: 1583 - 1588*.
4. The strange manner of Henry Cheke's death is reported in his entry on the History of Parliament website: https://www.historyofparliamentonline.org/volume/1558-1603/member/cheke-henry-1548-86.
5. This is the supposition put forward in my novel, *The Pearl of York, Treason and Plot*.